In Hitler's Shadow

Yaron Svoray
and
Nick Taylor

*With an Introduction
by Simon Wiesenthal*

An Israeli's
Amazing Journey
Inside Germany's
Neo-Nazi
Movement

In Hitler's Shadow

NAN A. TALESE

DOUBLEDAY

New York

London

Toronto

Sydney

Auckland

PUBLISHED BY NAN A. TALESE
an imprint of Doubleday
a division of Bantam Doubleday Dell Publishing Group, Inc.
1540 Broadway, New York, New York 10036

DOUBLEDAY is a trademark of Doubleday, a division of
Bantam Doubleday Dell Publishing Group, Inc.

Library of Congress Cataloging-in-Publication Data

Svoray, Yaron.
In Hitler's shadow: an Israeli's amazing journey inside Germany's
neo-Nazi movement / Yaron Svoray and Nick Taylor.—1st ed.
p. cm.
1. Nationalism—Germany. 2. Israelis—Germany—Politics and government.
3. Germany—Politics and government—1990– . 4. Germany—
Ethnic relations. 5. Racism—Germany. 6. National
characteristics, German. I. Taylor, Nick, 1945– . II. Title.
DD290.29.S89 1994
943.087′9—dc20 94-14775
CIP

ISBN 0-385-47284-6
Copyright © 1994 by Yaron Svoray and Nick Taylor
All Rights Reserved
Printed in the United States of America
October 1994
First Edition

1 3 5 7 9 10 8 6 4 2

Dedicated to Michal Svoray,
to Isaac Solomon Unger,
and to all people who believe that memory
is the seed of vigilance

Acknowledgments

A GREAT MANY PEOPLE were instrumental to the publication of this book. The authors wish to thank their families, the dedicated staffs of the Simon Wiesenthal Center in Los Angeles and the center's New York office, and the talented professionals throughout Doubleday, most especially in the office of Nan A. Talese.

Several individuals also deserve thanks, among them Sam Nyer, whose story was the genesis; Kevin Buckley, whose early encouragement was vital; Seymour Hersch, who provided valuable perspective; Ako Hintzen; Frauke Keller; Hannelore Kohler of the German Information Center in New York; Bernie Silverman; Hope Tudanger; Rabbi Samuel S. Kieffer of Temple B'nai Aviv in Fort Lauderdale, Florida; Francine LeFrak; Al Lowman; Jonathan Buchsbaum; and Frank Simmons. Rabbis Marvin Hier and Abraham Cooper, Mark Weitzman, Michelle Eisman, Rick Eaton, and Aaron Breitbart made valuable contributions to the narrative in which they figure, as did Mark Seal. In addition, recognition goes to a singular man, Assaf Heffets.

Special gratitude is due Enosh, Ellie, and Ohad Svoray, Yehuda and Rachel Svoray, and the late Dorit Yahalomi. They endured much, and have defined patience, love, and kindness during difficult times.

Historical data were drawn from a number of sources. Books used for background reference include *The War Against the Jews, 1933–1945,* by Lucy S. Dawidowicz; Martin Gilbert's *The Second War: A Complete History* and Gilbert's *Atlas of the Holocaust*; the *Encyclopedia of the Third Reich* compiled by Dr. Louis L. Snyder; Matthew Cooper's *The German Army 1933–1945*; *Hannah Senesh,*

Her Life and Diary; the catalogue of the historical exhibition in the Berlin Reichstag covering German history from 1800 to the present; and Michael Berenbaum's history of the Holocaust as told in the United States Holocaust Museum, entitled *The World Must Know.*

Introduction

OVER SIX DECADES AGO when I was a student, the initial reaction of myself and my Jewish peers to Adolph Hitler was to make jokes about a funny little man, a lunatic with a mustache. No one was prepared to take his bombastic threats seriously—until it was too late.

When Yaron Svoray entered the neo-Nazi subculture in the Germany of today, few were taking it seriously. The stirrings of extremism and hatred were decried but all too often accepted. Racist skinhead attacks against foreigners, firebombings, cemetery and synagogue desecrations—these sinister echoes of the past were, as then, written off as the work of elements at the fringes of society. No one thought they were a real threat. Yet the extreme right wing has tried consistently to penetrate the political mainstream of the Federal Republic.

Germany is not alone. Headlines from all over the world remind us that hate did not die in the bunker with Hitler. We are experiencing a new era of hate. People concerned about the world they live in must refuse, as did Yaron Svoray, to let these things incubate.

From the beginning, I have said that there is no need to pass any new laws for Germany to deal with neo-Nazi terror. The Federal Republic has established the toughest anti-racist and anti-hate laws in Europe. It is a model postwar democracy. What has been lacking until recently is the political will and collective consciousness to deal with the extremist movements and marginalize their ideas.

The most important aspect of Svoray's mission as related in *In Hitler's Shadow* is that it helped force people at the highest levels of the German government to confront a problem too many of them did not want to deal with. One can only hope that ordinary men and women, in every country where extremists would snatch liberty from any of their fellow citizens, will read the story of his mission as a cautionary tale as well.

History records that the people of Germany did not liberate themselves from National Socialism. It was destroyed from outside by the Allies. Today's younger generation has the responsibility of making up for what their grandfathers and fathers failed to do: recognize and fight National Socialism as an ideology based on contempt for mankind. For in the final analysis, the future will be determined not by how many Nazis there will be—or fascists or extreme nationalists or white supremacists—but how many anti-Nazis, people of goodwill, there will be to confront them. It is my hope that *In Hitler's Shadow* will help to motivate many thousands of anti-Nazis to stand up and be counted.

SIMON WIESENTHAL
Vienna
June 1994

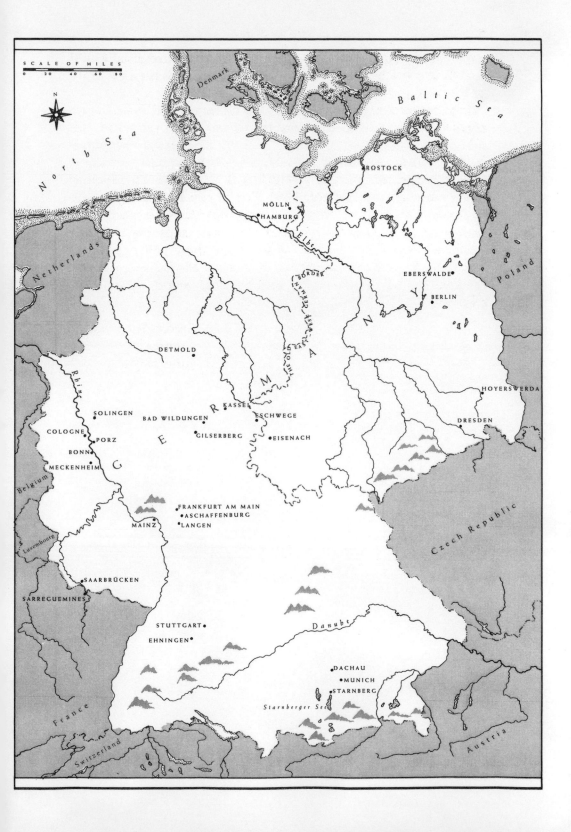

September
1992

One

YARON SVORAY crossed the Blies River into Germany in the late afternoon and headed toward the autobahn. As he drove he felt a shiver of excitement. Although nearly fifty years had passed since the Third Reich and the exterminations, it still was no small thing for a Jew to enter Germany. Svoray had never thought his diamond search would lead him here.

It had started at a bonds-for-Israel dinner in Bangor, Maine, four years earlier. Svoray was the guest speaker; having served in the Israeli army and the Tel Aviv detective force, he frequently spoke at these fundraisers on the subject of terrorism in the Middle East. He used his fees to support his family while he attended college in New York.

At that dinner, the chairman of the event, a World War II veteran named Sam Jacobs, told Svoray about a cache of diamonds he had hidden during the last months of the war. The diamonds had been found during one of Jacobs's scouting expeditions, in German-held Strasbourg. He had kept them on his person until reaching Sarreguemines, a small French town bordering Germany. Tunneling into the side of his foxhole, Jacobs buried the diamonds, intending to retrieve them when the final assault on Germany was over.

A mortar barrage upset his plans, however. Jacobs was wounded, hospitalized, and invalided back to the United States. Years later, Jacobs returned to Sarreguemines but suffered a heart attack as he was setting out to find the foxhole. That cursed the diamonds in his wife's eyes and she wouldn't let him look again.

Svoray had listened to Jacobs's story with interest. He was thirty-four then, married, and the father of two children. He had fought in the Yom Kippur War, made border raids as a commando, killed other men in battle, arrested drug dealers and murderers. Now he and his family were struggling, trying to pursue their dreams. The diamonds could be a way to finance their future.

A large man with a natural sense of self-confidence, a gift for talk, and a curiosity that sometimes outweighed prudence, Svoray knew he could locate the diamonds. As he continued to give speeches at bond drives, he repeated the story to anyone who seemed interested. Within a year, he had a small group of investors; Svoray added what he could from his speaking fees, from the money he earned as a limo driver and a roving reporter for Israeli newspapers, and also from the retainers he received from several law enforcement agencies that hired him as an undercover operative. By 1991, he had made several trips to Sarreguemines, had graduated from Queens College, and had earned a master's degree in media studies. But now, as he drove into Germany, he thought of the diamonds as his real lifework.

The man in Frankfurt could be the final link, the one whose information would take him to Sam Jacobs's foxhole.

Evening fell over the hilly western German Rhineland. Svoray reached the autobahn and made good time. He switched on the car's headlights as he changed from the A6 to the A67 and joined the northbound stream of traffic. The rented Peugeot was fast enough, but it kept getting passed by sleek BMWs, Audis, and Mercedes-Benzes, symbols of Germany's prosperity. The German economy was Europe's strongest. The Germans had the economic power the Jews always were accused of having, Svoray thought as he streaked along the autobahn. It was only since the fall of communism in the east that events had revealed an underside.

The month before, gangs of fascist skinheads had converged on a refugee center in the city of Rostock, a Baltic seaport in eastern Germany. Most of the refugees were Vietnamese, seeking asylum under a German constitutional provision that made the country a magnet for people fleeing war or poverty. The skinheads stoned buildings and terrorized the city's residents. They came again the next night, and the next, and the next. Spectators gathered to watch the sport. Police did not interfere. On the fifth night the skinheads threw firebombs and burned the complex. Television pictures of the youths, raising stiff-armed salutes in silhouette against the flames, faces twisted with hate as they chanted *"Ausländer raus!"* eerily recalled the Nazi era.

Svoray joined the A5 at Darmstadt. The darkness was complete now, and the lights of Frankfurt loomed against the sky. He passed the turnoff to the airport and switched to a road that took him toward the city center. North of the Main River, near the Hauptbahnhof, the main train station, he turned onto Wilhelm-Leuschner Strasse.

The Inter-Continental Hotel was one of the most expensive in Frankfurt. Svoray refused to stint when he was traveling. He didn't plan to stay long in any case. He'd hear what this new contact had to say and check it out back in Sarreguemines if that made sense. If not, he'd turn in the rental car at Frankfurt's airport and catch the first plane home to Tel Aviv.

He made the phone call from his room, afraid as he pressed the buttons that it was a flimsy possibility. The contact was the nephew of a German he'd met earlier that day, the latest in a chain of sources intrigued by the lie Svoray had concocted to explain his repeated trips to Sarreguemines. Svoray never said he was looking for diamonds. He said he was trying to find the buried diaries of a group of American deserters, from which he hoped to make a movie. The nephew was something of a military historian, apparently. It was a stretch; Svoray had come only so that, years from now, he wouldn't wonder if this was the one unchecked clue that might have led him to the treasure.

A woman answered in German. "Herr Müller, please," Svoray said. "His uncle called about me."

"Was? Was?" the woman said.

"Herr Müller, bitte. Herr Müller's uncle called. I'm the one he called about."

"Was?"

There was a sudden commotion at the other end as someone grabbed the phone. A male voice spoke in casual English. "Hold on." The voice screamed in German, and Svoray could hear the woman screaming back. After a moment the voice returned and said calmly, "Hello. Sorry about that."

"Is this Herr Müller?"

"I am Charlie Müller. Can I help you?"

"I'm the American your uncle called about. He told me to call when I got to Frankfurt."

"Yes. What was your name?"

Svoray hesitated. The name Yaron seemed distinctively Israeli. He did not want to deny being an Israeli or a Jew, but on the other hand he did not want those considerations to interfere with his gaining information. Then he realized that the villagers in Sarreguemines had provided a solution to the problem. They had simply condensed his name to something more familiar. "Ron," he said.

"You were looking into some war history or something," Charlie Müller said.

"Yes. I am trying to locate the American Sixty-third Infantry near Sarreguemines. I thought Germans who fought there might help. February of 1945, I'm talking about, when they were staring at each other across the river."

"Hm. Yes, I have someone in mind for you," Müller said, almost too quickly. "He speaks no English, though. Let me meet with you tomorrow. Then, if I think he can help you, I will arrange another meeting." He named a pub near the Hauptbahnhof. "What will you look like?"

"I look like a Turkish wrestler," Svoray said. He was pleased the arrangements were coming together so easily.

"Not too much, I hope," Müller said.

"In that case, I look a little like the Michelin man," said Svoray, referring to the plump advertising figure for the international tire company.

"That's better," said Charlie. "We want the Turks to all go home. I'll see you tomorrow."

Svoray spent the next morning at the hotel's health club for a sauna and a swim, followed by a large brunch. Around noon he got a map from the concierge desk and set out in the direction of his rendezvous. A clutch of dark-suited corporate travelers pressed into the revolving door ahead of him, as if his black Nikes and cotton slacks and leather jacket deserved a lesser status than their own. They testified to Frankfurt's rank as the German business capital.

But it was not to the business center that Svoray was headed. He walked north and east away from the river, toward the pedestrian mall called the Zeil.

Gradually he angled back to the west toward the Hauptbahnhof. As he approached the train station's Baroque facade along one of the main streets, the upscale shops, restaurants, and offices gave way to strip clubs, peep shows, anonymous hotels, and greasy food joints. Pulsing neon beckoned passersby into brightly lighted sex shops. Drunks and hustlers shared the streets with men and women wearing business clothes and clusters of sauntering young men on leave from the nearby military bases. When he was opposite the station, he turned and walked until he reached another intersecting street, and then turned back into the red-light district.

The pub Müller had named stood between a shop selling pornographic magazines and a club advertising "Live Sex Shows" and go-go dancers. Svoray was reaching for the door when it flew open and two men in grimy work clothes lurched into the street.

A din of voices and music and the sharp smell of cigar and cigarette smoke greeted Svoray as he entered the pub. It was a vast room with a bar down one side, heavy with smoke and the smell of beer. Bleary eyes flicked over Svoray as he stood inside the door, and he felt a mixture of suspicion and hostility.

A pair of small round glasses fixed on him from a table to his right. Opaque with reflection, they momentarily obscured the eyes behind them. The young face to which they were attached expressed arrogance. The head was shorn to a blond stubble. Two other young men, also with the close-cropped hair of skinheads, sat at the same table. All three watched Svoray as he approached.

"Charlie Müller?" Svoray said.

The one wearing the glasses spoke in English. "I thought all Turkish wrestlers had mustaches. Where is yours?"

"Good point," said Svoray. "I could never make it curl up on the ends, so I shaved it."

The man barked out a humorless laugh. "I'm Charlie," he said. He made no offer to shake hands.

"Ron," Svoray said.

The other two men nodded, but didn't introduce themselves or offer their hands, and Müller didn't introduce them. Svoray dragged a chair from another table, almost slipping on the damp, grimy floor. Empty beer mugs filled much of the tabletop, and Svoray pushed them toward the center of the table to make room for his elbows. Müller signaled a waitress and motioned for another round.

As they waited for the drinks, Svoray studied the men. Müller's faded blue eyes moved constantly behind his glasses, darting like a fly at a window. He wore a black T-shirt and jeans and a bomber jacket of shiny olive green nylon. His friends wore dark flannel shirts. One displayed filigrees of blue-black tattoos on the forearms below his rolled-up sleeves. The other had a boxer's battered nose. Neither of them had shaved that morning. "You have a last name?" Müller asked.

Svoray had thought about this, too. He took a notebook from the ballistic nylon shoulder bag he carried and ripped out a page, on which he printed a name in block letters: KRZYZEW-SKI. He'd always wondered why Duke University's basketball coach was known as Coach K, until he'd seen the name spelled out. "How would you pronounce that?" Svoray asked.

Müller looked at the name, then at Svoray. "Ach, Polish!" he said. He made a couple of lame attempts, then gave up and shrugged.

"It's pronounced 'Shuh-shef-ski,' " Svoray said.

Müller grunted.

"So just call me Ron."

The waitress arrived and slung four mugs of beer onto the crowded table.

"These troops you want to locate. What is so interesting about them?" Müller asked.

"I am researching a movie. The troop movements at the border near Sarreguemines are what I'm after. I want to be authentic."

Müller's transformation was immediate. His aloofness disappeared and he leaned forward. "A movie? You are involved with movies?"

"Yes," Svoray lied.

"Do you know anyone in Hollywood?"

Svoray borrowed the names of some of his limousine clients.

"Sure. Steven Spielberg, Woody Allen, Roy Scheider, Elliott Gould . . ."

"You only know Jews in Hollywood."

Svoray tried to keep his voice light. "Don't you know?" he said. "All Hollywood is run by Jews."

"So tell me," Müller said, "what kind of movies do you like?"

"I like old German movies, actually."

Müller brightened some more. "What is your favorite?"

"There are so many," Svoray hedged.

The two other men were trying to balance a saltshaker in a mound of salt they'd poured onto the table. Svoray leaned forward, and the table tilted on a short leg. The teetering saltshaker fell abruptly on its side. They started to protest and Müller angrily swept the shaker from the table in a spray of salt. It skittered across the floor and under an empty table. The skinheads got up, muttering, and walked to a row of video games and pinball machines at the back of the room.

"Idiots," Müller said apologetically. "They want only to fight. I'll tell you my favorite. It is *Triumph of the Will.*

Svoray's unease deepened. The Leni Riefenstahl documentary of the 1934 Nazi party rally was a militaristic pastiche of beating drums and marching troops and calls to arms by Hitler, set under omnipresent swastikas. It was a masterpiece, but a masterpiece of propaganda for the madness that Hitler would visit first on Germany and then on the rest of Europe and the world. He said, "I prefer *M.*"

"You know it?" Müller said delightedly.

"Of course." It was Peter Lorre's first film role, as an obsessed child killer stalked by both a band of criminals and the police.

For the next hour, Svoray and Müller talked about the heyday of German filmmaking and other titles, such as *Nosferatu, The Cabinet of Dr. Caligari* and Fritz Lang's *Metropolis* and *Dr. Mabuse, the Gambler.*

American movies, Müller said, had helped him learn to speak English after he'd received the basics in school. He'd learned more by hanging out with American GIs from the big army base in Frankfurt. Müller relaxed more as they talked. Finally he said, "What is the slant of your movie?"

"Well, it would be about a group of American deserters at the end of the war. That's why I talked to your uncle, and why he sent me to you. I'm looking for some diaries they buried. To find out why.''

''Maybe they thought they were on the wrong side.''

''Well, I don't know. Maybe so.''

''Maybe they thought the good guys were losing.''

''Look,'' Svoray said. ''I am not political. I don't want to refight the war. I'm only interested in what your friend remembers, however it can help me.''

''My friend was in the SS,'' Müller said.

Svoray froze at the name. The Schutzstaffel, the Black Shirts, had begun as Hitler's bodyguards and grew, as the Waffen or Armed SS, into the police and then the military arm of the Nazi party. Encouraged by Heinrich Himmler to regard mercy as a weakness and all blood but theirs impure, they considered themselves the ruling elite of Germany and the protectors of the German race. On the battlefield, the SS units were known as fanatic fighters, but tales of their atrocities—mass murders, executions of war prisoners—were legend. Their ''special duties'' included the extermination of the Warsaw Ghetto; sixty thousand Jews died in the ghetto's defiant death throes in the spring of 1943. The SS ran the concentration camps and carried out the ''Final Solution.'' The SS name has resonance with every Jew. Svoray gathered himself. ''So what?'' he said.

''You don't care?''

''Why should I care? I told you, I am only interested in finding my diaries and making a movie.''

''Do you have money to spend for information?'' Müller demanded suddenly.

''Some. A little. If it's good information.''

Müller nodded. He said, ''I like you, Ron. I think we might be able to do business.'' He pushed away from the table and stood up. ''Excuse me while I make a phone call.''

Svoray sat back and surveyed the room. Colored glass filled the windows, obstructing light and obscuring any sense of passing time. Behind the bar, bottles and a display of beer steins intruded into the mirror. Posters and signs in Gothic lettering covered the slatted wood walls. Caricatures of a man and a woman, with crudely drawn genitalia added courtesy of a graffitist, pointed the way to the bathrooms at a break in the row of game machines. Müller's friends still were bent over their game, jerking at the joysticks and slamming the buttons viciously. The men looked like the Rostock skinheads Svoray had seen on television, snarling their hatred to the cameras and giving their *"Sieg Heil"* salutes.

Müller returned, smiling. "Good news," he said. "Herr Schulz is going to meet us." He walked past Svoray to the skinheads and jerked his head toward the door.

Two

MIDDAY HAD SLIPPED into late afternoon unnoticed, bringing a chill. Svoray ducked into the collar of his jacket and thrust his hands down in his pockets. He was growing impatient.

"I want to show you some German history," Müller said. "Before we meet Herr Schulz."

The other two skinheads bowled into the street behind them, grinning wolfishly. Half a block away, a dark-haired prostitute appeared in a doorway under a sign that read "Sex Inn." She twisted slowly on her feet, hugging a short rabbit fur coat around her as she looked for prospects up and down the street.

Müller looked at her with scorn. "This is what they do," he said.

"What who does?" asked Svoray.

"Outsiders. Foreigners. They come to Germany and take jobs and housing and sell drugs and steal and prostitute themselves. They dirty the streets. And they are given money." He shook his head.

"And look. You see that?" he said sharply, pointing in the opposite direction to a line of people on the sidewalk. Svoray recognized it as a drug market, customers waiting their turn with a seller before retreating to doorways and then, in plain view, preparing and shooting heroin. Watchers—young men in modish clothes, lounging with belligerence—guarded the operation from across the street. It was a scene of predators and victims that fit Müller's prejudices perfectly, for the drug seller and his lookouts were dark and obviously foreign.

Article XVI of the German constitution guaranteed asylum to victims of political persecution. It was, in part, a way to repudiate the Nazi past by allowing Germans who had fled the Nazis to return, but a trickle of asylum seekers became a flood when the Iron Curtain disappeared. A quarter of a million applied in 1991. Most applicants claiming persecution were really looking for jobs. Fewer than five percent eventually qualified for political asylum, but the hearing process stretched on indefinitely. The asylum seekers in the meantime lived in hostels provided by local governments. They were given subsidies of twelve to fifteen hundred marks per month. At the same time many Germans, especially the young and especially in the east, could not find jobs. The government's treatment of the foreigners rankled. The asylum seekers inevitably committed their share of crimes and violations of the social order—drug dealing, prostitution, and petty theft among them—fueling the anger. Some adhered to strange practices, like begging and beating their wives, which fueled it more. Some had the audacity to take up with German women, to which the skinheads and the neo-Nazis responded by acting like the Ku Klux Klan.

Immigrants as well as refugees bore the brunt of right-wing anger. Officially, Germany had no immigrants, only permanent foreign residents. There were six and a half million altogether, of which the nearly two million Turks were the largest group. Living in Germany for a generation or more, speaking fluent German, working at the low-wage jobs that had helped West Germany prosper—none of this guaranteed acceptance by the German nation. Only by working in Germany for fifteen years and renouncing their national origins could foreigners even start the process of becoming German citizens. Meanwhile, anyone elsewhere in the world who could prove German ancestry was eligible to become a citizen. This was a concept of German "blood" dating to the kaisers, a concept warped by Hitler into the Third Reich's racial cleansing.

The demonstrations in Rostock had been only the most visible expression of anger against foreigners, the most dramatic and widely broadcast. Before Rostock there was Hoyerswerda, an eastern German city of dead coal pits, where hostels had been firebombed and stoned by skinheads in September 1991. In November 1990, a month after reunification, there was Eberswalde, also in the east, where neo-Nazis fatally beat an Angolan worker as police looked on. A favorite pastime was beating Turks and jumping on their heads. This was called "sidewalk cracking" or "curb jumping." Jewish cemeteries had been desecrated, gravestones destroyed, swastikas painted, a steady drizzle of hate behind the thunderclaps.

Most Germans were embarrassed by the attacks and the publicity surrounding them, and they refused to believe there was a Nazi resurgence. Germany's strict anti-Nazi laws made it illegal to publicly display the swastika, give the straight-armed *"Heil Hitler"* salute, or deny the Holocaust or advocate Nazi policies.

"Scum selling drugs," said Svoray of the scene in the street. It was a cop's response.

"Scum. You're right," Müller said. "I tell you, Ron, we are going to stop this one day soon, you'll see."

They walked two blocks, turned into a cross street, and at the next corner Müller entered a doorway. Svoray followed, ducking past a curtain into a long room where he found himself in a midden of pornography. Video boxes and magazines pictured men and women of every size and age and variety of sexual coupling. Male dummies modeled chains and handcuffs, backless leather pants, nipple clamps and penis rings; female dummies displayed garter belts and push-up bras and crotchless panties.

Müller led the way to a booth where change for peep shows was dispensed. A man with a straggly beard and lank, shoulder-length hair sat inside. He wore a black tank shirt under an open denim shirt, and an earring glinted at one ear. Müller talked with him quietly. The man slid a key through the small opening in the glass.

Taking the key and nodding at Svoray to follow, Müller entered a storage area and walked past shelves and stacks of boxes to a back door. The skinheads walked behind Svoray, closer now.

"Hey, have you guys got names?" Svoray asked.

They stared at him and kept walking, as if they would walk over him if he didn't turn and continue.

The four of them emerged into an alley. Broken glass littered the weed-sprouted concrete. Müller headed across the alley and a few doors down to a graffiti-covered metal door. He slipped the key in the lock and pushed through. Svoray followed, the skinheads on his heels.

They were in the back of an empty store. Construction dust clung to the walls and chunks of plaster and sheetrock lay on the floor. The door closed behind them, and one of the skinheads threw the bolt.

Svoray had supreme physical self-confidence, but he wondered now if the odds weren't against him. He clearly had misread Müller's apparent friendliness. Müller was tall, but skinny, the other two compact. Svoray could take any one of them, he was sure, and all three in succession, but he didn't know if he had the stamina for all three at once. He wondered if he was only going to be robbed.

A door against the far wall opened to a stairwell. Müller pulled a light cord at the head of the stairs and went down, his boots clumping on the wooden steps. As Svoray let the other two men precede him, he saw Müller open a door at the bottom and lean inside. A light blinked on beyond the door, and Svoray descended.

The sight as he entered the basement room sucked his heart into his throat. A huge Nazi flag, the angled black swastika in a white circle at the center of a blood-red field, covered an entire wall. Svoray's skin prickled and his shoulders twitched in an involuntary gesture of revulsion. Müller and the other two skinheads searched his face for a reaction. Svoray understood that he was being tested. What he didn't understand was why.

Beneath the flag, on tables, were spread the contents of a veritable Nazi supermarket. Some of the items seemed to be military reproductions: flared German helmets of the style worn in World War II, the hand grenades that resembled bowling pins, canteens, dress daggers engraved with swastikas. The rest came from an ideologue's souvenir shop. T-shirts, patches, flags, and stickers conveyed nationalistic vainglory, xenophobic hatred, and a sense of German martyrdom. A T-shirt displayed a three-armed version of a swastika with the words *Blut und Ehre.* Blood and Honor. It was the SS slogan. Others said *Deutschland den Deutschen,* Germany to the Germans; *Ausländer raus,* Foreigners out; and White Power.

Survival instinct propelled Svoray to one of the tables. He

picked up a T-shirt picturing a fist, middle finger extended, held it to his body as if checking its size, and turned. "How do I look?"

"Excellent," Müller laughed. "It looks good on you." The other skinheads laughed too.

"This is impressive," Svoray said, putting the T-shirt down and picking up another. He had gotten past his initial sick reaction and saw it as a story for one of his newspapers. It would help pay the expenses of his diamond hunt. "What is all this?" he asked.

"It's a good business," Müller said.

"Who buys?"

"Well, people like you who are interested in history, the true history of the war. And also people who believe in the Nationalistic Front."

"What's the Nationalistic Front?"

"One of our parties. Banned by the Jew-loving politicians who want to give our women to the niggers. But not just the Nationalistic Front. Orders come from all over. What do you think?"

"Very impressive," Svoray repeated.

"So you see now who will clean up the whores and the drug sellers."

"Yes."

Müller turned off the lights, and the ugly souvenirs and relics disappeared into a sanctifying darkness. The four men climbed the stairs, retraced their steps through the construction debris, and emerged into the alley. Svoray seemed to have passed the test and was beginning to have an idea of what awaited him with Schulz.

Gerhard Schulz was a scrawny old man, and he ate as if starving. Svoray sat across the table and watched him saw away at a huge bloody steak. Müller had generously told the man that his friend Ron would buy supper; Schulz had chosen a steak house called Churrasco, a chain restaurant with red tablecloths and napkins and a salad bar piled high with greens, sauerkraut, and a variety of pickles. It was just the three of them. The other two skinheads had gone on their way.

They ate in silence for a while. Svoray took note of the frayed collar on Schulz's white shirt, the narrow tie, the worn dark suit a generation old, the prominent nose, the gray-white stubble on his cheeks and chin. Schulz clutched his fork in his fist as he sliced the meat, but his hands were delicate. They were fine and slender, the kind of hands a musician or an artist would have.

At last Müller sopped up his steak drippings with a piece of bread, washed it down with a swallow of beer, and sat back. Schulz sat back as well. He sensed a ruby drop of steak blood trembling on the point of his nose, wiped it with the back of his hand, and looked at Müller. He nudged his empty beer mug and inclined his head toward Svoray with a question on his face.

"Sure," said Svoray, interpreting Schulz's expression for himself. He signaled the waiter.

When the beers came, Müller spoke to the old man in German. Svoray understood a little, and he caught snatches of his story about looking for buried diaries in Sarreguemines. Schulz seemed to listen carefully, nodding at regular intervals. Gradually his face wrinkled in a look of puzzlement. When Müller finished speaking, he shook his head and said something back to the younger man.

Müller said, "Herr Schulz says he does not know how you got the impression he was at the border near the end of the war. He was not close to the border and so he knows nothing at all about the fighting there."

"What?" Svoray was furious. "I don't believe this. It wasn't my impression he was at the border. You knew what I was looking for, and you said this guy could help. I came all the way to Frankfurt to get jerked around like this?" He looked at his watch, wondering if there was any kind of flight to Tel Aviv at this late hour. It was seven in the evening.

"But if you are interested in history he can tell you other stories about the war," Müller said, ignoring Svoray's outburst. "He can tell you about the Jewish-American propaganda that you call history."

"Propaganda? You're kidding."

Schulz spoke directly to Svoray in German. His voice carried an old, defeated bitterness. Müller translated. "He says he forgot you were American. You were raised on this propaganda."

"What propaganda? Does he think he won the war? I've got news for him." Svoray's temper was starting to get the best of him. The trip was a waste, he'd been dragged to some kind of

Nazi warehouse, and now this. He looked straight at the old man. "Let me tell you something, pal. You lost."

The young skinhead answered in a low but fervent voice. "Yes, the Reich lost and was crucified for it. Germany is still being crucified. But Herr Schulz can tell you that the so-called Holocaust is lies and propaganda. That's the propaganda that he means. There is much proof of this." He told Schulz what he had said, and the old man gave a vigorous nod.

"Why are you telling me this?" Svoray demanded.

"Because you are interested in history. Because you seemed to want to know the truth."

And because I said I would pay for information, Svoray thought. He tried to decide what to do. It was too late to catch a flight. This had nothing to do with the diamonds, but something in him wanted to know how far it would go. "How do you know all this?" he asked, with the innocence of an impostor.

Müller leaned close, then sat up sharply as the waiter appeared, hovered, and then moved on. Müller looked around to make sure he could not be overheard from other tables, then leaned in again. "Herr Schulz knows the truth because he served at a KZ during the war."

"A KZ?" Svoray was lost.

"A camp. A concentration camp."

Svoray stared at the old man, who, smiling a thin-lipped smile, tipped his fresh beer mug to Svoray in a kind of salute.

"He can tell you about the Totenkopf units of the Waffen SS," Müller continued.

The SS Totenkopfverbände, the Death's Head formations, were the concentration camp guard units, drawn from the toughest Nazi elements. Their commander, Theodor Eicke, preached strict obedience and suggested that SS men with pity in their hearts retire to a monastery.

"He served at a concentration camp, and he says the Holocaust is propaganda?" Svoray was unable to suspend disbelief.

Müller chuckled nastily. "You see?" he said. "You have been indoctrinated." He spoke to Schulz in an undertone, listened briefly, then turned back to Svoray. "The camps were for criminals and enemies of the Reich, not innocent people. Some were executed for their crimes. Others bore diseases. They were filthy.

Typhus, tuberculosis, dysentery. Nobody killed them. They died." He shrugged.

"Where was he?" Svoray asked.

Müller almost whispered, "Buchenwald."

Svoray dammed up a flood of emotions and forced himself to remain calm. He seemed to be in the middle of a nightmare evoked by the very name. Buchenwald was technically a concentration, not a death, camp, but the distinction hardly mattered. Prisoners had perished by the tens of thousands from slave labor, starvation, and disease. Gypsies were forced to drink seawater as a medical experiment to see how long they would survive. The commandant's wife, known as the Bitch of Buchenwald, brutally whipped prisoners as she rode through the camp on horseback. She made lampshades from tattooed human skin. Part of Svoray wanted to curse Müller and Schulz and walk away, but he was drawn onward by a grim fascination. There was no hint of remorse from Schulz, nothing of apology. Svoray felt that he had turned a kind of corner, away from the diamonds, to a destination that was unclear.

"Herr Schulz wants to know if you are interested in documents."

"Documents?"

"He wants to sell his *Soldbuch*. To help the movement."

"Does this movement have a leader?" Svoray was playing the moment now, seeing where it would go.

"There is someone. I don't even know his name, but he is waiting for us to gather strength."

"Tell me more about this book."

"Ron, are you sure you're not with the Verfassungsschutz?" Müller was talking about Germany's Office for the Protection of the Constitution. Charged with internal security, the agency monitored extremists from the Red Army Faction of left-wing terrorists, successors to the 1970s Baader-Meinhof Gang, to the skinhead and neo-Nazi groups.

"What is that, the cops? Of course not."

"His *Soldbuch*. Paybook, technically, but you could call it a soldier-book. It's a full record of his service," Müller said. "Many were destroyed after the war, when the Allies were hunting war criminals. Because of that it's very rare. So are you interested?"

"Yes, of course I'm interested in documents if they can help me in my research," Svoray said. "Does he have it? Can I see it?"

"Oh, no. He could not bring it out in public. Besides, it is too valuable. Worth many thousands of dollars. Are you still interested?"

"I don't know. Let me think about it." Svoray suddenly felt very tired. The evening had stretched into a long, gray twilight. His charade burdened him. It was becoming too difficult to keep silent in the face of Schulz and Müller, and he wanted to get to the hotel and take off his mask. He thought he might have to study himself in the mirror to understand who he had become. He stood up and, giving Müller his room number at the hotel, said, "Call me tomorrow."

Schulz stood too. He spread open his suit jacket, stuffed his shirttail into his pants, and adjusted himself before sitting down again.

Müller followed Svoray into the street. "There is a meeting of a movie group tomorrow night," he said. "You should come. They'll see a very special film that I helped edit. I'd like to know what you think." A blinking neon sign from somewhere shone on his scalp through the stubble of his hair and added a rhythm to the darting of his eyes.

"Let me sleep on it," said Svoray. He had to get away. The skinhead had begun to feed a turbulent emotion in him that he couldn't name.

Three

WHEN HE CALLED room service to ask for fresh fruit, the woman at the desk offered to send someone to the stand at the Hauptbahnhof. A teenage boy came to his door half an hour later and presented a bag containing bananas, apples, and a bunch of red grapes. As Svoray rummaged through his pockets looking for change he asked the boy where he was from.

"Turkey," he said, standing shyly by the door.

"When did you come?"

"Two years," the boy said in halting English, placing himself among the flood into western Europe from the east and northern Africa and, more recently, from the ethnic wars of what had been Yugoslavia. The Rostock firebombings had been aimed indirectly at the bellhop. It was he Müller wanted to exclude when he said "Germany for Germans." The Turkish bellhop and Svoray the Jew would go. How many others? And by what means? Svoray gave up searching for coins and gave the boy a bill, waving off his protests that it was too large. At the same time a starchily dressed couple came from the elevator past his door to the next room.

The boy took the money and headed for the elevator. The couple paused at their door. "You gave him too much," the woman said in English.

"It doesn't matter. I wanted the fruit," Svoray said.

"But he will expect more from everyone. And even more of them will want to come here. There are too many now."

"No, he won't. He'll just think I am a generous big tipper. Which at the moment I am." He closed the door on the couple's disapproval, drew the curtains, and fell onto the bed with his clothes on.

He reeked of stale cigarettes and beer from the pub. He was aware of an overpowering headache. He nibbled at the grapes the boy had brought, but put them aside and picked up the phone.

He dialed the number in Tel Aviv with anticipation. After nine years of marriage and three children, Yaron still loved Michal as he had when they first met. They were like one person; he was the schemer and dreamer, she reined him in with her reason. When he was away he called her daily and sometimes several times a day. They had just returned to Israel that summer because after eight years, they had had enough of life in New York. And he had practically left her at the airport with the children and the suitcases to renew his search for the diamonds.

"*Shalom,* Michali," he said when he heard her voice on the line. They spoke in Hebrew, the language of their youth. He pictured her brown eyes and auburn hair and easy smile.

"*Shalom,* Yaroni. Where are you?"

"Um, Frankfurt."

"Frankfurt?"

"Yes. There's someone here I had to meet."

"Is it bad?" she said.

"Why do you ask?"

"I don't know. You sound upset." She had always been able to read him in a few words.

"I've met people I cannot describe," he said.

"That bad?"

"Yes. Tell me, what are you doing? Are the kids asleep?"

"I've just put them to sleep."

"Wake them, will you? I want to be sure they're okay."

"They're okay," she said. "Let them sleep. Tell me about it. You sound terrible."

He told her he had met an SS guard from Buchenwald.

"I want you to leave," she said.

"I can't," he protested. "I can't get away until tomorrow."

"I want you to leave tonight."

"There's no way. No more flights. I have to stay tonight." Svoray could not explain what was keeping him there. He said, "I'll leave as soon as I can," then hung up the phone and fell asleep.

Svoray woke up in his stinking clothes, his head throbbing. He turned the shower on and stripped. He stood before the bathroom's full-length mirror, studying himself. A white coil of scar tissue shone below his right knee, a bullet hole from a raid on the PLO in Lebanon. He turned around to view the other bullet hole, this one in his right calf, from another raid against the PLO. The mirror also showed a shrapnel scar over his left eye. He was a survivor, and a child of survivors.

His father was born Heinz Sobersky in Berlin in 1925. Heinz's father, Carl, was a veteran of World War I who earned an Iron Cross fighting on the Eastern Front. By 1938 that no longer mattered, and the Soberskys fled Germany as Hitler stepped up his campaign against the Jews. They arrived in Palestine that September, two months before Kristallnacht unmasked the Third Reich's true intentions. Ten years later he married Rita Stern. Her family were Rumanian Jews from Czernowitz who had lived in Cairo and were Egyptian citizens. They naively returned to Czernowitz—now Chernivtsi in southwestern Ukraine—for their regular summer vacation in 1940. That summer Rumania joined the Axis and passed anti-Jewish laws, enforced by the Iron Guard. Germany occupied Rumania that fall, and the family was cut off. They remained for three harrowing years, protected by their wits and their Egyptian passports, until they managed to escape through Turkey to Palestine.

Heinz Sobersky became Yehuda Svoray. Rita Stern was known as Rachel. When Yaron, their first child, was born in 1954 they lived in a remote kibbutz in the Negev Desert near the Gaza Strip. Young Svoray was nineteen when he entered the Israeli Defense Force in 1973. Two months later he was fighting for his life in the Yom Kippur War. The conflicts and skirmishes that followed took him on raids into Syria, Jordan, Lebanon, and the Egyptian Sinai, and left their residue of scars.

Maybe today you'll figure out what you're doing here, Svoray thought. Then his image disappeared as steam crept across the mirror, and he climbed into the shower.

The pulsing water cleansed the smell of ashes that was in his nose and eased his headache. He let it run a long time, but it failed to cleanse his thoughts or provide an answer to his questions. Toweling himself afterward, shaving and dressing in fresh clothes, he still could not decide whether to stay or go. After calling Müller and receiving no answer, he decided to take his indecision to the streets.

Some kind of inertia was keeping him in Frankfurt. He believed now that Müller had known from the start that Schulz could not help him find what he was looking for. Müller had seen dollar signs, as much for himself as for any movement. But it was this so-called movement that now interested Svoray, and the shadowy leader to whom Müller had referred. He had seen the snout of something large and ugly. It fed his curiosity and sense of outrage.

Know your enemy, he thought. We can learn from our enemies. Learn—this time—to kneecap them before they grow too strong.

He picked his way toward the Zeil, where he bought presents for the children. If he was going to write a story, he would have to stay in touch with Müller. And what of Schulz's *Soldbuch?* Was the man a war criminal? Would the book expose him? He'd love to have a hand in bringing a Nazi war criminal to justice. How many were left, after all?

Laden with small packages, he returned to the hotel and inquired at the desk for messages. There were none. Forget it, he thought as he rode the elevator to his floor. I'm getting out of here right now, today.

He was about to call the cashier to prepare his bill when the phone rang.

"Ron, it's Charlie. What do you think? Do you want to buy the *Soldbuch?*"

An SS man from Buchenwald. Svoray's thinking changed again. "I still don't know. I don't have so much money with me. I think I could find a buyer, though. I'd like to keep in touch."

"That's good. That's okay. Will you come tonight to see the movie?"

Svoray drew a ragged breath. He didn't want to spend another night in Frankfurt. But Müller was his entry point, and Svoray would need him if he decided to do more. What was one more night?

Müller was wearing the same nylon bomber jacket he'd worn the day before, but instead of black jeans he had on camouflage pants stuffed into a pair of black paratrooper boots laced up high. He'd shaved his head anew. "This way," he said, and started walking.

They had gone several blocks from the meeting point—the same porno store from which Müller had led him to the basement stash of Nazi materials—when Müller turned past a steel gate into an alley. Svoray followed, wrinkling his nose at the odor of stale urine. Müller turned right, then right again, his boots clomping loudly on the concrete, and they emerged into a parking lot that appeared to be a cul-de-sac. Svoray looked for an escape route and saw none.

Three cars were parked beside a dark building that looked as if it housed insurance offices. A door at the corner of the building opened to a service stairwell, and they trudged up several unlit flights. Svoray's lungs were bursting before Müller entered the fifth-floor corridor and walked to the last door on the right.

He knocked and the door opened a crack, then swung wide. A young man, dressed like a waiter in black pants, a white shirt, and a bow tie, nodded them into the room. Beyond the entry foyer, Svoray saw identical high-backed chairs arranged facing a screen. Next to each, ashtrays and Styrofoam cups stood on small white-topped tables. The room resembled a reading room at a private club, oddly cheapened by the foam cups. A projection machine stood behind the chairs.

"Where is everybody?" Svoray wanted to know.

"They'll be arriving soon," Müller said. He looked at his watch. "Very soon. No one will be wanting to miss this." He leaned to Svoray and said confidentially, "We have the movie for only one night. They will be paying one thousand Deutschemarks apiece. Ah!" He turned to the sound of knocking.

The attendant opened the door and two men walked in. One was in his fifties, silver-haired, the other in his late thirties, with brown hair combed straight back from his forehead. The attendant took their coats and carried them somewhere to hang them.

Müller, acting deferential, offered the men drinks from a small bar. They both wore quasi-military dress, the younger man a military-style tunic belted at the waist, the other a tunic with a Sam Browne belt across his chest; both wore trousers with sharp creases. They looked at Svoray without curiosity.

Five more men arrived within ten minutes. They, too, were dressed in versions of military garb in khaki, black, and gray; two wore armbands with curious tilted crosses that were not quite swastikas.

Svoray watched from the back of the room with an observer's detachment. Each man paid his thousand marks in large bills, then took one of the chairs placed a discreet distance from the next.

As Müller moved from man to man, holding out a box of tissues, each man pulled several tissues from the box and then found somewhere on his person a tube of lubricating cream. Their mouths hung open with anticipation. The men clearly planned to masturbate. This is too weird, Svoray thought, as he heard Müller introducing him in German. Müller described him as an American filmmaker and an expert on German films.

"So perhaps tonight he will learn something new," he added in German.

The men laughed and nodded their approval. Müller, continuing in German, talked for a few minutes about film versus videotape editing, then motioned to the attendant to dim the lights.

Wagner's "The Ride of the Valkyries" swept into the dark room, faded, and then a scratchy black-and-white film came on the screen without a soundtrack or preliminary titles. Svoray's complacence died quickly as the screen reflected men in motorcycle jackets, wearing handkerchiefs tied as masks across their faces, and a terrified young girl. They were someplace in the American desert. The girl was dark, perhaps Mexican. She may have been eight, or ten, or a small thirteen, and she fought and dragged her feet, but she was helpless as the men yanked her like a rag doll into some kind of shack. They slapped her to quiet her. Svoray's knees buckled as the men began systematically to sodomize and rape her. He clung to the back of an empty chair, but he heard clearly the sound of zippers being lowered and felt the heat rise in the room and sensed the urgency of movement.

In response to the horror on the screen, Svoray began to hum silently.

He sang to himself, in Hebrew, a Jewish martyr's poem that had been set to music. Hannah Senesh was a Hungarian teenager who had escaped to Palestine before the war. She volunteered to parachute into Yugoslavia as part of the British army's Jewish Brigade in 1944. She was captured entering Nazi-held Hungary, where nearly three hundred thousand Jews had already been sent to the death camps; she was imprisoned, tortured, and executed. Every Israeli schoolchild knew "Blessed Is the Match," the brave, fatalistic poem she had left before departing, but Svoray sang words she had written earlier, to life:

> God—may there be no end
> to sea, to sand, . . .

In the corner of the screen a hand drew a long knife from a boot.

> water's splash,
> lightning's flash,
> the prayer of man.

Svoray sang the words over and over.

Some of the men waited to consummate themselves until the girl's blood spilled. It was useless for Svoray to close his eyes; the images of her violation burned inside his eyelids. He sang on silently. The scene shifted. The soundtrack of Riefenstahl's *Triumph of the Will*, with its stirring drumbeats and military bugles, poured into the room, and the image of Adolf Hitler appeared on the screen. The dictator's rantings were intercut with shots of young girls looking up adoringly, as if they were on their knees before him.

As in a dream, Svoray heard Müller beside him. "This is my editing. Pretty good, eh?" Nazi flags filled the screen, a passage from "The Ride of the Valkyries" repeated, and then, mercifully, it ended.

In the black silence, Svoray could hear rustlings as the men adjusted their clothing. His heart beat queasily high in his chest and he had almost vomited, but now he was choked with rage.

The men were standing when the lights came on. They clapped and stomped their feet and nodded their appreciation, as Müller retrieved their coats. The silver-haired man in the cross-belted tunic held out his hand to Svoray as he left with his companion. Svoray gripped his fingertips, then looked for a place to wash his hands. When only Svoray, Müller, and the attendant remained in the room, Müller said eagerly, "Well, what do you think?"

Svoray's detachment reappeared, settling over him in a blanket of calm purpose. Two days ago he had been concerned with finding the diamonds and making himself rich. Since then he had encountered monstrosities that had angered him beyond any thought of wealth. He saw with great clarity a new path that lay ahead.

"Excellent job, Charlie," he said, smiling. "Excellent job."

"Do you really think so?"

"Excellent job," he repeated. Shaking off Müller's suggestion that they go out for a beer, Svoray returned to his hotel, gathered his luggage, and checked out. He drove all night to Paris and caught a morning flight to Tel Aviv and home.

November 1992

Four

RABBI ABRAHAM COOPER cradled the telephone in his office in Los Angeles. He sat quietly for a moment, thinking. Then he picked up the phone again and punched the number of an extension on the floor below. "Is he in?" he said. Then, "Have you got a minute? I've got something interesting."

The wall beside him rattled with a burst of laughter. The adjoining room was filled with students of the yeshiva that shared the building with the Simon Wiesenthal Center. The center had outgrown the yeshiva that Cooper had helped found when he came to Los Angeles from Vancouver with Rabbi Marvin Hier in 1977 as a young man of twenty-seven. It had practically outgrown the building on West Pico Boulevard.

Classrooms and offices stood side by side within, engulfed by the comings and goings of students and the harried staff. Cooper walked down the dingy hall and descended an open staircase through the atrium-like lobby to the first floor. Two white-shirted young men rushed toward him, deep in a discussion about grades, fringes of their tzitziot flapping at their waists. He let them pass, and entered Hier's office.

Hier looked up, his face alive with curiosity. He was the Wiesenthal Center's founder and dean. The center existed in his image, which was single-minded and insistent. It carried on the work of its namesake, the baggy-eyed Viennese architect and Holocaust survivor who was legendary for tracking down hundreds of Nazi war criminals. The center also was an international gadfly that monitored anti-Semitism throughout the world. Its job, according to its mailings, was "like that of a forest-fire spotter who scans the far horizon for telltale wisps of smoke." Spotting the evidence, the center would create publicity, rouse public opinion, lobby politicians, whatever it took to call attention to the problem. Such loud activism was part of the mandate laid down by Wiesenthal in exchange for his good name. One of the center's first acts was assembling a lobbying blitz against a proposed West German statute of limitations on Nazi war crimes. The legislation was defeated.

"What?" said Hier. Even in the single syllable, his voice was gravelly and redolent of New York's Lower East Side and the Jewish tenement and street life that began there in a wave of turn-of-the-century immigration. Hier's parents came from Poland; his father worked as a lamp polisher after arriving in New York in 1917. When Hier was born, in 1939, the old tenements were closed but a large community of observant Jews remained. He grew up among thread shops and kosher delicatessens and attended the oldest parochial school yeshiva in the country, Rabbi Jacob Joseph, located on Henry Street, where he was ordained in 1962. It was a *hamische* neighborhood, warm, family-like, comfortable. But he abandoned it soon after ordination. At twenty-two, with a nineteen-year-old wife, the new rabbi left to serve the small Jewish community in Vancouver, British Columbia. They stayed for fifteen years and had two children. When he outgrew Vancouver, Hier, with his family, headed south to Los Angeles to start a small yeshiva and museum that grew into the Wiesenthal Center.

Large, squarish, gold-rimmed bifocals sat on the crest of his nose as he waited to hear what Cooper had to say. His face was elfin; his eyes were permanently crinkled at the corners in an attitude of mirth, and if he were a child you'd start looking for a match in the toe of your shoe. But it was a mistake to take Hier any way but seriously.

"I just had a call from Mark Seal at the JTA in New York," Cooper said. The Jewish Telegraphic Agency was the international Jewish wire service. "He has a guy he says we should meet, a journalist who came to him with an idea for a story."

"What's the story?" Hier asked.

"He was in Germany doing something else, and he met some neo-Nazis. He thinks he can find out more about them."

Hier ran a hand through his dark hair, a habitual movement that made his wavy forelock stand up over the rim of his black yarmulke. He said, "And he wants us to sponsor him, I bet."

People were always approaching the Wiesenthal Center with schemes for exposing some new facet of the Nazis; most of the schemes amounted to requests for paid vacations. In 1979, when the center offered a million-dollar reward for information that would lead to the arrest of Josef Mengele, fortune hunters appeared from everywhere saying they had seen the Nazi death camp doctor only yesterday and could track him down if the center would put them on retainer for unlimited periods of time. Mengele, as it turned out, had died that year.

Cooper fingered the corners of his short gray beard. He had known Hier a long time, trusted his instincts, his quick grasp of situations. Cooper had been a student at Yeshiva University when he was sent to help the Jewish youth program in Vancouver in 1971. It was his intention then to attend law school. Hier's charisma helped lead him instead into rabbinical studies. "I spared the world another Jewish lawyer," Cooper liked to say. Now, at forty-three, he was the perfect complement to Hier: Hier the often mercurial inspiration, Cooper the implementer who turned inspiration into action.

"Well, no," he said. "Apparently he'd only barely heard of us. He wanted to do stories for the JTA."

"So why doesn't he?" Hier fidgeted in his chair, holding his nervous energy in neutral.

"It's not really what they do," said Cooper. "They've got a few stringers, but they don't sponsor investigative stories. And this would cost some money, which they don't have."

"Money." Hier ran a hand through his hair again and steadied his yarmulke on the crown of his head.

"Somebody he met is peddling a document. An SS soldier-book. The guy served at Buchenwald. You know, Moish, it could be what we've been looking for." "Moish" was a nickname only Hier's closest friends could use.

Hier stopped fidgeting and looked at Cooper. They had talked about the explosion of neo-Nazi and right-wing skinhead violence in Germany. Since the Berlin Wall fell, it had been increasing. In the post-Communist euphoria, no one brought up the Nazi past. Hier was concerned about the oversight. As far as he could tell, the reams of reunification documents failed to mention the word *Nazi*.

"I am not among those in the cheering section applauding the rush to German reunification," Hier wrote in a letter to West German Chancellor Helmut Kohl, raising the spectre of a Nazi resurgence. Kohl, who had spoken at Simon Wiesenthal's eightieth birthday dinner in New York and was cordial with Hier, responded testily: "Relentless political pressures to combat right-wing extremism will continue in a unified Germany." The exchange made front-page news.

By 1992, it seemed as if Hier had been looking at a crystal ball. Foreigners were the new Jews, subjected to arson and sometimes bomb attacks, beatings, robbery, and abuse. The police moved slowly to protect them. In Rostock, for example, warnings that an incident was brewing were ignored. Hier believed that the string of incidents called Kohl's promise into question.

Wiesenthal Center researchers had learned during the past summer that a Ku Klux Klan organizer in Oklahoma, Dennis Mahon, had met in Germany with skinheads and extremist groups. Hier wondered if there was a connection. He wondered if there was some guiding hand at work. He and his staff had puzzled over the best way to approach the problem.

Hier's desk was piled as high as a medieval banquet. He pushed some papers out of the way and leaned forward as Cooper settled in one of the armchairs across from him.

"Does he have a plan?" Hier asked.

"The proposal he made to the JTA was to get back in touch with the people he met and just find out as much as he can," Cooper said. "The document could turn out to be a bonus."

"A war criminal?"

"Maybe."

"Who is the guy?"

Cooper's rounded, open face grew troubled. "That's a problem, Moish. He's an Israeli."

"An Israeli? A Jew? Never." Hier waved the idea out of existence. "We could never put an Israeli in that situation." He swiveled in his chair and faced the wall of books behind the desk. The value of a Jewish life was paramount. The history of the Holocaust echoed with the debates of rabbis in the ghettos over such impossible questions as whether to send some Jews for "relocation" in order to save others. But that same history also told the tales of martyrs such as Hannah Senesh and the heroes of the Warsaw Ghetto, to whom the struggle against Nazism was more important than their lives.

"I know," Cooper said.

"Does he have a wife? Kids?"

"I think so, yes."

"It would be wrong. He'd be in danger. These people could find out who he is and kill him. If anything happened to him, it would be on our heads."

"I know," Cooper repeated patiently. "But Seal thinks he could handle himself. Apparently he's done some police work. He says we at least should meet the guy and hear him out."

"He vouches for him?"

"Yes."

Hier leafed absently through some of the papers mounded on his desk. He picked up an architect's drawing of the center's new museum, Beit Hashoah–Museum of Tolerance, that was nearing completion next door. The fifty-million-dollar building of glass and pink marble was scheduled to open in February. It was already early November, and both Hier and Cooper were sandwiching their other duties among the museum preparations. Cooper waited. Hier stared at the drawing, then put it down again. "It won't hurt to have someone talk to him, I guess," he said. "Better do some checking first."

Svoray located the rental in the second row of cars, tossed his bag onto the seat, and climbed inside. Following directions from the guard at the gate, he found La Cienega Boulevard and headed north toward the Hollywood Hills.

Flying to Los Angeles had been an impulse, putting more stress on his credit cards and his bank manager's indulgence. But Svoray had been too troubled after the meeting in New York to do anything else. After almost two hours of answering questions for the man from the Wiesenthal Center's office there, what he had heard sounded like "Don't call us, we'll call you."

They had met at the Jewish Telegraphic Agency. A large bottle of antacid pills held center stage among stacks of papers on the desk in Mark Seal's office. The Wiesenthal Center's man was named Mark Weitzman, and he said that Yaron was the name he had given to his firstborn son.

"Do you speak German?" Weitzman asked.

"No. But my parents spoke it, so I understand a little. Don't worry. I can find translators."

"What are you going to do about your accent? Most people would mark you as an Israeli right away."

"Most native English speakers, but if English is a second language, no. Nobody picked it out when I was there."

"You don't look German."

"You noticed." Weitzman let the sarcasm pass. "No, I don't," Svoray continued. "I have an Australian passport, since I lived there with my parents. It's a continent of immigrants, and so I really could be from anywhere."

"You would use the Australian passport?"

"Yes."

"And your story?"

"Right-wing Australian journalist doing freelance reporting for the American market. In Germany to look at the movement and report the good news to the true believers at home."

"What do you know about the right? Do you know any of the players? And where have you been in the right wing? You'll be coming out of nowhere."

"My enthusiasm will make up for that. I'm a new convert. I'll be so over the top no one will question me. And if they do, I'll convince them. It won't be hard to learn some names. You have a research department, right?"

And so it went. Weitzman and Svoray had done the talking while Seal sat by proprietarily.

"I don't know," Weitzman had said, finally. "I'll talk to the rabbis in Los Angeles. It's up to them what they want to do. Then I'll call Mark and he can get in touch with you."

Now, driving through L.A., Svoray willed himself to overcome his impatience. He thought back to the time he had spent at home after leaving Germany. The image of the murdered girl in the snuff film had haunted him—even Michal and the children could see that he wasn't his usual self. Michal had agreed with him that he had to find a way to tell this story. If it meant the inconvenience of flying across the continent to be vetted by higher-ups at the Wiesenthal Center, so be it. He just hoped they wouldn't stop him.

Five

ABE COOPER drove to work after the Veterans Day holiday brimming with news. Mark Weitzman had wasted no time in calling him the day before. He hadn't walked the dog, lit the barbecue grill, or played catch with his son after he got home to Westchester from the meeting at the Jewish Telegraphic Agency. Instead, Weitzman had gone straight inside and called Cooper in Los Angeles. He said he'd been impressed.

"Tell me," Cooper had said.

"He's a serious guy. He's motivated. He's quick on his feet, smart. And he can handle himself. I thought at first he was fat, but he's more, I don't know, solid, like a bull. I think it's worth your meeting him."

"What's the down side?" Cooper had asked.

"Well, he's not the blond god of Hitler's dreams. He sounds like an Israeli. He doesn't know a lot of German, or much about the neo-Nazi movement. His plan's sort of loose. But it's worth a meeting whenever you can get him out there."

Cooper reached his office and immediately put in a call to Marvin Hier. The dean was out, but Cooper didn't have time to be disappointed. He spent the morning going over plans for his piece of the new museum, the multimedia center. As he pored over descriptions of the tens of thousands of photos, videotape segments, maps, and bits of text the computers would present at a click on the strange device known as a mouse or a fingertip pressed against the screen, he lost track of time. When his secretary rang him to say he had a visitor, he was surprised to discover it was early afternoon. In the next moment, a stocky figure filled his office doorway.

The figure, wide as a barrel, walked in and announced, "My name is Yaron Svoray."

Cooper was puzzled for a moment. Then his conversations with Weitzman and Mark Seal came to him. He said, "You're the Israeli guy, right?"

"Right," said Svoray. "Yaron Svoray."

"We didn't expect you. I'm very busy."

"That's fine. I'll wait."

Svoray returned to the corridor. The lobby was brightly lit and uninviting, so he wandered. Students brushed by him, fleeing between classes. Eventually he found himself on the ground floor before a set of double doors. They opened to a single large room, the museum that the structure next door was going to replace.

He was greeted by a legend printed against a splash of red: "To the memory of six million Jews, men, women and children murdered in the Holocaust, to the five million of other faiths who suffered a similar fate, to the heroes of the ghettos who fought for human dignity, to the few who risked their lives to shield them. To them we dedicate the Simon Wiesenthal Center for Holocaust Studies so that man's inhumanity will not be forgotten, so that it will not happen again. Remember."

The exhibit was more like a class project than a museum, crammed as it was into the one room. Svoray looked at old black-and-white photos of Jewish life in Europe before Hitler, then after the Nazis came to power. One in particular struck him forcefully: a small boy wearing a black coat stood with his hands raised while a hulking SS guard behind him held a rifle. It seemed to signify all the brutality the Nazis had brought upon the Jews.

Elsewhere in the museum were photos from the liberated concentration camps showing wasted corpses stacked like cordwood and a photographic roster of the murderers—Himmler in his glasses, with a mustache and goatee, had a special look of evil— and of the genius the Third Reich drove from Europe in such talents as Piet Mondrian, Arturo Toscanini, Marc Chagall, and

Walter Gropius. Svoray paused for a long time before a model of the Auschwitz II extermination camp at Birkenau, its vast scale almost beyond comprehension.

As he waited, he knew that he must not let the rabbis tell him no.

Returning to Cooper's office, he tapped on the door and opened it. Cooper looked up, and waved him in.

The rabbi's desk was covered with schematic drawings and the pink confetti of telephone message slips. He worked in shirtsleeves. He regarded Svoray with an expression that combined curiosity and frank amusement. "This is a surprise," he said. "Mark Weitzman said we should meet with you, but I thought you'd wait for an appointment. Sit down."

Svoray took a chair in front of Cooper's desk. "I wanted to talk with you directly. It is the only way you can understand what I saw."

Cooper held up a hand to interrupt him. "I got the basics from Mark Seal. You met some neo-Nazis in Germany that you can contact again. Maybe you can buy a document from a concentration camp guard. I have to tell you that with the increasing violence there, we've been looking for a way to find out more about it. Tell me, how do you know Mark? Have you worked with him before?"

Svoray choked back his displeasure at the renewed questioning. "We've talked about stories, but that's all."

"You're a journalist?"

"And an ex-cop. Detective. I've also done some investigation work."

"This can all be verified?"

"Of course."

"You have a family, Mark said."

"A wife and three kids. A girl and two boys. In Israel."

"Parents?"

"They live in Australia now. My father was born in Germany. His father fought in World War One and was decorated with the Iron Cross. They got out in time. My mother's family got trapped in Rumania under the Iron Guard and then the Nazis. It took them three years to escape. Their relatives went up the chimneys. My mother worked for Moshe Dayan when he was in the Knesset.

I could not believe these people still existed in Germany, with their swastikas and brown shirts."

"What's your interest in doing this?"

"If you had seen what I saw there, you wouldn't have to ask that."

Cooper leaned back and patted his blue knit yarmulke, as if he were smoothing his hair. When he turned back to Svoray, he said, "And how do you see our relationship?"

"I'll file dispatches for the JTA, which they'll run later. But I need help. You have people who can tell me who I'm dealing with. What I learn will go into your files. If I buy the document, it belongs to you. I'll need money, for the document and for expenses. Ten or twelve thousand should do it. I want no money otherwise."

"No money? How do you live?"

"I'll be paid for the story." Svoray felt it unnecessary to mention his contract with *Playboy*. The editor, Kevin Buckley, was a friend and had welcomed Svoray's proposal for a story on life among the skinheads. He had not objected when Svoray said he also wanted to approach the Jewish Telegraphic Agency. Such double-dipping—recycling a story for different audiences—happened frequently.

"How long would this take?"

"A week. Ten days."

"Do you have any pictures, papers, anything from this trip you were on that would indicate who you met, what you saw?"

"Nothing," said Svoray. "Either you believe me or you don't. But what do you think, I'm going to come in here like a schmuck just so I can go back to Germany to pal around with these people who masturbate watching a little girl get killed?"

Cooper's eyebrows lifted. People usually talked to rabbis more gently. He rested his chin on his thumbs and tapped the corners of his mouth as he studied Svoray. After a time, he said, "What do you get out of this?"

Before Svoray could reply, the door opened and an agitated Hier burst into the room. He glanced at Svoray, then cried indignantly, "Abe, there's somebody in my parking space."

Svoray looked sheepish.

Cooper said, "This is Rabbi Marvin Hier."

"Are you the dean?" asked Svoray.

"Yes."

"Then I'm in your parking space. I'm sorry. I thought you wouldn't be here."

Hier looked at Svoray with new attention. "This is the guy Mark Seal called about," Cooper said. "Yaron Svoray. He just showed up. But Mark Weitzman called me yesterday and said we ought to talk to him, so I guess it's just as well. What's your schedule like?"

"Don't ask." He shook Svoray's hand and sat down in the chair next to him, in front of Cooper's desk. "So tell me the story," he said. "So far I'm the only one who hasn't heard it."

"The story begins with a story," Svoray said. "I thought it would change my life."

He told Hier about meeting Sam Jacobs at the Israeli bonds dinner, about Sam's story and Svoray's subsequent search for the diamonds, the meeting that led to Charlie Müller in Frankfurt, his tour of the neo-Nazi warehouse, Schulz and his offer to sell his soldier-book to fund "the movement," and Müller's reference to a shadowy leader. Hier listened, nodding from time to time, exchanging glances occasionally with Cooper. As Svoray told about the snuff movie, Hier sat up slowly in his chair, shaking his head. Svoray finished by summarizing his background, including his police experience and undercover work for agencies that included the Bureau of Alcohol, Tobacco, and Firearms and the Drug Enforcement Agency.

"Why do you want to do this?" Hier said when Svoray stopped talking.

"I am the son of survivors. I hate what the Nazis did. This story came my way. It's a good one, and I don't think I can ignore it."

"Then I've got another question for you," Hier said. "Is this more important than your wife and three children, who you may never see again if you wind up in the hands of these neo-Nazis? Don't you think that's worth considering?"

"Of course," replied Svoray. "But you know, you choose a job, something that you want to do, it's your vocation. I've been in danger before, and I will be again."

"Yes," Hier said. "Certain people make their living walking a trapeze wire."

December
1992

Six

NEW YORK CITY was decorated for the Christmas season. A lighted snowflake hung over Fifth Avenue. Cartier was wrapped in its red ribbon, and the big tree at Rockefeller Center glittered with lights above the gliding skaters on the ice rink. A freakish snow of big, wet flakes had come down the day before. Its remnants lingered in the gutters, but the melting snow deterred few shoppers on the second Sunday before Christmas.

A month had passed since the rabbis had agreed to sponsor Svoray's return to Germany. Technically, he would be working for the Jewish Telegraphic Agency, but the Wiesenthal Center was putting up the money. Cooper had set a budget of twenty thousand dollars, far more than Svoray thought he would need. But some of it was for the million-dollar life insurance policy the rabbis had insisted he buy.

"If something happens to you, and your family is left alone, we would feel responsible," Hier had said.

Neo-Nazi violence in Germany had reached a new crescendo in the meantime. A Turkish woman, her ten-year-old granddaughter, and her fourteen-year-old niece were killed on November 22 in a skinhead firebomb attack in Mölln. Mölln is near Hamburg, and the attack there shattered the myth that right-wing skinhead violence was limited to eastern Germany. Nazi-style racism clearly had roots throughout the country.

The Mölln attack was highly publicized, drawing reaction from

Chancellor Kohl and newspapers across Germany and around the world. "There are more and more of the merciless among us, those who do not even find this appalling," wrote the *Frankfurter Neue Presse*. "What are these monsters doing to our beautiful country?" Less publicized were two other incidents on the same weekend, the stabbing death in Berlin of a squatter by a group of neo-Nazi teenagers and the identification of a corpse found in Holland as that of a middle-aged man from Wuppertal, in Germany, who had been beaten, burned, and dumped across the border. The skinheads who killed him thought that he was Jewish.

Kohl called the deaths in Mölln "a disgrace to our country." Significantly, however, he ignored their right-wing nature when he referred to them during a budget debate in the Bundestag later the same week, and he declined to attend the funerals of the victims. But statistics were accumulating that showed just how dramatic the rise in right-wing violence had become, on both sides of the former East–West German border. From January through November 1992, as refugees and asylum seekers poured into Germany at a rate of nearly forty thousand every month, the government counted twenty-three hundred violent acts, from property damage through assault, arson, bombings, and murder. Fewer than fifteen hundred had occurred in all of 1991. At the same time, nazism was creeping further from the closet in more swastika graffiti, straight-armed fascist salutes, and neo-Nazi posters, flyers, and T-shirts like those Müller had shown to Svoray. Such displays were occurring at a rate two-thirds higher than the year before.

"Look for the connections," Hier had said, hunched behind his massive desk and waving his arms like an orchestra conductor at Svoray. "Between the old Nazis and the young; one group of skinheads and another; the right-wing parties and the skinheads. See if there's anything going on between the skinheads and the Ku Klux Klan; we caught a Klan organizer over there last summer.

"Look for a computer game. There's one we've been trying to find, called KZ Manager. Players get points for gassing Turks. And try to buy that document. That could establish a continuum. A young skinhead and an old Nazi trying to get some money for a movement by selling the old Nazi's soldier-book. That's the kind of thing we're trying to find out about."

The meeting had ended with a handshake. "Come back in one piece," the rabbi had said.

Svoray had spent the intervening month in Israel, loving Michal, lavishing attention on the children, and dodging the newspapers that were trying to hire him. The time had gone too quickly. He had returned to New York to pick up the money the Wiesenthal Center was supplying through the JTA and to buy equipment he couldn't get in Israel.

Svoray's shopping took him to Times Square. Past the flickering neon and an undertone of chirps and bleeps that marked a video arcade, he stopped in front of a photo shop that advertised ID cards.

Inside, he found what he was looking for. A display of identification cards covered a Plexiglas room divider. Behind it, instant photo machines occupied a narrow work space. The cards bore official-looking headings like "Employee ID," "College ID," and "Student ID." One version just said "Official Identification Card"; another mimed importance with a pseudo-governmental eagle.

Svoray sat in one of the photo booths, pulled the curtain, and snapped himself twice, then twice more for good measure. He had given some thought to a false name and had already ordered business cards. "Ron" had worked well enough with Müller, and there were so many layers between Müller and the few people in Sarreguemines who knew his real name that he was confident he'd never be found out. But Ron what? It had hit him while he was glancing over comic books at a sidewalk table: Ron Furey. It mimicked his own name and would be easy to remember. It was ideal for the right-wing journalist he intended to portray, not least because *Furey* and *führer* sounded similar. The audacity of it was an added benefit. Svoray, holding the still-wet photos by their edges, chuckled to himself as he walked to the laminating machine to choose the cards he wanted.

Minutes later, he walked from the store with identification as Ron Furey, journalist, and Ron Furey, a writer for *News Time* magazine.

December had brought its early twilight down upon Times Square, brightening by contrast the tiers and cascades of neon

that rose above the streets like mountain walls in a fantastic
dream. Steam trailed from gratings in the street. In the triangle
between Seventh Avenue and Broadway, theatergoers lined up
for discount tickets and dodged the spray from passing taxis.
Pedestrians comprised two groups; the tourists turned their faces
upward to the lights, while the natives kept their heads down and
went about their business. Young men in groups of twos and
threes watched from corners and doorways. Svoray watched them
watching, registered a drug deal going down with the touch of a
hand between a man in a hooded sweatshirt and the driver of a
limousine, saw a pickpocket stalking the crowd around a three-
card monte game and an undercover cop shaking a begging cup
as he huddled in a blanket. He loved the street with a fond
disgust, saw the ballet of underlife to which the untrained eye
was blind. He'd need these instincts when he got to Germany. He
felt the eyes of the young men rake over him, assess him in a
glance for opportunity, reject him as too strong, not lost, not
hungry for some forbidden pleasure, and pass on to other possibilities.

Svoray turned up the collar of his coat and turned down Seventh Avenue. He dodged a tall black man standing with an open
tray of shiny counterfeit watches and walked into the seven-day
copy shop where, two days earlier, he'd placed an order.

"Business cards. Furey," he said to the clerk at the counter,
who wore the turban of a Sikh.

The clerk rummaged among the finished orders and brought
a small box to the counter. A specimen was taped to the top of
the box. Svoray looked at it for a moment and said, "Fine." Then
he looked at it again. "Wait," he said.

The clerk turned from a young woman who was ordering a
copy of what looked like a parking ticket. "No, no, no," Svoray
was saying. "This is wrong. Look." He shoved the sample card
across the counter. "You see?"

Ron Furey was spelled correctly on the card. The trademark
bunny with one cocked ear looked identical to the real thing.
Svoray stabbed a finger at the name. *"Playboy,"* he said. "You've
got *Play Boy."* The clerk looked at him uncomprehendingly. "It's
one word. *Playboy.* You've got two."

"Minute." The man shoved a pencil under the edge of his

turban. He made the woman's copy, handed it to her, and took ten cents.

The clerk stared down at the card and shook his head. "I don't know," he said.

"It's a magazine. One word. Don't tell me you've never read it in the bathroom, eh?"

"Ah, *Playboy.*" The clerk grinned, then shrugged. "I will make new ones." He consulted a calendar pinned beside the cash register. "You can get them Tuesday." He took the box and aimed it toward a trash can.

"No, I can't," Svoray protested. "I have to leave tomorrow night."

"Today is Sunday. Tuesday is the earliest."

"I need them tomorrow or not at all."

The clerk shrugged again and reached to retrieve the box. "I'm sorry. You want to take these?"

Svoray had no choice. He added a handful of the cards to the fake IDs in his green bag, knowing he would have to be careful how he used them.

On the street again, standing with his hiking boots in rivulets of melting snow, he contemplated his remaining tasks. Tonight he would scour all his clothes for laundry tags, removing anything with Hebrew or Israeli markings. Once he did that he could pack. Tomorrow he would make his final preparations.

The day started badly. Mark Seal had a check for him, not the cash that he'd requested. He wasted hours at the JTA's bank, first convincing a skeptical young officer that he was the Yaron Svoray to whom the check was written, then scrawling his cramped signature in cursive English on traveler's checks until his arm was numb. He wrote more fluidly in Hebrew.

It was early afternoon before he left the bank, with little time remaining to buy the gear he needed.

His mood was clouded as he stepped out of a cab on Christopher Street, the boulevard of gay New York in the West Village. It seemed an incongruous location for the Spy Store, but it was just off the West Side Highway, next to an AIDS hostel that a few years earlier had been a fashionable hotel.

He had expected something like the Sharper Image, a trove of toys he could pick through before finding the perfect equipment for his mission. He stepped instead into a small storefront with a few shelves and a couple of small display cases. A tall man with a long face stood behind a counter, talking quietly into a telephone. The sound of a television show came from a back room. A placard on the wall boasted, "If Nixon had come to us, he'd still be President." Another customer, wearing a long, duster-style coat, kept his face averted as he looked at bulletproof vests displayed along one wall.

The long-faced man hung up the telephone and straightened, adding inches to his height. "Help you?" he asked.

Svoray said, "I need something to record, and something to take pictures." He noticed himself in a small video monitor, and looked around for a moment before spotting the camera in what seemed to be a smoke detector.

"Undetected?"

"No, I want everyone to know. That's why I came to the Spy Store and not Forty-seventh Street Photo," Svoray said sarcastically, in the grip of his foul mood.

The man ducked his head and looked at Svoray as if from over reading glasses. He sucked his lips for a minute and then oozed down the counter to a display case. Scattered on a few glass shelves were high-powered binoculars, tiny lenses, multipurpose tools including pliers, knife blades, and the like in a single unit, and miniature cameras. The man slid open the case and handed Svoray a Minox camera. "Is this what you had in mind?" he said.

"I had in mind something invisible," said Svoray.

"This?" He bent down again and drew out what looked like a cigarette lighter.

"No, no, no." Svoray waved the lighter away. "I don't smoke. What would I be doing with a lighter?"

"You tell time, right?" Exasperation had entered the man's voice. He replaced the lighter and handed Svoray what looked like a bulky sports watch.

Svoray took the watch and studied it. He held it up to the Breitling he wore on his right wrist, then turned his wrist this way and that to mimic aiming and taking pictures. "No. Too obvious," he said, handing it back.

"Too obvious?" The man stared at him.

"Yes, because I'm always going to be looking at my watch and holding it at funny angles. Why am I going to be doing that?

Look, show me something serious. What about some kind of a recorder?"

The customer in the long coat pretended not to listen. The salesman replaced the camera-watch, closed the case, and moved back behind the counter to a wall shelf, from which he took a microcassette recorder and some kind of a base station and placed them on the counter. He said in a tight voice, "This is a body wire, the best there is. It's what the FBI uses. The microphone comes out and attaches to a wire. See? You can clip it to your tie, your shirt, whatever. No speaker, so nobody can hear what's on it. You've got an earphone, or there's a speaker in this base set. The tape is ninety minutes."

Svoray picked up the tiny black recorder, smaller and thinner than a pack of cards, and examined it. "How much?"

"Four twenty-five."

Svoray was determined to be displeased with everything he saw. "But it's just a tape recorder. I could get one at an audio shop for half as much."

"Not this one." The salesman's voice grew tighter. "You want serious equipment, this is it. If you don't think this is serious, you came to the wrong place."

"Any audio shop. Less than half."

The man stood to his full height. "You want an audio store, go find one. There's one on every corner."

Another man, compact and wiry, materialized in the door to the back room. "Problem?" he said to the tall man.

"Guy wanted an audio store. He's just leaving."

Svoray groped for a parting insult. He walked out snorting with disgust instead. He stood on the sidewalk puffing clouds of vapor into the cold air, calculating the time he'd need to get to Midtown and Forty-seventh Street Photo, where Hasidic Jews worked in a warren of boxes containing every camera and every tape recorder made and sold them at a discount. The body recorder had been a nice little piece of work. Svoray regretted leaving it.

"What's the deal?" The voice came from beside him.

Svoray looked. Standing there was the man who'd been studying the bulletproof vests inside the store. He was on the other side of forty, but trim, with gray hair and a mustache; he wore jeans and cowboy boots under the long coat. Svoray followed his gaze across the street to a red Porsche. There was something familiar about him, an attitude that separated him from civilians. Svoray took a guess.

"New York cops must do really well," he said. "Cops can't afford Porsches where I come from."

"Where's that?"

"Israel."

"Israel. You a cop?"

"I was a detective with the Central Police Command."

"What happened?"

"I came here and went to college. Then I got involved with other things. My name's Ron." Svoray stuck out his hand.

"Mike," the man said, shaking hands. "Ex-cop. Not New York, Newark." He waved in the direction of the Hudson River and New Jersey on the other side. "Got my disability four years ago in a shoot-out with a crackhead. Still got the bullet." He rolled his left shoulder and grimaced. "Went into security consulting. Maybe I can help you out."

"I'm doing some undercover work," Svoray said. "Not surveillance. I need a camera and a tape recorder I can hide and use while I'm talking to people. I can't say much more about it."

"Want to tell me where?"

"Germany."

"Is this a private deal?"

Svoray smiled. "If not, I wouldn't be here shopping."

Mike nodded thoughtfully, buffing his Porsche with his eyes. "If it wasn't, you wouldn't tell me, either. But listen, I know the guy you need."

"Where is he? I have to leave tonight."

"Over there. He's all over Europe." Mike reached into an inside pocket of his coat. He pulled out a palm-sized notebook and jotted down a number. "Take this," he said. "Ask for Johannes."

"I'm landing in Paris," Svoray said.

"No problem. He'll get to you."

"What about the price? I can still get to Forty-seventh Street."

"The best you'll get. And real stuff. Serious. Hell of a guy, too. Good luck." He stepped off the curb and strode across the street, folded himself into the Porsche, and gunned it as he drove away.

Seven

THE NEXT MORNING, Svoray woke to the sight of winter sunshine on combed hayfields. French villages rose and offered up their details: red tile roofs and church spires and cars crawling along roads set off by rows of trees. Then the concrete of Charles de Gaulle Airport swooped into view and the 747 settled onto the runway.

He made his call from the first phone he saw in the tubes and tunnels of the airport. People moved past him on conveyor belts, like ducks in a shooting gallery. He had thought the number was in Paris, but it proved to be in Switzerland. A woman answered, *"Allo!"*

"Hello," said Svoray. "Is Johannes there?"

She switched seamlessly to English. "Can he get back to you?"

Svoray gave the name Ron Furey and the number of the pay phone and waited restlessly. When the phone rang, he snatched it up and practically shouted into the mouthpiece.

The voice at the other end was young, calm, and uninflected, giving no hint of national origins. "Hello, Mr. Furey."

"I need some equipment," said Svoray. "How does this work?"

"The first thing is, it doesn't work over the phone," the voice said. "You are in Paris, I believe. Where are you heading?"

Svoray described his itinerary to Sarreguemines, from which he intended to enter Germany. Border checkpoints had fallen as

Europe moved toward a common marketplace. He felt safer renting a car and driving into the country than flying to Frankfurt and presenting his passport to German immigration. It was paranoid, he knew, but he thought the neo-Nazi network would somehow learn of his arrival. He had found in Sarreguemines a crossing point he knew would be unmanned; if he entered there he would be invisible. He would be invisible to the responsible authorities as well, of course, but this did not occur to him.

Johannes answered swiftly, apparently without referring to a map or mileage table. "It will take you four hours to get there," he said. "It will take me five. There is a café just on the German side, the Casablanca—"

"You're kidding," said Svoray.

"No." Johannes sounded mystified. "Why would I be?"

"You don't see the irony?"

"Actually, no," he said, a little sharply and sounding this time like an Englishman.

"Never mind," said Svoray. "How do I find it?"

East of Paris, traffic thinned and the highway rose and dipped in a series of furrows. Woods dotted the landscape between rolling farms. Silhouettes of trees on distant ridge tops stood up like rows of lollipops against the sky. Near Verdun, black pines replaced the open countryside. At Metz, there was a forest of transmission towers. Then Svoray was driving on the familiar streets of Sarreguemines.

Nothing had changed in the time since he had been there last, and everything had changed. Had it been only September? The restaurants and shops now were bright with Christmas decorations. The front windows of the Hotel Alsace glowed with warmth and cheer, while across the street, in front of the town hall, the fall flowers in a mounded bed were wilted and faded from the cold. The changes were not in what Svoray saw, but in his shift of purpose.

He drove the rented Fiat up the hill behind the town, out to the north. Where the road cut between cornfields, he turned off onto a deserted lane. The lane entered a forest of tall trees and twisted into a downhill grade that was carpeted with fallen leaves, then narrowed to a rutted track as the grade steepened. Vines and tree limbs clawed at the sides of the white car, until with a bounce and a last flurry of flailing underbrush Svoray steered onto a paved road that ran among farmhouses. He followed the road through a right-hand turn and over a narrow concrete bridge. A sign on the other side welcomed him to Germany.

The rendezvous point, five minutes away, was out of some Bavarian fantasy. A white chalet with dark beams, it stood by itself at the roadside. A sign at the front advertised a hotel, restaurant, and, in lettering that suggested it had been an afterthought, a pizzeria. Casablanca was the hotel's nightclub, with its own entrance to the side.

Svoray was early. He drove slowly past and looked around: a parking area in front, a driveway leading to the back, no other cars that he could see, no signs of activity. Down the road, a clump of trees cast a wintery filigree of shade from their bare limbs. He parked beneath their overhang and walked into a meadow, where he chose a spot from which he could watch the building unobserved.

The day was warm. Svoray took off his leather jacket and lay back on the grass, using his nylon shoulder bag for a pillow. Cows grazed in an adjoining field. Nothing stirred at the Casablanca. After half an hour, he got up to urinate. He was returning to his spot when he saw a big silver Mercedes turn up the Casablanca's driveway and park behind the building.

The man who climbed out of the car wore shades of violent red and purple. Svoray watched him for a moment, then approached across the field as the man busied himself in the car's open trunk. Svoray was thirty feet away before he was noticed. The man jerked upright. For a second Svoray thought he would produce a gun from the trunk and shoot him. Instead, he grinned.

"Mr. Furey, eh? You gave me a start. I'm Johannes."

He grabbed Svoray's outstretched hand in both of his and pumped it vigorously. In addition to his purple T-shirt and red blazer, Johannes' slacks and shoes were green. He had wavy blond hair and appeared to be in his thirties. He shifted a piece of chewing gum inside his mouth and looked intently at Svoray with deep blue eyes.

"Did you have any trouble getting here?"

"No. I used the bridge at the end of the farm road," said

Svoray. Johannes' wardrobe was distracting him. It was as if Bozo had retired from the circus and taken up golf.

"That's good. My favorite route. Better to avoid a border check with this kind of equipment." He swept his hand in the direction of the trunk. Svoray looked in at three large aluminum cases, one standing with its lid ajar. Wedged into niches in the dark gray foam were listening devices that ranged from small to microscopic.

"I guess most of the border checks are gone," Svoray said.

Johannes kicked a pebble with one of his green shoes, exposing a width of naked ankle. "Why take a chance?" he said. "Now tell me, what are you doing and what do you need?"

"I'm a journalist doing an investigation."

"Aha. The neo-Nazis," Johannes said.

Svoray was dumbstruck. "What makes you think so?"

"What else would it be? Who else is running wild in the streets attacking people and making everybody think of Hitler?" He sensed Svoray's dismay. "Don't worry. I'm a businessman, I don't get involved in politics. So let's see what you need. Do you always carry that bag?"

When Svoray answered that he did, Johannes leaned into the trunk and picked out what looked like a leather-bound datebook. Johannes moved his hands on it like a conjurer until the book opened with a series of clicks to reveal a microcassette recorder. "Where is your car?" he asked. "Can you drive it back here?"

Svoray jogged down to the thicket of trees where he had parked. Pulling up the narrow driveway and parking beside the Mercedes, Svoray noticed for the first time just how vulnerable they seemed. They stood on a patch of pavement at the back of the hotel, hemmed in by an annex that was a row of rooms over garages. Heavy trash bins blocked one end, leaving the driveway as the only route of escape. Although no one could see them from the road, they were visible from any of a dozen windows.

Johannes followed Svoray's eyes to the overhead windows. "We're perfectly safe," he said. "The Germans mind their own business." He peered into Svoray's car, then at him, and said, "I was looking for a coat or something. Is that the jacket you wear all the time?" When Svoray nodded, he said, "May I have it, please?"

Svoray handed him the jacket. Johannes held it up and moved his hands to the collar, where a button was sewn to hold a flap high against the neck. He took a knife from his pocket, snapped it open and cut the button off. Then, sitting in the open door of the Mercedes with an attaché case full of tools, he sliced the button into two wafers with a heated blade. Svoray watched, fascinated, for the next fifteen minutes as Johannes, sometimes peering through a jeweler's glass, fitted a matching button against the back half of Svoray's, inserted some sort of disc into the space between them, and, fumbling for the first time, sewed the button back into place.

"Done," he said, biting off an end of thread.

"What is it?" said Svoray.

Johannes smiled. "One of the simplest listening devices." The smile widened. "Also, one of the most expensive." He explained that the disc would serve as a membrane and its backing a transmitter that would bounce sound to a receiver in the datebook-recorder. "Here, put on the jacket. And the recorder in your bag. Always keep them close together. It hasn't much range." He pressed the upper part of the datebook binding. "Now, what shall we talk about? Not politics, remember. Let's talk about money."

"If this works, I'm going to be very impressed," Svoray said.

Johannes then took the recorder, opened it and rewound the tape, inserted an earphone into a tiny hole in the binding, and let Svoray listen to the conversation they'd just had.

"I'm very impressed," said Svoray.

Johannes gave him some additional cassettes and instructions for opening the recorder, and showed him where on the binding to press to begin recording. Then he opened the second of the cases in the trunk of the Mercedes. This was filled with camera gear. Svoray chose a faceless box that hid in the bottom of his bag, its lens at the end of a flexible wand. Johannes rigged the lens into the clasp attaching one end of the strap of his green bag. "To take a good picture with this, pretend your belly button is your eye," he said.

"Like shooting."

"Yes." Johannes finished with the camera. "Now." He leaned into the trunk, shifted the cases around, opened the third one, and stood back. Handguns and machine pistols nestled in the thick foam pads of the Haliburton case. Svoray identified a nine-millimeter Beretta with a fifteen-shot clip, a long-barreled Colt Python, and a stubby Glock with clips in three sizes. A mini-Uzi with a wire stock completed the arsenal.

"I see why you like unguarded border crossings."

"Oh, I don't cross borders with the guns," Johannes said. "I keep some here, some there. It's bad enough with the cameras and the listening devices. I'll be happy next year, when the borders are gone."

Several knives, both switchblades and fixed-blade models that were sharp on both edges—good for throwing—gleamed in other foam niches. Johannes pulled out a beeper that concealed a twenty-two-caliber three-shot pistol. Other assassin's pistols hid in the barrel of a Mont Blanc pen and in a marine emergency flare gun.

"Do you need one of these?" Johannes asked.

Svoray glanced up, imagining for an instant that something had moved behind one of the overlooking windows. But it was the reflection of a tree limb, pushed by a gust of wind. He looked back at the guns. The temptation was strong to take one from the case, the Beretta, say, and show that he knew how to handle it. But getting caught with a gun could kill the mission and land him in a German jail. A cold shadow of fear suddenly passed over him. He realized he didn't know this man, with his hustle and his splashy clothes, at all. For a brief, panicky moment, he wanted to get out of there. He forced himself to think rationally.

"I don't think so. If I get into a situation that is so dangerous I have to use a gun, then I think it will be too dangerous to use it."

Johannes nodded sagely. "How about this?"

Svoray took the knife Johannes handed him. It was a sturdy switchblade that felt cool and heavy in his hand. He flipped it open. The blade locked. He measured the gleaming steel across his palm; it overlapped by the width of a finger.

"Why not?" he said. "If I get in a knife fight I'll be in deep shit, but at least it's legal."

"Good," said Johannes.

The salesman closed the case, spun the dials of its combination locks, and then closed the trunk. He returned to the front seat and pulled out a calculator. "Tell me," he said, "do you want to buy, or rent?"

A few minutes later, poorer by several hundred dollars for temporary use of the equipment and his credit card imprint taken to ensure its return, Svoray watched Johannes drive down the driveway of the Casablanca and disappear from view.

He spent the night in Saarbrücken, waking twice from a restless sleep to wonder what he'd done in giving Johannes the imprint of his credit card. He drifted away again each time, convincing himself there was no way to connect Yaron Svoray with the character he intended to be, Ron Furey. In the morning, he found a bank branch where he opened an account with his traveler's checks and rented a safe deposit box. For these transactions he presented his Australian passport and used the address of an Israeli he knew who lived in Saarbrücken.

A clerk took him into the vault. She wore a tweed skirt, a fawn-colored sweater, and a scarf artfully draped over one shoulder. Their keys together opened the box in a ritual that was intimate and almost sensual. Then she left him with the open tray, her heels clicking out of earshot on the marble floor.

Pulling a straight-backed metal chair around to a scarred metal table, Svoray emptied his wallet and the pockets of the green shoulder bag onto the table.

As he looked at the markers of his life, he tried to anticipate the days ahead. To be found out as an Israeli would be fatal. He separated his Israeli passport and driver's license and his airline ticket, which was round-trip New York to Israel, and placed them to one side.

His Australian passport, the New York driver's license he had used to rent the car, and the rental papers could be explained in an emergency, he thought. A name change. A pen name. He placed these with his Bank Hapoalim credit card, the fake IDs, and the defective business cards that divided *Play* and *Boy* into two words, and restored them to the green bag.

What remained were more credit cards, video club cards, his *Hadashot* press card, a membership card from the library in Tel Aviv, his ID from the Jack La Lanne health spa in New York, his army reserve card, and the photographs he carried of Michal and the children. The Jack La Lanne membership had lapsed. He crumpled the card and threw it away. The rest he slipped into a manila envelope that he laid in the safe deposit tray. Hesitating, he reopened the envelope, retrieved a photograph of Michal with all three children, and placed it with the items in the shoulder bag.

Now Svoray turned his attention back to the first items. Unfolding a square of heavy aluminum foil, he placed the passport, license, and ticket in the center and wrapped them tightly. He placed that bundle into first one and then a second plastic sandwich bag, folded the bags close and stretched rubber bands around the package.

The tapes were left, and for a long moment he couldn't decide what to do with them. The Israeli music on the cassettes would give him away as surely as his passport with the menorah. He had dubbed Mozart and Bach at the beginning of each tape as a precaution. The kitschy, warbling folk songs of Shlomo-Artzi and Aric Einstein were at least five minutes in. They reminded him of the kibbutz and sing-alongs and the tug of young romance. He threw them in the bag.

He was ready to call the bank clerk back, but something stopped him. He thought for a moment. Then, in the silence of the vault, he dug a notebook out and began to write.

"Will of Yaron Svoray," he wrote in Hebrew. He crumpled the paper and started again with "To my family:

"If anything should happen to me, I want everyone to know I love you.

"To Michal, I know I have not made our life easy, but I don't think if it had been easy it would have been any more fun. You light my way, and when this is through I will follow your light home.

"To Enosh, if you are to be the man of the family, you must be strong and take care of your mother. Try to help her all you can, and remember your father loves you and is proud of you.

"To Ellie, you have to also help your mother and your brothers. And it will be your job to make everybody laugh, which I know you will do because you are so happy.

"To Ohad, you are the baby but you won't always be, you will grow up and then you will have to do your part to help take care of the family, too.

"To my parents and my brother Ori, I want you to be proud of me.

"I am doing this because I think it is important. Because we cannot forget that there are those who hate us because of who we are, and what can happen if we let them get too strong. I don't have much to leave you. Just my love. I'm a little scared. But sometimes you have to do things that make you scared, because they are important.''

Svoray looked back over what he had written. It was maudlin, blushingly sincere, not much as a last will and testament. It made him feel good, though. He folded the paper, wrote ''To my family'' again on the outside, and placed it in the safe deposit box with the envelope.

The clerk was sitting at her desk, a china cup of coffee resting in its saucer at her fingertips. ''I would like my wife to have access to the box,'' he said.

She gave him a paper, which he filled in with Michal's description. Then she returned with him to the vault and they locked the box with the same coordinated turn of the two keys.

Back on the street, he found a post office where he bought a phone card. It was one of the great inventions, the cost of calls automatically deducted from the card as it was used. He called Michal from the first card phone he could find.

''It's starting,'' he said. ''I may not be able to call you every day.'' He told her that a safe deposit key and the address of the bank were on their way to her by mail.

When he returned to the car, he opened the hood and wiped an old T-shirt in engine grime. This he wrapped around the bundle containing his Israeli passport and license and the ticket. Finally, he opened the trunk, lifted its carpeted lining and the cover over the spare tire well. Spinning off the wing nut that held the spare, he raised the tire and placed the grimy T-shirt underneath it with the tools.

He reached Frankfurt two hours later, accompanied by a cold front that rattled the gold weather vane atop the spire of the Katerinenkirche, which stood by the entrance to the Zeil. It was December 16, a Wednesday, nine days till Christmas.

Eight

T HE WIND WAS BITTER. Not everyone had fled the cold, however. At the escalators leading to the U-bahn and S-bahn interchange under Hauptwache Square near the Katerinen-kirche, a group of skinheads huddled out of the wind against a wall. They were drinking beer from large brown bottles.

Svoray stood watching them. He had forsaken the luxury of the Inter-Continental for the more modest Hotel Scala, located on Schäfergasse just off the Zeil. Failing to get an answer at Charlie Müller's number, he had decided to go out. Shoppers were hurrying from store to store along the pedestrian strip, bundled against the knifelike gusts, ignoring the skinheads. After a moment Svoray tugged on his baseball cap and swaggered up to the skinheads. "Hello," he said. "May I talk to you?"

The sound of English caught their attention. They looked at him suspiciously. They seemed to range in age from late teens to mid-twenties, and two or three women were part of the group. The men for the most part wore bomber jackers and black jeans bloused into black combat boots, although two or three wore long field coats in concession to the weather. Their faces were red; whether from the wind or alcohol was hard to tell.

"Get out," one of them snarled in German. Turning to the others, he said, "He's a journalist who got lost looking for Mölln." They laughed at that. Another one said, in English, "We talk when we finish our drinking." This one was tall and loose-limbed. He wore two days' growth of beard, a watch cap, and an army field jacket over a black turtleneck sweater. The laces of his combat boots were white.

"When will that be?"

"Morgen. Tomorrow." His grin dismissed Svoray, and he turned back to his friends.

"What about now? I'm a correspondent for *Playboy.* Ron Furey."

"Playboy." The tall fellow looked at the card Svoray handed him. Speaking to the others in German, he held out his hands to indicate breasts, provoking more laughter. A girl in black leather rocked her hips and vamped with a hand behind her head.

"I'm doing a story on the skinheads," Svoray said.

The tall one leaned into his face. "We are not skinheads. We are students."

Svoray held his ground. "Students? Why aren't you in school?"

The tall young man turned to his friends, again repeating in German what Svoray had said. They responded with derisive laughter.

"Vacation. Christmas. Don't you see?" He turned back to Svoray, waving a hand at the decorations and then getting into his face again. "You're not a Jew, are you?"

The others surrounded him in a close circle. He heard someone whisper, *"Juden?"*

"What if I were?" said Svoray. He shifted his feet to gain a little room.

"You would be rich. All Jews are rich." He looked at Svoray in his parka, his cotton slacks, and his black Nikes. "I don't think you're a Jew," he concluded. He turned to his friends and said in German, "He can't be a Jew. He's not rich."

The girl in leather sneered as if she wasn't convinced. At that moment one of the men pointed across the square. *"Aus-länderin,"* he said. Svoray looked to see a Peruvian flute band, four men and a woman with coal-black hair and bronze faces, wearing heavy thick-knit sweaters, beginning to tune up near the Katerinenkirche. The wind that had peeled away the early clouds from a remote sun and deep blue sky now seemed to be dropping as the day receded. Svoray tried to take some pictures with his hidden camera. When he leaned against the wall that marked the U-bahn entrance, it was possible to actually feel warmth where the sun struck the grainy surface of the concrete. Several of the group moved off in the direction of the Indians.

Svoray breathed easier. "Now that we've cleared that up, let me buy you a beer," he offered. "What is your name?"

"Wilhelm." He peered at the brown bottle in his hand, tipped it up, and watched a trickle of foamy dregs splatter on the paving bricks, then tossed the bottle in the general direction of a trash can.

The two of them drifted to the side door of a tavern that opened onto an alley. Svoray gave Wilhelm some money. He disappeared inside and emerged a moment later with four bottles of beer that he set upon a window ledge. With a Swiss Army knife he produced from his coat pocket, he flipped the caps off two and sent them flying.

Svoray took the bottle Wilhelm offered and felt cold all over again. He took a small swig and set it down.

Wilhelm drank deeply. He moved down the side of the building into a patch of reflected sunshine and turned his face upward.

"So you tell me, Wilhelm," Svoray said. "Are you a skinhead or not?"

Wilhelm lifted his watch cap, revealing a stubble of blond hair.

"Are you a Nazi?"

Wilhelm pivoted his head and stared. "A Nazi?"

"You wanted to know if I was a Jew."

"You know that here in Germany, Nazis are an embarrassment."

"Of course. You killed half the world."

"No." Wilhelm shook his head. "The word. It is an embarrassment like *nigger*. I am not a Nazi. Politics is shit. I am a good German."

"What is a good German?"

A good German, Wilhelm explained, hated Germany's asylum policy and the foreigners it attracted. A good German wanted a clean Germany, one with pure air and water and, especially, streets cleansed of dirty foreign rabble who stole and peddled their women and children, shit in public parks, and cooked their dogs. Wilhelm's Germany was a land of heroes and suffering, a fairy-tale place of industry, towheaded children, and braided pigtails. As he talked, he drank steadily, replacing each empty bottle with a fresh one from the window ledge. Finally he drank what was left of Svoray's.

The sun's reflection passed and the alley fell dark and cold again. Svoray stomped his feet for warmth.

"Here is a piece of information for you," Wilhelm said. He pointed down and said, "My boots, you see the laces? White. That is how we know each other."

"Why white?"

Wilhelm shook his head at such a stupid question. "White is the best color for Germany," he said.

"What group do you belong to?" Svoray asked. "Are there groups? Are you organized? Or is it just something you believe?"

Wilhelm studied the empty beer bottle he held in his hand. He said, "You know, you ask many questions. You should pay me if I am giving you the answers."

"Of course. But what is the story?"

"How do I know you are telling the truth, anyway? You could be with the police."

"That's silly."

The tall youth looked at Svoray almost lazily. His voice took a calculated, nasty edge. "Maybe you are a Jew after all. You ask funny questions. Americans are big friends of the Jews. Or a Turk. Actually, you know, you look like a Turk."

"I'm from Australia."

"You live in America, I think. I bet you love Jews." Just then a shout came from the head of the alley.

"Wilhelm! *Komm!*"

Wilhelm waved his companions into the alley instead. They came in a military trot, just two of them. Wilhelm spoke to them in rapid German. Svoray felt the bricks of the wall against his shoulder blades as one of them, moisture pearled in the fine hairs of his mustache, stepped up to him and swung a fist into his stomach.

The blow took his breath away and froze him. He tried to scuttle sideways, but a second blow landed, digging upward into his solar plexus. As he doubled over, clutching himself, a knee caught his forehead, knocking his cap off. Wilhelm brought the bottle down across the back of his head. Miraculously, it didn't break. Svoray tried to stay conscious and protect himself as someone kicked him once, twice to the stomach. Then a flurry of kicks rained on his back and legs. A moment later he heard their running footsteps and the bottle clinking to the paving stones.

His breath returned in a series of hacking gasps and he tried to sit up. He was alone in the alley, although he could see people passing on the Zeil. No one looked in his direction. He touched the rising knot on the back of his head and looked at his fingers, sticky with blood. The whole thing had taken less than two minutes, the attack startling for its sheer speed, its violence for the sake of sport.

A wave of nausea hit him when he tried to stand. He tried again, more slowly, steadying himself against the wall. In his bag, the recorder and camera seemed intact, though he realized he hadn't been running the recorder. His clothes had scuff marks from the pavement, and there was the print of a dirty boot sole on one pants leg. His cap lay upside down across the alley. Suddenly he realized he was sweaty and shaking, from fear, anger, and the cold.

"Shit," he said. "Shit."

He pulled his coat around him and moved cautiously toward the entrance of the alley. His back was throbbing, his belly tender where the kicks had landed. The clotted blood on his head felt gummy and cold. As he entered the square, he saw the Indians in their richly colored sweaters kneeling around one of their number, who lay sprawled on the pavement. One large drum was turned on its side. A small crowd of bystanders was gesturing angrily and pointing, others were trying to help the shaken band members. Some policemen were approaching at a walk. There was no sign of the skinheads, but he felt their presence.

Back in his hotel room, he stripped and took a hot shower. Afterward, he explored the damage. He had a knot on his head, but no more bleeding. A yellow bruise on his thigh would be blue by tomorrow, but the boots had missed his kidneys and his spine. While he tried to decide what to do, he called Müller again. There was no answer. After several minutes of thinking, he took the phone book from the night table. He looked up the number for one of the Frankfurt papers, *Frankfurter Rundschau*, called, and asked for the police reporter.

The operator spoke English. She asked him to hold. Eventually, a man's English-speaking voice came on the line.

"Yes?"

"My name is Ron Furey. I'm a writer for *News Time* magazine. I'm working on some story possibilities and I need some help. Could we meet?"

There was a long pause. *"News Time,* you say?"

"Yes."

"And what is the story?"

"An investigative story. I'm on a tight budget and you could save me a great deal of time." The silence told Svoray it wasn't working. "I've heard your sources are impeccable. The best. And I'll be glad to share if I learn anything. I just need a starting point. Some names."

"Names of who?"

"Police contacts. I'd like to leave it at that for now."

The reporter reluctantly conceded. "Well, I will be free around seven. There's a pub near the newspaper office. What do you look like?"

"Burly." The reporter's acceptance restored his sense of humor. "Like a Turkish wrestler, I've been told."

"Don't say that. They're not so popular."

The pub was on a street off Hauptwache Square. As he walked stiffly among the package-laden shoppers and crowds hurrying toward the U-bahn, he pondered Müller's disappearance; two more calls had gone unanswered. The few blocks were enough for the cold to seep in again. He almost passed the place before he caught the glow of light and weave of shapes behind a multipaned, steamed window.

He had gained the refuge of the vestibule and was rubbing his hands to warm them when a man in his mid-forties, with thinning hair and a salt-and-pepper beard, came through the door. His clothes were a rumpled caricature of a reporter's. Svoray introduced himself.

The reporter's initials were J.S. "Keep my name out of this," he said.

They fought through the crowd of after-work drinkers at the bar and found a table near the back. The first thing J.S. wanted was to see Svoray's credentials.

"Credentials?" said Svoray.

"Yes. Your press credentials."

Svoray tried to think. His Times Square ID cards weren't made for sophisticated scrutiny. He took one of the *Play Boy* cards from his shirt pocket and slid it across the table. He started to make up an explanation for the typo, but the reporter looked at the rabbit logo, not at the words. He nodded and handed the card back.

"A good magazine. But I thought you said you wrote for someone else."

"*News Time.* But *Playboy,* too. Actually, several magazines." Svoray was beginning to see a slapstick quality in his multiple identities. He would have to settle on one or another. It was too confusing.

But J.S. apparently was satisfied. "Good," he said. "What would you like to know?" He signaled a waiter and ordered a carafe of white wine.

"I'm trying to do something on the far right wing. Basically, I'm looking for a connection between the World War Two Nazis and the neo-Nazis, skinheads, whatever, who are causing all the trouble against the refugees."

"A connection? Interesting. But you know, we don't cover that so much."

"You're kidding. Even after Mölln?"

The waiter arrived with their order. J.S. poured a glassful of wine and lit a cigarette. He studied Svoray through the smoke. "We covered Mölln, of course. But with the lesser incidents, it's more or less a policy," he said.

"What kind of policy?"

"These are publicity seekers, these people. To put them in the paper every time they do some cruel or stupid thing only encourages them to do more."

"But it's a problem, don't you think?"

"Of course, but it will only get worse if they get publicity. Many papers take similar positions."

"So you ignore it?"

"Don't blame me. It's not my policy," the reporter said. He was a personable man. He smiled as he refilled his glass with wine.

Svoray trawled several lines of inquiry during the next hours. He learned that Himmler's daughter, a so-called icon of the neo-Nazi movement, was thought to be living in Munich. One of Frankfurt's neo-Nazis was the son of an ex-Nazi who owned an army-navy surplus store in the city; J.S. didn't know where, but he had heard it looked like a Wehrmacht museum. A woman named Margitte would know; she worked at a tavern on the outskirts and knew the right. J.S. had heard of, but not seen, computer games like the one Rabbi Hier had asked Svoray to look for. No, he didn't think Germany was turning back the clock.

Svoray was calling the waiter for the bill when J.S. snapped his fingers. "Do you know who Michael Kuhnen is, was?"

"Is he the one who died of AIDS?" Svoray tried to remember all the names the Wiesenthal Center researchers had thrown at him during the quick briefing he'd received once the rabbis had approved his project.

"That's right. His best friend lives near here, in Langen. Heinz Reisz. You should try to speak to him."

Svoray wrote down the name. Five minutes later, after he had said goodbye to J.S. in his wrinkled trench coat, he dashed to a card phone he'd located on the Zeil and called New York. He caught Mark Seal just as he was leaving the JTA offices for his commuter train to Princeton, New Jersey. In another minute, he was patched through to the Wiesenthal Center in Los Angeles.

"Remind me about Michael Kuhnen," he said.

Aaron Breitbart, head of the center's research department, paused a second before answering. "He's dead."

"I know. But tell me about him."

"Led the German Alternative, a party that's now banned. He died of AIDS in 1991. It was a blow to the neo-Nazi movement, because he was the smartest and most articulate guy they had. Wore an SA uniform, brown shirt, belt across his chest, the works. Went to prison for it, among other things, like denouncing the state and distributing Nazi propaganda. Probably got AIDS in prison. The crazy thing is, he was a Communist once. Why?"

"The name came up. In reference to a friend of his."

"Who?"

Breitbart spoke to a dead phone. Svoray, seized with cold, had hung up and was hurrying toward shelter.

Back at the hotel, another call to Müller went unanswered.

In the first instant of waking the next morning, he didn't remember the beating he'd gotten in the alley. Then he moved, and gasped with pain. He hobbled to the mirror to see that the bruise on his thigh had deepened. The knot on his head still was tender, but as he moved, the stiffness in his muscles eased and he felt better.

The first thing he did when he went out was buy a set of long underwear. Fortified against the cold, he set out in the rental car to find the tavern and the woman Margitte whom J.S. had mentioned. He lost his way in a maze of one-way streets, however, and soon the streets bore no resemblance to the directions he'd written in his notebook. Then he discovered he'd neglected to write down the name of the tavern. He had felt no need to record last night's interview. He called *Frankfurter Rundschau* from a phone booth and asked for J.S., but the reporter had gone to Wiesbaden. Angry with himself, Svoray started back toward the skyscrapers clumped against the sky.

He found his bearings when he reached the Hauptbahnhof. On an impulse, he parked the car and headed toward the pornography store where Müller had taken him.

Browsing businessmen filled the aisles. The long-haired clerk sat in the change booth outside the peep shows. He still wore a black tank top, but with the change of seasons he had replaced the denim shirt over it with a tight red leather jacket. Svoray peeled a ten-mark note from his money clip.

"Have you seen Charlie Müller?"

The clerk stared back, stone-faced. Svoray added a bill to the one in his hand and slid them through the window. "I'm looking for Herr Müller," he said.

The clerk shook his head and pushed the money back at Svoray. "I don't know him," he said in German.

Svoray understood this. "The hell you don't know him. You gave him a key. I was with him."

"Sie haben sich geirrt." Telling Svoray he was mistaken, the clerk shook his head again and pushed the bills until they were suspended on the edge of the counter. "Take the money," he said in English, surprising Svoray. "There is no Herr Müller here."

Svoray returned to the street and wondered what to do next.

In daylight, Frankfurt's red-light district had almost achieved the appearance of respectability. Men and women crossed the streets in business dress. Whores were absent from the doorways. The fast food shops catered to lunching office workers. Only the signs—"Sex Inn," "Peep Show," "Non Stop Sex"—informed those entering the district that it was different from other sections of the city.

His gaze passed over, then returned to a green and white police van parked a block away. He walked toward it.

A female officer was in the driver's seat, a male sergeant riding shotgun. They were drinking coffee from paper cups. Svoray made a tourist's gesture of helplessness. The driver rolled her window down, and waited for his question.

"I'm an American journalist," he said. "Maybe you can help me."

She responded in English. "I will try."

"I'm here to do a story on the neo-Nazis. I wonder if there's a problem here in Frankfurt."

She and the sergeant conferred, apparently deciding what to say. She turned back to Svoray. "We don't see too many. A few skinheads, but mostly drunks. Not dangerous, usually. Sometimes they harass foreigners they see."

Svoray fingered the knot on his head and decided not to argue. "Where are the neo-Nazis, then?"

She looked at the sergeant. He nodded. "In Langen," she said.

"I've heard that. Where is Langen?"

"Near the airport. You should try to find a man named Reisz. He is the best-known neo-Nazi now."

The officer started the car. "Good luck," she said, rolling up the window, and backed into the street. Svoray stood at the curb and scribbled the name Reisz in his notebook for the second time in twelve hours.

Nine

GOETHE UNIVERSITY was only a few streetcar stops from the Hauptbahnhof, according to his map. One of the boxy, high-windowed cars came into view around the silvery curve of track. Svoray boarded when it stopped. He was still forming the plan by which he would approach this friend of Kuhnen's, Reisz.

Standing in the aisle and clutching an overhead support, he looked around the car. A pair of matrons sat near the front, wool coats tucked around their knees, purses firmly clutched between forearm and torso. Midway back, a man in a raincoat read a book. There were businessmen and women with shoulder bags and briefcases, workmen, waitresses and shop clerks, students: the democratic jostle of public transportation. Seated next to where he stood, a young man read a newspaper, the English-language *International Herald-Tribune.*

"I see you read English," Svoray said.

The youth looked up, startled. His face was a long, soft oval in which wide-set blue eyes under heavy brows gave an impression of naiveté. His upper lip was trying to sprout a mustache, and blond hair spilled past his shoulders. He looked to Svoray like Jesus Christ, all wrong for the idea he was forming. Svoray saw his Adam's apple bob as he ducked back into the paper.

"Can you tell me which stop is the university?"

The bland face looked up again reluctantly. "You get off at the Marriott."

"I'm a journalist," Svoray confided. "My name is Ron Furey. Australian, but working in America. Do you mind if I talk to you?"

The young man looked around. He seemed to feel conspicuous. "It is a public streetcar," he said uncomfortably.

"I'm looking for the young person's viewpoint," Svoray continued, bracing himself against the car's rocking. "What young people think about current events, particularly Mölln and the skinheads. Everyone has heard from the politicians, but what do students think?"

The two stiff-backed matrons were staring openly. The youth folded his newspaper and stood up. Svoray looked out to get his bearings. "Is this the stop?" he asked.

The youth nodded. The streetcar's bell clanged and it glided to a stop. As he paused at the door, he turned back and made a face at the women, sticking out his tongue. Then he leaped from the car. Svoray followed, glimpsing the women open-mouthed as he stepped down.

"You shocked them," he said to the young man.

"Everything shocks them." He began walking with long strides. Svoray hurried to catch up. "I was buying water at the grocery store today when a man yelled at me. An old man." He waved his arms in imitation. " 'You should be thrown out. Longhairs. Gypsies. You are ruining the country.' " He stopped abruptly. "You are a journalist? That is what you should write. All that craziness. What was your name?"

"Ron. Are you going to the university?"

"Yes. My name is Stefan."

"Listen, Stefan, I agree with you. But you know, all the news coming out of Germany is about the right."

"That is not representative," Stefan said firmly.

Svoray's plan grew clearer. "Is there a student center? Some place where students put up notices looking for work? Or a school for languages? I'm looking for a translator, too. I will pay. I have to interview someone."

"I have some friends who may help you."

"What about you?"

The young man glanced at him quickly. The modern tower of

the Marriott was behind them now, along with the bustle and glitz of the financial district. The campus was a place apart, a conglomeration of bland modern buildings along narrow streets, now and then set off by walks and grassy plots. "I don't know," he said. "I'm very busy."

A scattering of students lounged, played cards, watched television. Stefan said many already had left for the Christmas holidays. Those who were left had late exams or professors who were sticklers for attendance or, like him, lived in Frankfurt and hung around the student center in preference to home.

Svoray found an empty table, sat back, and surveyed the room, a bulky figure in a baseball cap. He chuckled to himself. The center looked as if it came from another time and place. Posters of Che Guevara and Mao stared down from the walls. A crudely drawn swastika, crossed out with a diagonal line in the international symbol, was taped to a window. Jeans were the uniform of choice, except for a few young women who wore long dresses in flower prints with incongruous lace-up boots—the latest antistyle. Along one wall, machines dispensed coffee and hot water. On the counter beside them, cello-wrapped muffins and cakes and various teas were for sale on the honor system, the cash drawer a cardboard napkin box. Svoray got up and counted some change into the box for a muffin; he would have preferred a cheeseburger, but he'd missed lunch and wasn't picky. It was almost three o'clock.

Stefan was moving from group to group, talking quietly. Some of the students shook their heads no and went back to what they were doing. A few others looked in Svoray's direction. When Stefan was through with his rounds, they came with him to where Svoray was sitting.

"Did you tell them what I want?" he asked Stefan, dabbing away muffin crumbs.

"He told us you are a journalist who wants student opinions about right-wing violence, and also that you are looking for a translator." The speaker was an attractive young woman of average height, with light brown hair and high cheekbones in a mobile face. Her flawless English had a British accent.

"That's right."

"We are very against the skinheads," another student interrupted.

"Yes." A third student spoke up. "This week is a march in
Bonn against the violence. I am going. You should come. You
would meet many Germans not in favor of what is happening."

"I am going, too," said Stefan.

"How much will you pay?"

Svoray turned toward the British accent. The young woman
stared back at him. "Do you know where Langen is?" he said.

"It's very close. Ten minutes on the S-bahn. What is at
Langen?"

"A neo-Nazi I have to interview."

A buzz went around the table. Several of the students shook
their heads. "I thought you wanted the other point of view," one
said accusingly.

"I think if they talk they will look like idiots," said Svoray.

"Who is it?" The accent again.

Svoray consulted his notebook. "His name is Heinz Reisz. He
was a friend of Michael Kuhnen's."

"How much will you pay?" she repeated.

"Whoever comes with me, I'll give one hundred Deutschemarks and buy the train ticket."

"When?"

He shrugged. "Now."

"Now?"

"Sure. Why not?"

While the other students hesitated, the young woman said,
"Stefan, will you go if I do?"

Svoray appreciated the Frankfurt Hauptbahnhof for the first
time. Behind its facade of hybrid styles topped with a statue of
Atlas shouldering the globe, the station was a world unto itself.
An underground shopping mall occupied its lowest level, fed by
pedestrian passages under the busy street that curved past the
facade and its flag-lined plaza. The station's main level was an
explosion of space, lit by high arched windows near the ceiling
and filled with shops, stands, restaurants, and hurrying people.
Svoray felt as if he had stepped into a movie set. A *Fruchtshop*
displayed bright oranges, bananas, and red and green apples,
while the misted windows of a florist's kiosk were lush with roses

in all colors and tiny purple orchids. Opposite the row of shops and restaurants, the train platforms extended under a curved skylight toward a great arch that was the station's portal to the world.

The young woman had come with him from the campus. Her name was Kristina. Stefan had run some kind of errand and was going to meet them. He loped into sight, and the three of them descended from the main station to the U-bahn and S-bahn interchange beneath. A train arrived within minutes.

As the train rocked out of the underground into twilight, Kristina asked a question Svoray had been pondering himself. "Do you know how to find this Mr. Reisz?"

"No, but it won't be a problem."

"Why not?"

"He seems to be well known. We'll ask somebody, a cab driver or a cop."

The light was gone when they reached Langen, lost to the approaching winter solstice. Tall lamps on the platform cast the station building in a yellow light in which it seemed to huddle, reminiscent of another time. On the street to the right, several cabs waited in a line.

Stefan fretted as they headed toward the taxis. "How will they know? This is a big town."

But one did know. The driver wrinkled his nose at the mention of the name, as if smelling something bad, and jerked his head toward the backseat in brusque invitation.

Svoray took one window seat. Kristina crawled into the middle, conceding the other window to Stefan. Svoray was conscious of the warmth of her thigh alongside his as the car's motion jostled them together. The streets of Langen were anonymous, suburban—rows of shops interspersed by apartment blocks, cars, and people hurrying as if to escape the dark. The driver turned into a wide street, Darmstadterstrasse, with two lanes in each direction, and stopped.

"This is it," he said in English.

"Where?" Stefan asked. There were several apartment buildings on the long block, one a high-rise with at least ten stories.

The driver shrugged. "One of the low ones," he said. "His name is on the mailbox. He is a Nazi pig. That's all I know." He refused to take a tip, and drove away.

They tried several times before they found the mailbox, the lowest of three to the left of a door at one end of a long three-story building. Three more mailboxes were inset to the right of the door, their positions apparently corresponding to the apartments inside. The entranceway was obscured on either side by shrubbery, and the door was of thick, translucent glass through which only light and shadow could be seen. There seemed to be a further set of steps inside. Svoray looked at his two young companions, took a breath, and rang the bell.

At first there was no answer, then the sound of a door chain rattling, then forms moving down the steps accompanied by a deep-throated barking.

"Oh, God," Kristina breathed, clutching Svoray's arm. "I'm afraid of dogs."

Then the door opened.

A buxom woman with fluffy blond hair held a German shepherd by its collar. The dog erupted into barking. *"Nero, nein!"* she said, swatting it on the nose with the palm of her hand. The dog subsided. She looked at them inquiringly.

"We are looking for Herr Heinz Reisz," Stefan said in German. Kristina was hanging back behind Svoray, away from the dog.

"This is where he lives. You are . . . ?"

"Tell her I am a journalist who wants to interview him," Svoray said.

Stefan conveyed this in German, adding that he and Kristina were students who had come as translators. The woman nodded. "Please, come in," she said in German.

They followed her to a door on the first landing, still holding the dog by the collar. "Heinz?" she called into the open door. Then she turned and beckoned them.

Ten

T HE FIRST THING Svoray noticed was not the man but the portrait of Hitler on the living room wall. It hung on light wood paneling next to a copper pressing of a swastika surmounted by the SS slogan, *Blut und Ehre*—Blood and Honor.

"*Willkommen,* my friends. How can I help you?" a voice rumbled in German.

Turning, Svoray expected to confront a black uniform and polished leather. Instead, he saw a barrel-chested, middle-aged man whose brown hair and thick Stalinesque mustache were shot with gray. He wore an old cardigan sweater, plaid shirt, corduroy pants, and a pair of battered slippers. He regarded them cordially, his eyes bright and curious.

Svoray fished for the *News Time* press card he'd had made in Times Square. "I've heard a lot about you, Herr Reisz, and I would like to do an interview. My name is Ron Furey. I come from Australia but I write for an American magazine. I want to hear what you have to say."

Reisz listened, his expression polite but uncomprehending.

"Do you speak English?" Svoray asked. Turning to Kristina, "Does he speak English?"

Kristina spoke, listened to Reisz's response, and said, "Herr Reisz regrets he speaks only German. But he is glad to meet you and answer your questions. He says we have already met his wife, Renata."

"Tell him," Svoray said, "that I regret that I speak only English, though I understand some German. Tell him he can be candid. I have no problem with any of his opinions. My magazine is very receptive to what he has to say. I am an empty glass. If he fills it with water, it's water. But if it's wine, it's wine."

Kristina translated this for Reisz. As Reisz answered, Stefan translated simultaneously. "Herr Reisz is used to people disagreeing with his opinions. But he is used to giving them anyway."

"Good, we understand each other," said Svoray. He was finding Reisz hard to dislike, felt even, despite himself, a fondness for the man's unguarded candor. "Does he feel he's taken over the job of Michael Kuhnen?"

A smile of sadness and affection crossed Reisz's face as he listened to Kristina relay the question. "Michael was a genius," Stefan translated. "Herr Reisz says he is not on the same level. Michael was born under the wrong star. His death was a great loss."

"Does he now speak for the neo-Nazi movement?"

"He can speak only for himself."

"But he knows the movement. Is he its leader?"

Reisz, lighting a cigarette, laughed at the question. "Oh, no. He is only a friend," Stefan translated. "Anyway, there is no one movement at the moment. It is a problem. That was what Michael was trying to address."

Dishes rattled, the sound of preparations. Reisz's wife called from the kitchen. He stood up and as he spoke, Stefan said, "He is offering us refreshments and asks us to excuse him while he helps his wife."

As soon as he was out of the room, Svoray said, "Do you take him seriously, or is he a nut case?"

"All these people are crazy," Stefan muttered. Kristina made a sound of disgust.

Reisz returned carrying a tray with cups and saucers, a pot of coffee, and a plate of cookies. Renata came into the living room and sat to one side. The dog hovered near Reisz, who sat on a sofa next to a bookcase that contained a television and stereo gear. As Svoray looked around the room, he noticed metal braces fixed on either side of the front door and a length of wooden

two-by-four leaning against the wall, so the door could be barred
from the inside.

"Ask him," Svoray resumed, when everyone was settled, "what
is his attitude about the Jews?"

"He says Germany is a country, and a people, who have been
raped by the Jews, by the dirty Jewish state."

"Germany has been raped by the Jews?" Svoray was incredu-
lous.

"Billions we've been contracted to pay up, blood money for
the six millions we have killed," Stefan translated. "He says for
that kind of money you have to find a lot of people, not fifty or a
hundred thousand."

"Does he believe in the Holocaust, by the way?"

Reisz answered himself. *"Nein. Nein. Propaganda."*

"He thinks it's propaganda?"

"He says the Jews themselves don't believe it."

"Auschwitz?"

"Propaganda."

Svoray remembered his kibbutznik childhood. Many hands
cradled and tossed him from time to time, childrearing, like
farming, being part of Kibbutz Gvulot's collective enterprise.
And of those hands a surprising number bore a tracery of numbers above the wrists. Once he had thought everyone had them,
and wondered why his parents and grandparents had been left
out. Later, he understood that the tattoos were part of his exposure to the Holocaust.

Despite this vivid memory, Svoray felt a growing affinity for
Reisz. Sitting there in Hitler's shadow, Svoray found himself
drawn to the man in a way that went beyond their different beliefs. Reisz was open and friendly. Svoray had met criminals he
liked in the same way because they were similar to him, men
without pretension or apparent guile, who were what they were
without apology. It saddened rather than angered Svoray that
Reisz denied the Holocaust. He didn't detect meanness in Reisz;
the man was deluded.

"Does he think being a Nazi is a badge of honor?"

"He says the Nazis didn't kill more people than the Americans
killed Indians."

"I tend to agree," Svoray said, drawing a sharp look from Kristina. His next move was perilous, he knew. It would draw him

closer to Reisz, but alienate the two students. It couldn't be helped. "Besides being a journalist, I tend to agree with his ideas. One of the basic problems of my country of Australia is foreigners. Does he think one of the solutions is actually killing people?"

"Nein."

"Well, is there any contact between the new right and the old Nazis? Because the neo-Nazis seem to be disorganized hooligans. My problem, I see Germany from the outside. Are they organized, these attacks?" He continued as Reisz was trying to answer. "Tell him I also think the problem is overplayed by the world media. It's an internal problem to do with Germans that we shouldn't be caring about."

Kristina gave him another strange look, then turned to Reisz and repeated what he'd said in German.

Reisz nodded vigorously. "We are not only skinheads. You see?" As Stefan translated, Reisz grinned and lifted his thick shock of hair. When he released it, it fell back across his forehead in a way that mimicked the portrait of the brooding Führer.

"Ha, ha. Very good." Svoray laughed. "You know, your hair makes you look a little like Hitler." He gestured to the wall where the portrait hung. "Do you get many compliments?"

Reisz answered, *"Ja, ja,"* nodding with a smile. He was warming to Svoray as well.

Their growing camaraderie was having an effect on Kristina. She looked at Svoray, with her face set in accusation. Stefan, too, seemed troubled. Svoray ignored them.

"Is he frightened to be speaking out like this? It must take courage." When Kristina hesitated, he urged her, "Go on, ask him."

"Kristina is getting upset," Stefan whispered, then translated Reisz's answer: "That is a problem. Right now, the government wants to stop him from speaking." Reisz pulled his hand across his mustache. Stefan continued, "They want to zip his mouth. He is spied on and raided. He is attacked."

Reisz got to his feet and moved to the door, where he placed the wooden stave in the metal arms by way of demonstration.

"He has to bar himself in," Stefan continued. "And when they go out . . ."

Reisz moved to the side of the bookcase and pulled from behind it a large square piece of metal. This he took to the window, which he opened inward on a vertical hinge. He brought down with a clatter a set of aluminum shutters from above, then hoisted the metal plate into the frame and closed the window, turning the small room into a sealed chamber. Kristina looked with alarm first at Svoray, then at Stefan. She started to stand, then changed her mind. Reisz gestured at the outside and listed his enemies.

"Communists, Zionists, ANTIFA, longhairs, dirty people, black people who come out of the trees like apes."

"ANTIFA are militant antifascists," Stefan added to the translation.

"They shoot through his windows?" Svoray asked.

"Shoot. Throw rocks." Reisz removed the plate from the window and slid it back behind the bookcase, then unbarred the door. He took from a cabinet a small, lethal-looking metal crossbow, cocked it, showed it to them, and returned it to its place.

"But some people must agree with him," Svoray said. "I mean, he's living in this town and he's quite open with his views. Let him tell us about the people who like him, who find him a good German. Can he introduce me to people younger, who can give me an idea of the connections?"

"He says five hundred people meet every two weeks. He has friends he could call."

"How is it paid for, the meeting hall, the lights? That's what I mean by asking him if they are organized." Svoray shook his head at the answer. "He pays for it out of his own pocket? He is a true soldier."

Reisz conveyed in a palms-up gesture a state of poverty.

"And is it growing? Does he think that next year it will double, the movement? Is it the economy, or because they are right?"

"He says it is growing for all reasons. It would grow more but it takes money to organize. Right now most of the money goes to fighters in Croatia."

"Where?"

"Croatia. They have young men in training, skinheads who will come back knowing how to fight."

Stefan almost choked, and Svoray could hardly believe what he was hearing. Meanwhile, Kristina was glaring at Stefan, and he was avoiding her eyes. Neither of them had bargained for the warmth between this man with a portrait of Hitler on his wall and the voluble journalist they'd met just hours earlier, who was sounding like a Nazi himself. Svoray, seeing their distress, couldn't blame them. He and Reisz had become friendly very quickly. They communicated at a level independent of translation, each understanding enough of what the other said to catch the drift if not the details. Their familiarity excluded the two students. It was beginning to seem that Kristina and Stefan, not Svoray, were strangers in Langen. He had not expected to like Reisz, either. Now this disturbing piece of information. But there was opportunity in the chemistry between them. Svoray saw how he could use it.

"Tell him I could get the money," he demanded of Kristina. He rubbed his fingers together in the universal sign.

She was furious now, and she spat out the translation. She had trusted him to take them on a lark, and he had taken them instead into some dark lie. Too bad, it can't be helped, Svoray thought coldly. He prayed she wouldn't challenge his metamorphosis.

"Tell him my magazine has a certain audience," he continued. "The reason I took this assignment was to meet some serious people. Now, talking to him, I realize the movement is not made up of crazy people but people with coherent ideas of what should be done. I have a check for fifteen thousand dollars waiting to be written. But I'm not going to give it to him so he can go and drink beer. It must go to the cause. He has to take me and show me that this is where he's putting it."

Kristina spoke in rapid German but refused to look at Reisz. Instead she turned to Stefan. Her face said she had had enough.

Svoray caught the look. He pulled up his sleeve and peered at his watch. *"Ach,* almost eight," he said, rising and reaching for his coat. "My friends must get back to Frankfurt. Let me take them to the train station."

Reisz looked like a child whose toy was snatched before he'd begun to play with it. He began to protest.

"But I would like to come back, if you will be here," Svoray continued. "I think we understand each other well enough, don't you?"

"Ja, ja. Bitte," Reisz said. He went to call a taxi.

———

Kristina dragged Stefan down the stairs and into the street when they heard the taxi's horn. She refused to sit next to Svoray, forcing Stefan into the middle seat. They rode to the station in silence. The streets were dark and quiet. When the car stopped in front of the station, Kristina flung the door open and stalked around the building to the platform. Svoray asked the driver to wait and hurried after her.

She turned on him as he approached, brushing tears from her cheeks with the back of her hand. "You lied to us," she cried. "You're as bad as they are. You are them."

Stefan caught up and tried to comfort her. She shook his hand away.

"I'm not," Svoray said. "Listen, both of you. I was lying to him, not to you."

"No, no." She shook her head violently, casting off the thought. "You liked him. You were like . . . You were like lovers."

"Oh, my God," Svoray said, exasperated. He turned and walked to the end of the platform, where the tracks disappeared into the darkness. Next to him, dim forms of bicycles hung in vertical racks under corrugated metal inside a wooden fence. Signal lights glimmered in the obscure distance. Far away down the line of tracks, a single dot of white appeared and grew into the headlight of an approaching engine.

Fuck it, he thought.

He walked back to Kristina and Stefan. They watched him as if he were some ragged urban beggar approaching with a cup outstretched, who might transform before their eyes from harmless lunacy to violence. He reached into his pockets and withdrew his driver's license and his Bank Hapoalim credit card, which he had decided to keep on him in case of an emergency.

"Look at this," he urged Kristina, thrusting them under her nose. "Look at my name. Yaron Svoray. And the card, from Israel. Take it. See? I am an Israeli. He is not my friend. I can't tell you more than that."

She took the items from his hand. She looked at them, then at him with shock and horror. Her expression was so exaggerated he had to stop himself from laughing. "And no, I'm not in the Mossad," he said. Stefan took them from her and looked at them with interest.

The train neared. "Listen, both of you," he continued. "Tell no one about this. Promise me. It's very dangerous. Do I have your promise?"

Stefan responded first. "Of course." Kristina nodded mutely.

The train was almost at the station. He gave each of them two hundred Deutschemarks, twice the amount he'd promised at the university, pressing the bills into their hands when Stefan protested. With Kristina he knew it was useless, but he asked Stefan if he would be willing to come with him again.

"I don't know," the young man said. But he wrote his number on a page from Svoray's notebook.

When Svoray looked back from the taxi, they were a single silhouette against the lights of the arriving train, huddled together against the dread of their new knowledge.

Reisz was outside walking the dog. He broke into a wide grin when Svoray got out of the taxi. "Ron," he said, wrapping his voice around the name in pear-shaped tones that were a caricature of German. He sounded like Sergeant Schultz in "Hogan's Heroes."

"Nero?" Svoray said, pointing to the dog. He thought he remembered what Reisz's wife had called it.

"Ja, ja. Nero," Reisz said, patting the black and tan beast on its thick neck. Nero looked at Svoray and tensed, baring his teeth. *"Nein, Nero. Er ist ein freund,"* Reisz said. "Friend," he repeated in English.

"Friend," said Svoray.

They grinned at each other like two idiots. Reisz tugged the dog to the door of the building, motioning Svoray to follow. When they were inside the apartment, Reisz went into the kitchen and got on the telephone. Reisz's wife smiled and motioned to a chair. She appeared top-heavy in her thick sweater. *"Kaffee?"* she asked.

She disappeared when Svoray shook his head. He sat down and studied his shoulder bag with its hidden camera and tape recorder. He had left it in the apartment deliberately, knowing it would disarm Reisz and also tempt him. He had tried to leave the strap caught between the zipper teeth in a way to let him know if the bag had been inspected. He didn't think so—Reisz seemed to operate at some primitive level of trust—but it was hard to remember just how he had left it.

"Yes, Ron. Ron Furey. An American journalist, but a friend," Reisz was saying to someone on the phone. Svoray understood the German surprisingly well. Reisz had converted him to an American already. It must be the money. The conversation went on for a few moments. When Reisz returned to the living room, he picked up his gray parka and handed Svoray his coat.

"Where are we going?" Svoray asked.

Reisz understood him reasonably well, too, for he answered, in German, "To meet friends."

They walked along the main road after leaving the apartment building, then turned down a side street where there were more apartments. The street was empty of pedestrians, the air sharp and clear. In one high apartment window, Svoray thought he saw a lighted Hanukkah menorah but decided he must be mistaken; Hanukkah hadn't started yet. As they walked, Reisz spoke and Svoray gathered that he was on the dole and worked for the movement because nobody would hire him. His views were too radical. His wife, Renata, shared his views, but quietly; she worked as a supermarket cashier. He had four children. One son was also a Nazi, either in prison or recently released, Svoray couldn't tell; his crime was attempting a robbery to help fund the movement. The movement needed money—that was very clear.

At an opening between buildings, they came to a low frame structure fronted by a gravel lot. Four or five cars were parked outside. Neon beer signs lighted the windows. Reisz clapped Svoray on the shoulder and steered him toward the door.

The bartender, bald except for a horseshoe of dark hair, looked up as they entered. He saw Reisz, lowered his head, and returned to the glasses he was polishing. The place was quiet in the middle of the evening. It was too late for early drinkers and too early for late ones. The undercurrent of conversation was a remove from the Frankfurt beer hall where Svoray had first met Charlie Müller. He wondered if he would ever see Müller again.

Reisz led the way past the bar to an alcove that branched off from the main room. There, two casually dressed young men sat at a round wooden table, their fingers hooked into the handles of large beer steins.

"Ah, Heinz," said the larger of the two, rising to greet the older man with an embrace. The other, a wiry man with a thin, sharp face, took the occasion to order more beers. Both studied Svoray with open curiosity.

They had a smattering of English, and combined with Svoray's German he gathered that the thin man was a roofer who laid terra cotta tiles. The big man was a mason. Both were sons of old Nazis. The roofer, grinning, said he would like to fly over Israel and drop a bomb.

"Ha, ha, yes. Boom!" said Svoray, swooping with his hands. There was much laughter about that. Reisz laughed indulgently; he was proud of his new friend.

The two workers were on show. Reisz wanted to prove that working Germans, not just drunken, jobless skinheads, supported neo-Nazi aims. For a while they talked about those aims. Svoray had heard them before: Germany for Germans; toss out the foreigners; get rid of the Jews.

"But the skinheads give you a problem. Bad publicity," Svoray said. "They can see only the building they want to burn. They see nothing long-term."

"Our youth is very exuberant," Reisz said in German. "Too exuberant sometimes. But we are stronger and better than the police want anyone to believe. They say we are smaller than we are. If we had money to organize and recruit, we could be a force by the next election. We could produce our leader."

"Is this someone who could unify the right?" Svoray asked.

"Oh, yes."

"I'd like to meet him," Svoray said.

He was on display as well. It emerged that some sort of movement gathering was taking place that weekend. Reisz was thinking of inviting him, but wanted the two men to size him up. Reisz was pleased that someone from the outside had come to learn the truth. If Ron would tell the truth, rather than the lies most journalists told, that was all anyone could ask. But Reisz had to be careful.

"He should perhaps pay," said the wiry roofer.

Svoray said he would pay what he could to help out, but not to meet a bunch of drunken skinheads.

"Nein, eine Feier der Natur." It was a celebration of nature, the Day of the Winter Solstice, an old Nazi holiday with Teutonic origins. It would be held in Mainz, a short drive away.

Svoray made a lame joke about blond men cavorting in the woods with blond women, which no one understood. But the men were serious. He could not go as a journalist, or take pictures or make recordings. Being a stranger, he would in all likelihood be searched. But many good friends would be there, Reisz assured him. He would see the face of the new Germany.

"What will you tell them about me? Who will you say I am?" Svoray wanted to know.

Reisz considered this with his chin in his hand, worrying his mustache with a blunt, tobacco-stained finger. Then he turned to Svoray and said happily, *"Mein Neffe."*

"Your nephew?" Svoray was astounded.

It was a long story that Svoray barely made out. The gist was that Reisz had a sister who was married to an American and lived in the South, near Atlanta. She had a son about Svoray's age. He would be that son.

They all agreed it was worth the subterfuge to give an American sympathizer like Ron Furey a true picture of the right.

"I don't know," Svoray said. He thought too much interest might betray him.

"But you must," Reisz insisted.

"I'll think about it and call you tomorrow." The conversation in the pub had gone slowly, protracted by the awkward translations. It was now after eleven. Svoray was sure the trains back to Frankfurt would stop running shortly. He begged to be excused, saying he had much to think about after such an exciting day. The sharp-faced roofer went to ask the bartender to call a cab.

Shortly there was a honking in the parking lot, and Svoray rose to leave.

"Boom," said the roofer.

"Boom, boom," said Svoray, to more laughter. They were blowing up Israel together.

Reisz followed him outside. Before Svoray could escape into the cab, Reisz caught him by the shoulders. The burly German held Svoray at arm's length, gazing at him fondly, and nodded with the satisfaction of a teacher who recognizes that he has found at last an apt and willing pupil.

Svoray, looking back at Reisz, knew he had found the key to his mission.

Eleven

MARK SEAL was leaving for Pennsylvania Station and his commute to Princeton, New Jersey, when his private phone rang. He paused, listened to the message, and then picked up the receiver. After talking to Svoray and taking a few notes, Seal returned to his office to draft a letter to one of the Jewish Telegraphic Agency's trustees. Theo Klein was a corporate attorney who lived and worked in Paris. As a Jewish activist and onetime head of the European Jewish Conference, he had contacts throughout Europe.

"I can't go into any details, but one of our correspondents is working on a special project," Seal wrote. "It may bring him into contact with elements in Germany whose activities may be subject to arrest. Please recommend an attorney in Frankfurt he can contact in case of trouble."

He left instructions that the letter be faxed to Klein in Paris.

The JTA's role in Svoray's mission had so far been limited and somewhat confusing. Svoray had called every day, pulling Seal out of meetings and conferences. He had air-expressed two shipments of tapes, which Seal had had copied for the Wiesenthal Center and transcribed. Seal hadn't known what to make of the transcripts when they landed on his desk. Svoray talked about Johannes and his Mercedes full of gear, the weather, Frankfurt's street life, the porno shops, his search for Charlie Müller, the drunks and skinheads on the Zeil, the comfort of his new long underwear, the pictures he'd taken with his spy camera, which seemed to be mostly of his legs and belly. He talked about his preparations for his mission and his sense of himself as a warrior for peace. He was embarrassed to mention he'd been beaten up. Seal read the transcripts as an unconventional travelogue that could not be run, in any case, until Svoray was out of Germany.

Seal found it awkward to be Svoray's main contact, when Svoray was really working for the rabbis in Los Angeles. He seemed to be spending most of his time taking Svoray's calls, or passing Svoray's messages along to the West Coast. He sighed, looked at the clock, and composed another message to be faxed.

This one went to Abe Cooper at the Wiesenthal Center: "YS advises he has met a neo-Nazi named Heinz Reisz. Plans attending Nazi celebration over weekend where others to attend. Wishes any information."

At a little after four, Los Angeles time, Aaron Breitbart looked up from his cluttered desk to see Abe Cooper standing in the doorway. Cooper said, "Who's Heinz Reisz?"

Breitbart cocked his head. The name sounded vaguely familiar. As head of the Wiesenthal Center's research department, Breitbart was in charge of keeping track of anti-Semitic organizations and activities around the world. He and his colleague Richard Eaton worked together in a cramped office that was barely big enough for their two desks, a few bookshelves, a Xerox machine, and Eaton's computer, monitor, and printer, which were jammed into a corner. Breitbart found a folder filled with clippings and dispatches, opened it, and said, after a moment's scanning, "Heinz Reisz? He must be somebody. He just got banned."

"Banned?"

"The Interior Ministry wants to take away his right to speak. They've petitioned the courts to limit his civil rights. The bastard is an agitator, apparently. It says here he's a notorious anti-Semite who's connected to several right-wing parties."

"Ah," said Cooper. He looked on Breitbart and his tumbled desktop with the admiration reserved for hidden genius. Nothing could be extracted from that incredible confusion, and yet Aaron had done it.

"He's gotten quite a bit of coverage lately," said Breitbart, excitement entering his voice as he shuffled through his clippings. Breitbart, big and soft-spoken, liked nothing better than nailing a bigot to the wall. "It looks like he's a big dog on the hill since Michael Kuhnen died. Why?"

"Our man's in touch with him. He says Reisz is going to take him to a neo-Nazi celebration and introduce him to more people."

Breitbart made a note on a yellow pad that seemed to promptly disappear into the confusion on his desk. He rubbed his large, soft hands together in anticipation. "Do we know who?"

"Not yet."

Eaton, meanwhile, tapped a note into his computer. "Reisz. How do you spell that again?" he asked. "Just so we'll have some way of knowing in case Aaron gets hit by a truck on the way home."

Svoray awoke with the feel of Reisz's hands still on his shoulders. The gray behind the room's sheer undercurtains told him it was early. He groped for the remote control, turned on the television, and flipped channels until he reached CNN. Nothing interesting. It was midnight on the East Coast of the United States.

He rolled on his side and looked at the telephone: no message light. There were no messages at the desk, either, when he called. He had hoped to hear from Seal about a lawyer. It was Friday; the solstice celebration was tomorrow and for his peace of mind he needed to believe that he would not be clapped into jail with a bunch of neo-Nazis.

A long shower erased the sensation of Reisz's touch. Svoray toweled and dressed, planning to spend the day in preparation. He decided to find another hotel. He had the vague sense of needing to keep moving, to stay one step ahead of anyone who might be trying to find out more about him. Before checking out of the Scala, he called Mark Seal and left a voice mail message saying he was changing locations and would be in touch.

The hotel he chose was closer to the Hauptbahnhof and the red-light district. The Parkhotel catered to business travelers. It offered luxury and discretion, and the police station across the small park from its front door was reassuring. Upon checking in, he gave the concierge a hundred-Deutschemark tip.

The concierge drew the note across the counter of his station, glanced at its denomination, and raised an eyebrow at Svoray. The man wore a dark suit with a name badge pinned to the breast pocket and had a self-assurance that came from speaking several languages and dealing with impossible demands.

"I have just checked in," Svoray announced. "I will be here for a week, and I want to be anonymous. My name is Ron Furey. But if anyone comes looking for me, you will not have heard of me."

"Of course," murmured the concierge in Italian-accented English.

"The rest of the staff also. I will take good care of them, too."

"Very good, Mr. Furey."

He delivered on the promise right away, placing twenty marks into the hand of the bellman who brought his bags upstairs and turned on the bathroom light. When he went out again, he gave an attendant in the lobby ten marks for opening the door and, seeing the attendant who had parked his car, tipped him twenty marks. Returning after a few minutes with a bubble pouch for mailing and a roll of silver duct tape, he lavished another ten marks on the doorman. On his way through the lobby, he saw the staff's heads turn in his direction.

From the desk in his small, sleekly modern room, he placed another call to Charlie Müller's number and was encouraged to hear a busy signal. Then he set about repairing some of last night's damage.

Stefan's mother answered the phone. "You must be the journalist from America," she said in English after he had introduced himself. Her voice bore disapproval. "He told me you had a very interesting time. In our house we're not very happy about him going to such places."

"I didn't like it either," Svoray said. "Stefan was brave. The impression is that the youth is only right-wing, but that's not true."

"No, it's not," she said.

"I was hoping he might go with me again."

There was a cool, extended pause before she answered. "Here, I'll let you talk to Stefan."

"Hallo!" said Stefan casually. "I thought you would be eaten by the dog."

Svoray relaxed a little. "Have you talked to anyone?"

"Only to Kristina and my parents. Why?"

"I mean about me. Where I am from."

"Only Kristina."

"That's good. Listen, Stefan, you must help me." He heard caution in the young man's voice and bulled forward. "There is a meeting. I want you to come with me."

"What meeting? I don't know."

"It's in Mainz. Some kind of celebration. I will pay you, but it's not just for translation that I need you. You know who I am and what I am doing, and I think you are my friend. I think I will need a friend when I am with these people."

"I don't know," Stefan repeated.

"Don't you think it's important to expose these people?"

"Yes, it is, but . . ."

"Then come. It will be more important than your march. I can't tell you how much, but trust me."

"If I come with you, I'll have to cut my hair."

"Why?" Svoray asked, sensing victory.

"Won't we be with skinheads?"

Bless Stefan, Svoray exulted as he hung up the phone five minutes later. He called Reisz in Langen to let him know he would be coming to the Day of the Winter Solstice.

Next, Svoray again tried Charlie Müller's number. This time there was no answer. The frustration of failing to contact Müller was starting to build, but Svoray was less worried than if he hadn't met Reisz. He called *Frankfurter Rundschau* and asked for J.S. When he was told the reporter had begun his Christmas holiday, he made a list of army-navy surplus stores from the phone book and went out in the afternoon to see if he could find the one with a neo-Nazi connection. On the way, he dropped the bubble pouch with last night's tapes—one from Reisz's apartment, a second containing his reflections on the meeting—with the concierge for overnight shipping, along with a fifty-Deutsche-mark tip.

The three stores he found within walking distance of the U-bahn—two in seedier districts of Frankfurt, one across the Main in Sachsenhausen—were the kind of surplus stores he had come to expect in the United States. They sold work clothes, camping and hunting gear, foul weather clothing, knives, and tools, but none displayed the Germanic paraphernalia that J.S.

had told Svoray to look for. Leaving the Sachsenhausen store, he decided to walk back across the river on the Eiserner Steg, the iron footbridge. When he reached the north side of the river, he headed for the Zeil.

Wilhelm and his friends were clustered at the U-bahn entrance in Hauptwache Square, where the Zeil slithered off to the east. They were drinking their large brown bottles of beer. The Christmas shoppers and commuters thronging to the U-bahn and S-bahn trains below the square ignored the group of perhaps ten. Svoray watched from a shadow of the church, thinking of revenge. There were several groups of uniformed police, where there had been none the other day. Svoray thought he saw some in plainclothes as well. A pair of entertainers in medieval costumes was trying to attract an audience. When one of the group of skinheads moved in their direction, the uniforms would pay attention. When they retreated to the group of drinkers, the uniforms relaxed.

After he watched for several minutes, Svoray caught a taxi back to his hotel.

Twelve

DECEMBER 19 DAWNED without sun. For a moment after he woke, Svoray did not remember the solstice celebration. When he did, apprehension gripped him. The feeling heightened when he remembered trying to reach Seal the night before.

Svoray had called him from the card phone in the Hauptbahnhof to avoid placing a suspicious number on his room bill, and heard the now familiar message of Seal's voice mail. Seal was often in meetings, and Svoray had the impression he did not like being interrupted. So he had left word that the neo-Nazi meeting was tomorrow. Instead of leaving his number, he said he would call back for the lawyer's name and contact information.

But when he returned to the hotel, he had fallen asleep watching television.

After he showered and shaved, he checked the action of the switchblade, flicking it open several times, savoring its heft and the way the blade sprang into place and locked with a businesslike click. He peeled a length of duct tape from the roll he'd bought the day before and taped the knife inside his right ankle, in the hollow behind the protruding bone. Winding off more duct tape, he taped his Bank Hapoalim card and the laminated photo of Michal and the children to his left ankle.

One weapon, one lifeline, one talisman; other than his clothes and his green bag, he was ready.

Stefan arrived at the hotel as Svoray was finishing a substantial breakfast. He had crammed himself with eggs and sausage, fruit and yogurt, rolls and butter, and orange juice, because he was not sure when he would eat again. Eating with neo-Nazis was not palatable, if his experience at Reisz's apartment had been any sign. The cookies had tasted like sawdust. Svoray was sure it was his imagination, but it would be easy enough to plead that he needed to lose weight.

"What do you think?" the student said.

"I think we will have an interesting day," Svoray answered.

"No. I mean about my hair."

Svoray peered. Stefan would not be mistaken for a skinhead, but his hair no longer reached his shoulders. In fact . . . "I see you have ears," he said.

Stefan smiled nervously. "I hope it is enough."

Svoray gave him a spare baseball cap just in case, and also supplied him with a denim jacket. He still looked like an antifascist student even with his shorter hair. Svoray feared for him when they reached their destination.

As they left the hotel he slipped the concierge fifty Deutschemarks and asked the man to book him on an evening flight to Munich. The attendant who brought the white Fiat with the French plates to the Parkhotel's front entrance was rewarded with twenty marks. The hotel staff was starting to rush ahead of Svoray and open doors.

The road into Langen took a dogleg and bore through a tunnel of woods. Svoray found Darmstadterstrasse and Reisz's apartment building, pulled off the street, and parked.

Reisz must have been looking out the window. He stepped out the glass door a moment later, his arms flung wide in greeting, dressed as if for a trip to someone's country house in a gray turtleneck and dark corduroys. *"Herein! Herein!"* he said, inviting them into the apartment.

Svoray and Stefan followed him inside. Renata was also dressed for a day in the country in walking shoes, slacks, and an oversized sweater that failed to disguise her ample bosom. The dog bristled and issued a low growl.

"Hush, Nero," Reisz said in German. "They are friends."

He took the metal plates from their storage place, pulled the windows open, drew down the outside shutters, and inserted the plates, until the apartment was sealed and dark. Finally, muttering in German about "gorillas in the trees," Reisz kissed the German shepherd on its forehead and pulled the door closed.

They walked around the corner to Reisz's car, parked on a side street, everybody squinting in the light at first. Svoray's car was nearby. Before he got into the old blue Mercedes, Reisz motioned Svoray and Stefan close.

Stefan said, "He says we may run into Communists and AN-TIFA, who don't like what their celebration is about. Police will be at the entrance, but if we stay close behind him they will probably wave us through together. That is, if they are good cops. If not, we shouldn't worry. They will just harass us for a little bit." The worry in Stefan's voice contrasted with Reisz's burst of laughter.

"Why is he laughing? Why is he winking at us?" Svoray wanted to know. But Reisz, still chuckling, got into his car.

"He's funny," Svoray said when they were on the road. In the car ahead, Reisz was an animated silhouette against the windshield, speaking to Renata as he drove. "He takes himself so seriously. I even like him. What is not funny is the consequences if they got power."

Stefan agreed. "Yes, you could like him personally except for the Jews, the way he feels. He likes you very much."

"I know he does. He's a total nut case, but he loves me."

"He says you are simpatico. And if you write even fifty percent of the way you appear, it will be the greatest thing he's ever read."

"It's going to be a very interesting day," Svoray repeated. Pretending the event would be merely interesting was a way of hiding his anxiety from Stefan.

Then Stefan asked, "Will it be dangerous?"

"Dangerous? No," Svoray lied. "But I think we will see many things to upset us."

Mainz was a short drive of some forty kilometers from Langen, part of the same urban sprawl. The city's clustered buildings and its nine-hundred-year-old Romanesque cathedral came into view when the road dipped toward the valley of the Rhine. Mainz was known for the cathedral and for its famous native son Johannes

Gutenberg. Lately, however, it had gained a reputation as a neo-Nazi hotbed.

Reisz crossed the river, left the autobahn, and steered away from the city center into a tangle of suburban neighborhoods. At times it seemed Reisz didn't know where he was going, and Svoray quickly lost his bearings. When Reisz stopped at last, they were on a residential street in front of a modern two-story house that perched a few steps up a hill. Reisz and Renata got out of the Mercedes. Reisz walked back to them, leaned into Svoray's window, and spoke in German.

"He apologizes for taking those wrong turns. He says he is not good with directions," Stefan said. "But we are at the house of a friend he wants you to meet."

"This is not the celebration?" Svoray asked.

"That is later."

Svoray slung his green bag over his shoulder. They climbed to the front door, where Reisz rang the bell. A slight man with tousled dark hair, a thick mustache, and large glasses opened the door a moment later. He had a restless manner that reminded Svoray of a caged rodent. A woman emerged behind him and they exchanged greetings with Reisz and Renata.

When they were through hugging and kissing, Reisz placed a hand on Svoray's shoulder. "He is saying that you are the man he told him about," Stefan translated. "He says you want to tell the true story of the movement and that you have friends in America who want to help. He wants you to know that this man is a star politician, a member of the Republican party here in Mainz. His name is Bernd Thrun."

Thrun appeared flattered by the praise. The Republikaners were the spearhead of the German extreme right, a party of over twenty thousand members. Like the National Front in France and Austria's Freedom Party, the Republikaners whipped up intolerance and hate by blaming refugees for their country's economic woes. The party was formed in 1983 and emerged in 1989 in West Berlin, before the Wall fell, when its members won eleven seats in the city parliament. Republikaners won fifteen seats in the parliament of the southwestern German state of Baden-Württemberg in April 1992. More recently, they had taken nine percent of the vote in Frankfurt's municipal elections. So far, although the party had not received the necessary votes to be represented in the Bundestag, the national parliament, it held seats in more than thirty German cities. Its leader was Franz Schönhuber, a white-haired, dark-browed former Waffen SS volunteer who spoke proudly of his wartime service. He publicly disavowed skinhead violence and neo-Nazi elements, but some members wanted to embrace those elements and take the party even further to the right.

Thrun invited them in. The house was ordinary, and they sat down at a round table outside the kitchen. Apparently, a lunch had been planned, for Thrun's wife brought coffee and bottles of beer, then returned to the kitchen for plates of cold cuts and sliced bread for sandwiches. Svoray saw that she was younger than Thrun, perhaps a second wife.

"Politics is not for all of us," Thrun said in German as he laid an affectionate hand on Reisz's shoulder. "My friend Heinz can never be a political animal. He is too honest, too much out on the limb for what he believes. But I have learned"—this he said sagely, with an upraised finger—"that to get where you intend to go you cannot always show your real colors."

Svoray agreed. "At least until you get there."

"It's true," Reisz said in German. "Bernd would like to come with us today, but he can't be seen there because it would harm his aspirations. He can't even be seen with me, poor fellow." He laughed and thumped the table so the plates jumped.

Svoray managed to excuse himself from eating, pleading that he had had a big breakfast. He drank only soda, while Stefan had a beer. Reisz, as he ate, predicted the movement would coalesce and take power in two to three years.

Afterward, Thrun invited Svoray and Stefan to see his World War II memorabilia, which included a collection of weapons. They ascended a spiral staircase to a study on the second floor. Thrun said his uncle had been a Gauleiter, a Nazi district leader just below the top Reich leadership. They oversaw political and economic activities, civil defense, and, in the quaint doublespeak of Nazi rule, "mobilization of labor." This meant funneling Jews, Gypsies, and other victims of the Nazi's into slave labor camps. His uncle, Thrun said, had been hanged for war crimes.

"He left me this," he said proudly.

He took from a shelf a small jewelry box and opened it. A

silver ring gleamed against a black velvet lining. It bore the death's head of the Totenkopf SS.

"From Himmler. See? It is inscribed."

Svoray looked inside the band to see a feathery inscription that was hard to read without a magnifying glass. It appeared to be a stamp of Heinrich Himmler's signature.

"His daughter is still alive, you know," said Thrun. "Married now, and very quiet. But very much admired."

"Really?" said Svoray. "I heard she lives in Munich."

"That's right. Her name is Burwitz."

"I bet she'd like to see this, eh? From her father."

Svoray made a mental note of the name. He thought, perversely, that he'd like to meet Himmler's daughter. He wondered if his crimes haunted her, or if she saw him only as a father. She had been sixteen when he killed himself by swallowing cyanide after his capture by the British. Even better than meeting her would be to have a photograph with her; Svoray thought that for an Israeli to stand next to Himmler's daughter in a photograph would be like spitting in the face of the Final Solution.

Reisz's big, smoke-roughened voice floated up the stairs as they started back down. Svoray picked out the word "Croatia." Back at the table, he said, "Heinz, I just heard you say 'Croatia.' You mentioned something about it the other day, that there were fighters there. What was that?"

A thick quiet fell when they heard Stefan's translation. Thrun looked at Reisz and Thrun's wife looked at Thrun, warning him.

"You must have said something wrong," Stefan said quietly. "They're very uncomfortable."

But Reisz was unfazed, and said in German, "Tell him. Tell him. He is a friend."

Thrun drew himself up. His wife turned away and entered the kitchen. Stefan reported, "He says he and Heinz and others have been collecting food and clothes for the good boys in Croatia." He added, "I don't believe this."

Thrun was pleased at Svoray's palpable reaction. "Five hundred of them," he continued. "From Frankfurt, Hamburg, Dresden, Berlin, and other places. Even France. They have joined the Croatians fighting for their land."

"Why?" asked Svoray.

"They were with us in the war."

Croatia, which then encompassed Bosnia-Herzegovina, was a Nazi puppet state during World War II. Bosnian Muslims were part of the Thirteenth Waffen SS division. The Ustachi, Croatia's version of the SS, murdered or deported forty thousand Jews during four years in power. They killed twenty thousand Gypsies and seven hundred thousand Serbs. Since the fragmenting of Yugoslavia, the Serbs had been extracting their revenge against Muslims and Croatians both.

"Also a small stipend," Reisz added. "We manage to send them one hundred seventy-five Deutschemarks a month. Nothing, really. But they are supposed to get five hundred acres of land and a house in the territories when the war ends."

Stefan continued the translation. "He says they see them as soldiers of the revolution. If they come back from this war, they will know how to fight. They will know the taste of it. They will know guerrilla tactics. They can train others. Then, when they are ready . . ."

Stefan began coughing as Reisz let the thought trail off. He went pale, gulped, and his eyes bulged. Svoray steered him roughly toward the door. "I think Stefan is not used to the beer in Mainz. I'd better take him outside."

When they were outside, Svoray said, "Get hold of yourself or we're going to be in big trouble."

"I'm not ready for this," Stefan said.

"You have to be."

"I thought this was over, these people."

"You're a student. You're smart. You read the papers. You know there are people throwing firebombs. Wake up. And you heard this before, remember?" Svoray shook him hard.

Stefan shook his head. The motion spun his cap to the ground. He took a deep, strangled breath. "You're right. But to be with them . . ." He picked up the hat, put it back on, took another breath. "Okay. I'm okay."

Renata was peering from the front door. "He's okay," Svoray said. He made an *O* with his thumb and forefinger, and tried to joke. "He's like me. He can't drink too much beer."

Stefan coughed again and managed to get a laugh from the translation.

"Come with me, then." Thrun, together with Reisz, led them to a garage door set into the basement level of the house at the head of a driveway. The door was fitted with three formidable locks. Thrun unlocked them, and opened the door.

A Volkswagen van, painted a ghastly shade of yellow, was parked in the dim garage bay among piles of boxes and bulging plastic bags. As Svoray followed Thrun to the back of the van, he saw that the boxes were filled with canned goods, the bags with clothing. Also scattered around were digging tools, knives, and kits of adhesive tape and bandages.

Thrun reached the back of the van and opened the doors. It was half full of the same materials, loaded as if for a trip.

"He says these things are for the fighters from their friends in the Fatherland," Stefan said. "He plans to drive the van to Croatia himself and hand it over to the boys at the front. He says—I don't think he is serious—he is trying to get Heinz to go with him."

"This is very impressive," said Svoray, triggering the shutter of his hidden camera and trying hard to keep his body, for a change, from intruding in the frame. But it turned out Thrun was glad to pose, as Svoray learned when he pulled out his pocket-sized snapshot camera as a contingency.

"May I?" he said. Thrun stood proudly by the van as Svoray took more pictures, saying how glad his friends would be to see all this.

Thirteen

THEY RESUMED THEIR JOURNEY in the pale light of the
December afternoon, the sky brushed with thin clouds,
Svoray following the blue Mercedes and feeling a quickening of
anticipation.

This time Reisz had good directions. He headed toward the
outskirts of Mainz. They entered and quickly left an autobahn,
following the surface road past stores and restaurants into an
area where the land was cleared and streets built, but there were
no buildings. It seemed to be a district for new development, a
prow of the city pressing into the surrounding farmland.

Stefan fell quiet. Svoray worried anew that the student's tem-
perament would fail. He let Reisz pull ahead until there was
some distance between them.

"Okay, Stefan?" he asked.

Stefan nodded, his jaw clenched.

Svoray slowed a little more, thinking to give himself time to
talk some enthusiasm into the young man. Ahead, the Mercedes
disappeared around a bend.

Accelerating to bring Reisz into view, Svoray was startled to
come on a police checkpoint at the entry to a side road. Reisz
had already passed through. Suddenly unnerved by the cluster of
police cars, vans, and uniforms, Svoray kept straight instead of
turning to follow the Mercedes through the checkpoint.

A police car pulled out immediately and fell in behind him.

The streets were a maze and there was no use trying to escape, since the police were between him and where he wanted to go. He slowed for the police car to pull alongside. Its driver motioned him to follow. He turned back toward the checkpoint.

"What are we going to do?" Stefan asked.

"Nothing. Don't worry. What law did we break?" Svoray said. A pinprick of fear entered his mind: Yaron Svoray had rented the car. The police could learn that with a simple license check, even if he could keep them from looking at his documents. The next question was, Did the neo-Nazis have a pipeline to the police?

He parked and jumped from the car before anybody could approach. There were more police than he could count in one glance. The vehicles made a chicane of the entrance road, so that a car would have to swerve around one police car and then another to get beyond the checkpoint.

"What's going on?" he demanded.

A policeman in the green uniform of the federal police was nearest. He was startled to hear English being spoken.

"Who are you? What are you doing here?" he demanded, also in English.

Svoray produced his *Play Boy* card. As the policeman peered at it, Svoray waved at the sky. "It's going to get dark. I'll lose my light."

"Who is he?" the cop asked, nodding toward Stefan, who had been walked by another officer to one of the vans. The other police were standing around in groups of two or three, watching but, so far, not interfering. Svoray could see Stefan talking and gesturing in an attitude of helplessness. Svoray had told him to leave his identification cards at home, saying it was better if the skinheads had no way of knowing who he was.

"My translator."

"What is his name?" the cop said.

"Stefan." Svoray realized he didn't even know Stefan's last name. "He is a student. I only met him on Thursday. He's not a Communist or ANTIFA. He's not even a neo-Nazi. Hurry, will you? I want to get pictures."

The two policemen conferred, and the first one returned to Svoray shaking his head. "You'll have to come with us. There is no confirming this."

"Wait," said Svoray. "Wait a minute. I have his phone number

here. Check it with him.'' He dug into his pockets and produced
the notebook with Stefan's number.

The cop took the number and walked to the van. Returning
again, he said, ''He knows the number you have. But what does it
prove?''

''That I'm telling you the truth. Come on. It's going to get
dark.''

''It only proves you know the same number.'' The cop paused.
''But what else could he be but a student, dressed like that?'' He
shrugged and nodded Svoray to the car.

Svoray had the car rolling before the cop could change his
mind, moving past Stefan and calling to him to get in. Waving his
thanks, he steered through the obstacle course and out the other
side onto a hard-packed dirt road that led past a farmhouse.

Reisz was waiting anxiously by an open auto gate in a high
wooden fence. Svoray found a space among the cars parked up
and down the road. He decided against taking his green bag.
The hidden camera and recorder were clearly for spying, and
therefore too dangerous to use. He'd stand at least a chance of
explaining more conventional gear, and wanting snapshots was
part of Ron Furey's personality. Most of the hidden camera
photos had been disastrous in any case, featuring arms, legs, and
couch pillows rather than revealing scenes. He got out of the car
laughing at the irony.

Stefan caught his eye. ''I'm okay,'' he said.

''Good.'' He stuck his handheld tape recorder in his jacket
pocket and handed Stefan the small snapshot camera. ''You be
my cameraman. Put it in your pocket, though.''

Two skinheads were lounging outside the gate. They wore camouflage fatigue outfits, high black boots, and the black peaked
caps reminiscent of the Waffen SS. One nudged the other as
Svoray and Stefan walked toward them, and started to laugh.
They moved to bar the gate.

''Hello, Ron. No trouble with the police, I hope,'' Reisz called
in German. He swept up Svoray and Stefan and led them
through the gate, nodding at the skinheads.

The house inside the gate resembled a high-sided Swiss chalet,
though no mountains were in evidence. The fence stretched out
of sight behind the house. Trees and bushes disguised it from the
inside, creating a garden.

Reisz steered them toward a man whose pants were stuffed into calf-high boots and whose brown shirtwaist jacket sported an armband. He wore weird glasses and an obvious hairpiece and seemed at least sixty. Renata waited beside him.

"He is introducing Herr Curt Müller," Stefan said as Reisz boomed the name. "Herr Müller hosts this party every year and also one for Hitler's birthday. He is telling him you are his nephew, Ron. The son of his American sister. And I am your translator. So even though he doesn't like Americans much, he will like you."

"I hope so," said Svoray. "Why doesn't he like Americans?"

Stefan asked Müller the question. "He says when he was a boy during the war he was almost killed by an American bomb that fell on Mainz. And also Americans are friends of the Jews."

"Tell him not all Americans," Svoray said. *"Nicht alle Amerikaner,"* he added on his own.

Reisz laughed at this, but the host still looked suspicious. Svoray asked if he could take his picture. When he heard the translation, Müller scowled. He shook his head furiously and spoke in rapid German that needed no translation. Reisz spoke to him.

"You are only a tourist, and you meant no offense," Stefan said. "But you are also a believer who can be trusted. Herr Müller isn't sure he trusts us."

Reisz steered them away toward the back of the house, whispering that Svoray had almost gotten all of them in trouble. He then turned back, saying he would stay behind to help Müller greet the arriving guests, most of whom he knew.

Renata hurried after them. Through Stefan, she added to her husband's warning. "Herr Müller hates journalists. He hates them worse than Jews. If he finds out you're a journalist, he'll kill you. Don't let him see you taking pictures."

Svoray said, "Ask her what happens if he finds out I'm a Jew."

Renata listened, her eyes widening. Then she laughed to show Svoray she recognized his joke. "She says he would know if you were Jewish," Stefan reported. "That's because he can smell them."

Behind the house, the fenced compound stretched toward an outbuilding nearly a hundred yards away, where people were gathered. They went toward it along a rough asphalt walk. On either side, a thick blanket of turf looked ready to be cut and transplanted.

"Give me the camera," Svoray said quietly. "We're going to forget what he said about the pictures. Don't be obvious."

Stefan slipped him the pocket camera. "I will forget I know you if you get caught."

"No you won't. Anyway, I won't get caught. Look at this. Look at these idiots. I don't believe it."

The scene was another newsreel image, or a still taken from a dusty Nazi party file. Several dozen people were standing around outside the building, a rough wood structure. Most seemed young, and they were all drinking beer. Some wore black or brown uniform shirts with belts, the SS or SA paramilitary look. Others wore neatly parted haircuts and white shirts and ties with dark coats, calling to mind either the Gestapo or the *Clockwork Orange* Mods—natty people who were about brutality. Some of them, too, had belts draped diagonally across their chests under their open overcoats. Skinheads sauntered about in their green bomber jackets, combat boots, and bloused fatigues, dragging along girlfriends in leather and black. Everyone looked hard at the outsiders.

Svoray knelt to tie his shoe. He wanted to feel the reassuring weight of the knife taped to his ankle.

Moving inside the building, they found a single high-ceilinged room ringed by a narrow balcony. The floor was hard dirt, covered with gravel chips. More people—and now Svoray saw there were older men as well as young, but few in their thirties and forties—clustered near several beer kegs set against one wall. A large portrait of Hitler hung from the balcony.

Stefan had managed to relax. He introduced himself to the nearest group, two men in black coats and two young women. "Hello, I'm Stefan. This is Ron. He is Heinz Reisz's nephew from America."

"Ask them why their hair's like that, so many alike," he said to Stefan. The men's haircuts were preternaturally neat, shaved above the ears and usually brushed to one side.

"Hitlerjugend," said the young man. Stefan listened and explained that their hair was cut to Hitler Youth tolerances.

Svoray reached for the camera. "The girls. They look pretty," he said. "Can I take a photo? Look at me." Stefan explained and they began shaking their heads and waving him off. At that moment he happened to glance toward the edge of the crowd.

He met a pair of eyes that frightened him as much as anything he had seen in his life. Cold, penetrating, utterly dead, they stared contemptuously from behind small round glasses, the Himmler style except for their gold rims. The man himself was young and gaunt, his dark hair slicked back from a high, thin forehead, his nose blade-thin, his carriage arrogant, his aura deadly. He wore a long black leather coat. He just stood there, studying them, and Svoray felt like a ghetto Jew who had been noticed, when life depended on escaping notice.

"Stefan, come on. I want to go outside," he said.

They escaped into the gray afternoon. The skinheads were drinking and playing games in which they punched each other or threw knives. New arrivals approached along the asphalt walk. Svoray was relieved to see Reisz. His sponsor was in animated conversation with an older man, a beefy fellow with a gut that strained the buttons of his flannel shirt. He wore, in addition, bleached jeans, a parka, and a black military beret.

"Ah, Ron," Reisz exclaimed as they approached, and began introducing Friedhelm Büsse.

"Herr Büsse has been a leader in the movement for over twenty years," Stefan said. "He has gone to prison for his opposition to world Jewry. It hardened and strengthened him. The government banned his party, so he started another one. They want to ban it, too. It is small, but not as small as the government thinks. Now he is telling him you are his nephew, and a friend."

Svoray pumped Büsse's hand and told him how glad he was to meet him. Büsse nodded gruffly.

"I'm very impressed, Heinz," Svoray said. "You said you would introduce me to some serious people, and here they are. And such an impressive place."

Reisz, talking in his booming voice, beckoned them around a corner of the building. "He wants to show us something," Stefan said.

As they rounded the corner the elements of a Nazi shrine came into view. First, a semicircle of stones, at its center a German helmet emblazoned with a swastika and an SS emblem, the letters stylized to look like lightning bolts. Behind it, against the fence, a stone pillar set between flanking evergreens. This Germanic altar was marked with Teutonic runes and hieroglyphics. It was topped by a metal fire bowl whose flame, when lit, would cast torchlight on the swastika banner that hung above and behind it, above the level of the fence.

The light was fading now. Svoray pulled the camera from his pocket and handed it to Stefan. "This is beautiful. I've got to get a picture. With Heinz and Herr Büsse."

He hustled Reisz and Büsse into position under the swastika, where he joined them in a pose: Svoray in his suede-brimmed baseball cap directly under the swastika; Reisz in the middle, bareheaded, hair falling across his forehead; Büsse on the left in an aggressive stance, right hand half-bunched in a fist, staring defiantly into the camera. Stefan snapped the shutter, catching the scene against a milk-white fading sky, with a small, gnarled, heavily trimmed tree at the right of the frame.

The party was continuing to build as they returned to the front of the building. Büsse went back inside to replenish his beer. Reisz indicated he was going to the toilet and wanted Svoray to join him.

"He says you have not seen everything," Stefan said. "He will show you one of Herr Müller's greatest treasures."

"What, his dick?" Svoray bellowed. "Heinz, I love you, but I don't want to see your dick."

"Oh, no, no, no," rumbled Reisz.

Reisz led them to what looked like a military guardpost, with a peaked roof and an arched entrance door. A cardboard sign tacked over the door pictured a Star of David hanging from a gallows and several lines of crude printing in German. Reisz opened the door with a flourish, revealing a toilet. Its raised lid and seat were scrawled with more writing and Stars of David.

"Oh, this is priceless," enthused Svoray. "What does it say?"

"Here is where we defecate on the Judas star . . ." Stefan said.

Reisz placed himself before the bowl and began to urinate. Svoray took a quick, surreptitious picture, then stepped back and took another of the entrance to the outhouse.

Reisz zipped up his pants and asked Svoray with a gesture if he wanted to use the inscribed toilet.

"No," he said. Not even passing as a neo-Nazi would he urinate on the Star of David. But he did feel a need, and when Reisz headed inside to draw himself another beer, Svoray pulled Stefan with him in the direction of the shrine. He looked behind to satisfy himself that no one was coming.

"Watch for me," he said.

He walked to the fence, drew down his zipper and aimed at the Teutonic altar.

"What are you doing?" Stefan asked in a panic.

"If anyone asks, I'm pissing in the bushes," said Svoray.

"You're crazy. Someone could come."

"Nobody will come. They're all too busy in the other place, pissing on the Jews."

Stefan peeked around the corner. Svoray leaned back on his heels and took pleasure in the arch of his stream. The student turned back to him, his face white. "Hurry," he pleaded. "Someone is coming."

"You're kidding."

"I'm not kidding. Please!"

"You are too nervous," Svoray said. Then he heard voices and laughter heading toward them around the corner of the building.

Fourteen

S VORAY WILLED HIMSELF to stop. He was still hauling up his zipper as they rounded the corner of the building and met the approaching group. There were six of them, three skinheads, two girls, and—Svoray saw the glint of gold-rimmed glasses in the dimming light—the blade-thin youth in the black leather trench coat. Svoray sidestepped to avoid them, but one of the skinheads moved into his path and pushed him against one of the women. "Fat pig," she screamed in German. "He's broken my foot."

Jumping back from her, Svoray caromed into another of the skinheads. This one reeled like a tenpin, but the third struck Svoray with a vicious elbow low on his left side above the kidney. He righted himself and spun to face them. Stefan shrank behind him.

"Tell them we are friends, Stefan," Svoray said. "We are friends and we don't want to fight."

The one who had pushed him first, whose big, stubbled head seemed too large for his body, stepped up and leaned into Svoray's face. *"Verfassungsschutz,"* he hissed in a voice that stank of beer. He unleashed an angry string of German that bulged the veins of his neck and rippled a blue lightning bolt tattooed on the side of his neck below one ear.

"He says we are fucking spies," Stefan said.

"What are you talking about? Are you crazy? We are friends," Svoray shouted. "Stefan, tell him we are friends."

Stefan replied. The girl jumped around on one foot, still cursing. Behind them, toward the front of the building, a pyramid of wood was stacked in preparation for a bonfire. The leader spit disgustedly in its direction. The second woman was holding a paper cup of beer and he took it from her, took a long drink, and tossed the dregs at Svoray's feet. Then he paused, waiting for some sign of fear, the bully's signal to attack.

Svoray measured them in return. They all were drunk, except perhaps for the youth in the trench coat. Finding him and Stefan alone, out of sight of the crowd, had been an unexpected bonus in their afternoon of drinking and Nazi celebration. They hadn't anticipated fighting when they headed off behind the building. They were probably just coming to look at the shrine, and it would take a moment for the relish of real violence to seep in. Svoray knew he had to take advantage of that moment.

He stepped up to the lead skinhead. "You are lucky, my friend," he said, not caring whether the other man understood English. "My shoes are dry."

He put his arm around the skinhead's shoulder and moved him in the direction of the shrine. When they were where they could see it in the half-light, Svoray threw out his arm like an impresario introducing a star act.

The transformation was immediate. The skinhead beckoned his friends. They stood and murmured with approval. Only the gaze from behind the gold-rimmed glasses showed suspicion. Svoray slapped the leader on the shoulder. "Excuse me," he said. "We have to get back to our dates."

"It's not safe to be around you. You could get us killed," Stefan said when they had rounded the corner.

"Stop worrying, Stefan. You're going to make me as nervous as you are. We're doing fine."

Svoray nonetheless was glad to see Reisz, standing in the light spilling from the door of the outbuilding. He was nodding and exchanging greetings with the skinheads and Nazis entering to replenish their containers of beer from the kegs inside.

"Nero," Svoray called, using Reisz's nickname, the same as his dog.

Reisz beamed at seeing him, and asked where he had been.

Svoray gestured to the back of the building. "Admiring the shrine with some new friends."

Reisz said he and Stefan were just in time to hear his speech. He followed Müller to a small platform set up before the wood-pile for the bonfire. He was an energetic speaker, and his rumbling voice and litany of hate drew loud applause. "He is talking about how they have all been bled by world Jewry and sent to jail and persecuted for their views," Stefan said. The crowd roared at his refrain: "Many enemies, much honor."

When he stepped down, in the deepening twilight someone crouched and struck matches to light the bonfire. At first it flickered from within, like lightning in a thunderhead. Stefan walked a few steps away and stood by himself. The flames struggled to start and then broke out, licking up from the base of the wood-pile and casting long, shuddering shadows. The fire threw a ring of warmth and drew a crowd. The drunker they got, the more violently the skinheads played their games. Two would pair off, remove their belts, and wrap them around their fists. Then one would hit the other on the shoulder. The man throwing the punch won if he moved the other man, but lost if the receiver stood his ground. The blows sounded like truncheons smashing into slabs of meat.

Svoray moved to watch a group of knife throwers. Two men stood facing each other inside crudely marked circles. They began throwing bayonets into the earth at each other's feet. Each throw reduced the opponent's "territory," until one of the skinheads tried to throw his bayonet while standing on one foot. The game was called Conquer the Universe.

With the men slamming each other and the thrown knives slicing into the turf, the skinheads and neo-Nazis pressed around. They began singing the "Horst-Wessel Song," the official Nazi party marching song, swaying together in front of the fire. Cries of *"Heil Hitler"* were raised. Scuffles began to break out.

Reisz headed off to the main house after half an hour, saying he wanted to help Müller greet the late-arriving guests. Svoray stood alone, watching the figures against the firelight, feeling their suspicion, and began to think about leaving. There was too little restraint now, and he thought he had learned all he could.

He went looking for Stefan. The boy was talking to a group of black-clad men and women. He held a beer, and seemed a little tipsy.

"It's time to go," Svoray said. Stefan looked disappointed for a fraction of a second.

As they passed through the crowd, they saw Renata. She was talking to a little old man who looked lost within the fabric of his overcoat. He had sparse gray hair, a trim white goatee, a scrawny neck that rose from his coat collar in a sag of wattles, and enormous ears on which were hooked a pair of steel-rimmed spectacles. Svoray interrupted them.

"Renata, we must go. Please say goodnight to Heinz if I don't see him. I'll call when I get back from Munich."

She pulled a disappointed face. "She says you must meet Herr Wilhelm Köberich," Stefan said as she pulled the small man to her bosom. "He is known as *'Kampfhahn.'* It means fighting cock. She says he was the valedictorian of the Hitler School."

The Fighting Cock blinked. Köberich was aptly named. His head protruded forward like a bird's about to peck the ground, and his pale eyes shone with a bird's wariness to danger. It was an intelligent wariness, and Svoray took note of it.

"The Hitler School?" he asked. "For the best and brightest of the Nazis?"

"Yes," Köberich responded. He added in halting English, "But I must correct. All were bright. I was not smarter than the others."

Svoray remembered the movie *Europa, Europa,* about the efforts of a Jewish boy to pass for Aryan during the war. Recruited to the Hitler School, he went to painful lengths to hide the circumcision that labeled him as Jewish. The Hitler School was the Eton or Andover of the Third Reich, a prep school for the purest young Germans who were supposed to be the Nazi leaders of the future. Here was one still faithful to its teachings.

"I'm sorry we must go. But I'll see you again, I hope," he said.

The Fighting Cock spoke to Renata, she in turn to Stefan. "He hopes so, too," Stefan said. "She and Heinz told them much about you. You have asked about unity. He has someone he wants you to meet.''

More guests passed them as they returned to the main house. They were either skinheads in their fatigues and bomber jackets or neo-Nazis wearing versions of Third Reich military garb. Svoray turned for a final look at the bonfire. A hundred or more were gathered around it, black silhouettes against the orange flames, moving as if joined together.

Neither Reisz nor Müller was at the gate. The two skinheads were still there, less sober and more jovial than earlier. When Svoray found his car, to his horror the Fiat was hemmed against the fence. Two other cars, at least, would have to be moved before he and Stefan could escape.

"Maybe those guys have the keys," he said to Stefan. "Ask them if they have any keys."

"Keys? *Nein.*" The skinheads laughed at the preposterous request.

Svoray was heading back inside the gate, Stefan following, when they ran head-on into Müller. The host of the solstice celebration was shouting angrily and gesturing.

"He wants to know why we are leaving, the party is just starting. He wants to know why his party is not good enough for us," Stefan said.

"Tell him you are not feeling well."

Müller snorted, and continued ranting. "It is not expected that we leave so soon," Stefan translated. "He is offended in his hospitality."

"Tell him I have to catch a plane to Munich," Svoray said.

"München?" Müller said.

"Yes. I am going to meet Himmler's daughter," he lied. The truth was he had arranged to meet an old Waffen SS man whose name had come to him in Sarreguemines. He hadn't forgotten entirely about the diamonds. Maybe he would try to meet Himmler's daughter too.

Müller paused at this. His agitated face relaxed. "This he can understand," Stefan said. "He hopes you will say hello for him."

"Tell him that our problem is that our car is blocked."

Müller sent the skinhead parking lot attendants to retrieve keys and move the cars. Reisz appeared, waving frantically and calling, "Ron, Ron," as they were about to drive away. He came to the car, speaking in a tumble of words.

"He is disappointed that we are leaving so soon," Stefan said.

"I am, too, but Himmler's daughter . . ."

"He understands, but he is still disappointed."

Svoray rolled down his window. Reisz leaned into the car and kissed him roughly on the cheek. He smelled of tobacco and beer and a cinnamon-scented aftershave. Stefan said, "He wants to know when his American 'nephew' will be back, so he can introduce you to more people," Stefan translated.

"I'll be back after the first of the year," Svoray said. "I want to tell my friends about all the good people he has introduced me to, and then see where we go from there."

Svoray had no wish to return. His mission, as he saw it, was accomplished, and he had no further need for Reisz. He knew now that links existed between generations, with Nazis of the Third Reich passing their hatreds along to the receptive young; that various neo-Nazi groups and even the "legitimate" Republikaners were in close contact, aided by gadflies like Reisz; that German skinheads were learning the basics of ethnic warfare in Croatia; that the violent right was looking for money to organize and was eager for outside support. Rabbis Hier and Cooper had suspected much of this; now their campaign to force the Kohl government to respond to right-wing violence might gather momentum. All Svoray had left to do was find Charlie Müller and buy the soldier-book.

Reisz said goodbye with a mock *"Sieg Heil"* salute.

Then they were free, past the skinheads, past the parked cars, past the police checkpoint, out of the grid of unpopulated streets and on the autobahn headed for Frankfurt.

Svoray was ecstatic. "We did it, Stefan. We did it, my friend!" He drove with one hand on the wheel, the other pounding Stefan on the shoulder, the speedometer showing one hundred twenty kilometers per hour as they streaked along the autobahn. "Do you believe it, all those idiots? The Fighting Cock, my God! Pissing on the altar. That was a close call. The skinheads throwing knives. Did you see the guy standing on one foot, about to get a bayonet between his toes? The only one who really scared me was the one who looked like a Gestapo agent. Didn't he look just like one, in that leather trench coat? His eyes, that's what scared me, eyes like a dead man's, the little fuck. I'm telling you, my friend, we are going to blow the lid off this. It will blow sky-high and maybe the government will have to do something. Then we will really have accomplished something."

Stefan grunted. He turned away and stared out the window at lights along the highway.

Soon Svoray picked up the signs to Frankfurt's airport. He planned to leave the car there while he flew to Munich; Stefan would take an S-bahn train from the airport home.

"Stefan, what's wrong? You should be cheering for joy that we got these fuckers. We can put a big crimp in them. Believe me, you should be proud. You did a good job tonight. I couldn't have done it without you. You're not still scared, are you? Or drunk? Not too much to drink, I hope."

Stefan shook his head.

"What is it, then?"

The student turned toward him and in the highway lights Svoray saw that his eyes were glistening. "Of what should I be proud?" he said. "That these people exist?"

"Listen, Stefan. You were very brave. That's what you should be proud of."

The airport, the largest on the European continent, came into view in a blaze of lights. Svoray followed the signs toward the parking areas. Stefan laughed once suddenly, then fell again into silence.

Svoray parked and grabbed his green bag, into which he'd stuffed a change of underwear and a fresh shirt. "Stefan, you can find the train okay, right? My flight is at eight, and I still have to pick up the ticket. Listen, you earned your money today. Here." He pulled out his money clip, peeled off a wad of bills and thrust them at Stefan.

Stefan pushed the money back at him.

"Stefan, this is ridiculous. Snap out of it. And take the money. You worked for it."

"I don't want it."

"Tomorrow you will want it." Svoray took the bills and tucked them into Stefan's shirt pocket.

The student rubbed his eyes and expelled a long, shuddering

sigh. He said, "This is not my country. This is not happening in my country."

"This is unbelievable." Aaron Breitbart sat at his prodigiously cluttered desk at the Wiesenthal Center in Los Angeles. A large red heart was visible outside the window, the sign for the restaurant next door, Love's. But Breitbart's attention was on the fax before him, the latest from Mark Seal. He rubbed the blue shadow on his cheeks, plunked his elbows on chair arms worn through to the stuffing. "Just unbelievable. This is like a roll call of the extreme right wing.

"Büsse. Listen to this, Abe," Breitbart said. "Büsse's a real hard-line Nazi. He founded the People's Socialist League Party of Labor in 1971. Substitute 'National' for 'People's' and you get the idea. It was banned, and Büsse went to prison for inciting racial hatred. Now he heads the Freiheitliche Deutsche Arbeiterpartei, the Free German Workers' party. A hundred fifty members, according to the watchdogs. All he wants to do is go back to National Socialism."

Rick Eaton, at the adjoining desk, busily typed this information into his computer.

Abe Cooper, standing in the doorway, found Breitbart's enthusiasm incongruous. The message from Seal contained important names that Svoray said he had met. But Seal himself seemed oddly indifferent to the information coming from Germany. He was unimpressed with Svoray's reportage. The rabbis had little to rely on but Seal's interpretation, since he was the only one regularly in direct contact with Svoray, and the transcriptions and tapes were days late coming from New York.

Questions nagged at Cooper. Svoray had linked young and old Nazis, but had he uncovered a plot or an affinity group? Was the police roadblock he had encountered for preventing trouble or gathering information? How much information was needed before the Germans could prevent the kind of carnage that had happened in Mölln? Did Heinz Reisz's connection with Bernd Thrun mean the Republikaners were a neo-Nazi party? It was frustrating not to have the tapes and transcripts; without them, there was no directing Svoray toward useful inquiries. He was on his own in Germany, while Cooper could only relay his questions through Seal, too late for Svoray to react. Cooper wished the center was dealing with Svoray directly.

"I can't find this one," Breitbart was saying. "Köberich. I'll have to call some people. If he went to the Adolf Hitler School somebody will have something on him. We'll put him on hold."

Eaton raised a hand. "Slow down, Aaron," he pleaded. "Spell it, okay?"

Breitbart spelled the name, and Eaton's fingers tapped at the computer keyboard.

"Anything else?" Cooper asked. "What about the host?"

Breitbart riffled through his mound of papers. "Curt Müller. No big name, just another fixture. He and his wife, Ursula, run something called the HNG. The Support Organization for National Political Prisoners and Their Families. It's like a Nazi help group."

Eaton paused from his typing. "What do they do, send care packages to Nazis in jail? Bake files into cakes?"

"Write letters to the Bundestag, probably. Müller's also a kind of recruiter, with this shrine of his. It gets young neo-Nazis all starry-eyed about the cause."

Cooper said, "What's missing?"

Breitbart paused. Eaton looked up from his keyboard. "Well, these are all known names," Breitbart said. "No real surprises."

"Didn't he say they needed money?" Eaton said. "It would be nice to find out what they want it for."

Cooper sat impatiently through a meeting that roughed out the opening ceremonies for the Museum of Tolerance. Gerry Margolis, the museum's director, was presiding. The building was finished, but raw gashes of earth indicated the landscaping still to be completed. Inside, the museum's slide and video displays were up and running. But its interactive research areas on the second floor remained tangles of unconnected wires. It was a *ba'al hagan* up there, a crazy zoo. No air conditioning, and they had to use portable phones. The Apple Computer people were urging Cooper to wait, wait, wait; the longer he waited the more up-to-date the technology—the touch screens and the database that included the Time-Life history of World War II—would be. Cooper's mind swam with the new language of information streams. The rabbi envied Aaron Breitbart's gift, his ability to search unerringly the database that was his desk and shelves. But he held in his hand a printout from Rick Eaton's computer files.

He showed it to Marvin Hier as soon as the last meeting guest had filed out of the rabbi's office. "Moish, look at this," he said.

Hier looked down through his bifocals at the paper Cooper thrust in front of him. When he looked up, Hier said, "He met these people? What did they say?"

"I don't know. We don't have the tapes yet."

"Where are the tapes?"

"They're still in New York. It takes a few days."

"Why?" Hier asked, brushing his forehead and raising the permanent wave of hair against his yarmulke. "We don't need transcriptions, only dubs. Machines do it."

"I don't know."

Hier looked down at the paper again. "This is impressive," he said. "Is this impressive?"

"I don't know. There's nothing new here. No new names. No grand scheme. Seal's not impressed with the narrative he's getting."

"Are we wasting our money?"

"Maybe. I don't know."

"There's some kind of scheme, Abe. I'm telling you. Look at the figures." Hier walked away and deposited himself behind his desk. He found the sheet of paper he was looking for and scanned it. "Over two thousand incidents of right-wing violence so far this year, and the year's not even over. Last year there were less than fifteen hundred. Seventeen murders. Those poor Turks in Mölln. And one poor schlemiel in Hamburg who committed the unpardonable sin of saying Hitler was a criminal. A German, too. A sea captain. Beaten to death."

"I agree," said Cooper. "It can't all just be random."

"Even if it is, it can't go on. It's the attitude that lets it happen that has to stop. The Republikaners are getting elected everywhere, when they should be banned. Kohl is not helping. You heard what he said. The same as when I wrote him."

Kohl, the chancellor, had insisted after the firebombing deaths in Mölln that the German democracy was "willing and able to fight violence and extremist terror with all the means at its disposal." Nonetheless, in the shrinking days of 1992, Kohl and his Christian Democrats maintained a policy that was a vestige of the cold war. They considered left-wing violence a greater threat than violence from the right and worked harder to prevent it. This, in Hier's view, was intransigence and a failure to accept the full weight of German history.

"If an Israeli can get close to these people, why can't the Germans do something about it?" Hier asked.

"That's the question, isn't it?" said Cooper.

"What's he doing now?"

"He's still there. This message is the last we've heard."

"Did he buy the thing yet, the document?"

"The soldier-book? I guess not. He didn't mention it."

Hier, with his love of documents and their potential for nuance and revelation, looked disappointed. "I thought that was the main point of this whole thing."

"A big part of it," Cooper agreed. "And his general impression of what's going on over there."

Hier seemed struck by a sudden thought. He chewed on a knuckle, then brushed a hand across his independent-minded forelock. "If he met these people and they trust him, think what he can learn."

"If," said Cooper.

"If he proves out, maybe we should think about keeping this going."

Cooper looked at Hier sharply. He had gotten used to the way his friend and mentor's mind worked. A question didn't have to be answered, an issue settled, before Hier moved on to the next one.

Fifteen

SVORAY RETURNED to Frankfurt on Monday, intent on finding Charlie Müller. Leaving the airport, he decided on impulse to detour to Langen and visit Reisz.

He had wasted two nights and a day in Munich. He had managed to ship his tapes from the airport. But when he got to Munich his bad German pronunciation had misled his taxi driver, who took him to a gay hotel and restaurant on the outskirts instead of the hotel he had reserved. The proprietor, an old drag queen, had chuckled understandingly; it was a common mistake. He finally reached the right place. By the time he found a card phone and called Michal, and then Mark Seal at home to get the name of the lawyer in case he needed it again, he was exhausted. A day of conversations with the old SS man proved useless, a smorgasbord of war memories, Holocaust denial, and vague yearning for a "proper" German leader. He did not see Himmler's daughter, but got her address.

When he returned to the hotel that night, he realized it was the first day of Hanukkah, the eight-day Jewish festival of lights that was pegged to the twenty-fifth of Kislev in the Jewish calendar but veered all over the Roman calendar. The holiday had revolutionary overtones, for it commemorated the rededication of the Temple in Jerusalem following the victory of Judah the Maccabee over the oppressive Syrian king Antiochus. Hitler sometimes was compared to Antiochus. This aspect of Hanukkah had special appeal for Svoray on the day following the solstice celebration. He left the hotel to find a card phone.

"Happy Hanukkah," Michal answered, as if she knew who was calling.

"Happy Hanukkah, Michali." It was a comfort to speak Hebrew.

"What new Nazis did you meet today?" she said.

"Only one, an old man who thinks Germany needs leaders who are 'correct.' But I'm almost finished here. Tomorrow I go back to Frankfurt and buy the soldier-book. Then I'm coming home."

"Can I believe that? Should I tell the children?"

"Yes," he said. "Tell them. Tell them it's a promise."

Reisz and Renata were home; Svoray saw the old Mercedes when he parked around the corner between rows of small apartment buildings. Reisz opened the door, and his face broke into an expression of delight when he saw Svoray. Svoray pointed to his watch and said he had only a short time. He wondered if Reisz knew Charlie Müller.

Reisz's hospitality was irresistible. In a moment Svoray was in the cramped living room and Renata was serving coffee and soft drinks. Reisz made a great fuss about excusing himself. He returned moments later with a package wrapped in tissue paper, which he handed to Svoray.

"Ein Geschenk," he said, beaming.

"A gift? For me?"

Svoray was nonplussed. Reisz was tipping the balance of friendship. It made him feel uncomfortable. He tore the paper away to reveal an old, hefty book, bound in cardboard, the size of a school textbook. Under a soldier's profile on its cover was a title in the requisite Gothic lettering: *Deutschland erwacht,* Germany Awakened, and inside a subtitle, *Werden, Kampf und Sieg der NSDAP.* The book was a tract about the rise of the Nazi party. Among its reams of text were picture cards pasted to the pages. Each showed Hitler or an event in the Nazi emergence. It was dated 1933.

"Heinz, I'm overwhelmed," said Svoray.

Reisz explained that the cards were collectibles before the war; young people bought the books and tried to fill them with the scenes that corresponded with the captions. He opened the book to an early page, which he had inscribed. Translated, the inscription read: "For Ron, from a convinced Nazi from Germany. Heinz Reisz." He had added his nickname, Nero.

"I'm overwhelmed," Svoray repeated.

He left an hour later with Reisz's gift tucked under his arm, but with no new information. Reisz had never heard of anyone named Charlie Müller.

Müller had vanished. Svoray began to doubt his existence. His calls produced the same chorus of unanswered bleeps that German phones made or, equally frustrating, a busy signal. He returned to the pornography store once on Monday afternoon, and twice again that night. Three different clerks, only one of whom he'd seen before, said they'd never heard of Müller. The change vendor at the entrance to the peep show shrugged and shook his head.

On Tuesday morning, Svoray stalked the shopping district and the Zeil. Wilhelm and his friends were drinking at the entrance to the U-bahn, and he avoided them. He returned to the steakhouse where he had eaten with Müller and Schulz, thinking they might somehow reappear.

He continued calling all the while. At five that evening, someone picked up the phone. "Charlie? Charlie, it's me, Ron," Svoray said. He heard silence, then a click as the receiver was replaced.

By late that night he was desperate enough to compromise his cover. He wrote "I have a buyer. Ron Furey" on a hotel notepad along with his room number and placed the paper in a hotel envelope along with two hundred Deutschemarks. Then he wrote "Charlie Müller" on the envelope, and headed for the porno store.

The red-haired clerk began automatically to shake his head when he saw Svoray. Three American GIs came out of the hall of peep shows and headed down the street talking about finding a beer hall. Svoray slipped the envelope through the window with another hundred-mark note. The clerk took it, and placed it to one side.

Svoray returned to the hotel. He spent another hundred marks at the concierge's desk. He was registered as Svoray, but he told the night concierge that he might be getting a call for

Mr. Furey, and to make sure it went to him. In his room, he stripped to his T-shirt and boxer shorts, lay down on the bed, and took stock. He was homesick and tired, but he could not leave without the soldier-book. Rabbi Hier had placed great importance on it. Svoray now felt as if his mission was only for the rabbis. It seemed to him that doing a story for *Playboy* compromised his purpose. Even filing dispatches for the JTA seemed a dilution of his mission. It seemed like profiteering. And he had seen enough resurgent Nazism to believe that stories alone were not enough.

He fell asleep with those thoughts. The next morning, he rose and showered. When he came out of the bathroom, the message light on his telephone was blinking.

"Ah." The concierge, wearing a hotelier's look of bland discretion, inclined in his direction. "Do you know someone named Müller?"

"Yes. What did he look like?"

"Ah. He was young, with his hair short. Perhaps he was a skinhead." His face showed distaste. "Little round glasses, and light eyes that . . ." The concierge darted his eyes around. "He came asking for Mr. Furey. He had a note on hotel paper." The man paused, waiting for Svoray's reaction. "So I, ah, suggested he leave some way of contacting him, in case you did happen to be here. He gave me this."

Svoray took the paper the concierge held out to him and read a name. "Where is this?" he asked, as he dug into his pocket for his money clip.

"Ah. It is in Sachsenhausen. On the other side of the river. Not far. He said he would be there tonight at ten o'clock."

The taxi driver crossed the Main at nine forty-five and wound among streets of half-timbered houses, narrow alleys, and small squares. There were people in the streets despite the hour and the nighttime chill, couples and groups strolling, convivial in the Christmas season. The taxi stopped in front of a small hotel. A sign at its corner advertised the entrance to a pub.

Müller had picked the only unpopular bar in the district. He was sitting at a table next to a window, illuminated by a stained-glass lamp that hung from the ceiling. Two men whom Svoray had not seen before were with him; they wore black jeans and fatigue jackets, but no obvious skinhead tattoos or paraphernalia. The three of them were drinking beer from long-necked bottles, not using glasses. Two other men were playing pinball at a machine against the wall. They paused when Svoray entered, and watched him walk to Müller's table. At the end of the bar, a waitress was smoking a cigarette while the bartender replaced glasses in an overhead rack. The place was empty otherwise.

"I thought you had been swallowed by the earth," Svoray said. He dragged a chair from another table and sat down.

Müller was more somber than Svoray remembered him. His nervous eyes held a suspicion of Svoray that had not been there in September. He pulled two hundred-mark notes from the pocket of his shirt and put them on the table.

"What was this for?" he asked.

"A down payment," said Svoray. "I have a buyer who wants the soldier-book."

"Oh, no," Müller said. His eyes paused on Svoray, then fled to the lamp, to the window, to the pinball players. "No more. The soldier-book is not available."

Svoray was stunned. "You mean you sold it?"

"No. It just is not available. Not for sale."

"What do you mean, not for sale? I told you I would get the money. I came all this way. I've been looking for you for the last week. Ah, I see you have the grace at least to look embarrassed."

Müller shrugged. "It's not me. Schulz is worried," he said.

"About what?"

"Secret police. Verfassungsschutz. Zionist agents."

Svoray burst into laughter. "You're kidding me. Zionist agents?" He turned to the other two men at the table. "Do I look like a Zionist agent? Listen, Charlie, I'm dealing with collectors. I have buyers and they're eager. You can't tell me you have nothing to sell."

"Who are they? Zionist agents?"

Svoray stopped laughing and leaned across the table until he was in Müller's face. His two companions tensed. "You're paranoid," he growled. "You used to be a happy-go-lucky guy. We saw your little movie together, remember? You introduced me to Schulz and said he had the book to sell. It would help your movement. I don't care about that, frankly, one way or the other.

But I went home and found someone and got the money. You set me up, you cocksucker. You owe me two thousand dollars right now for wasting my time and taking me away from home at Christmas. My kids are crying at home because daddy's not home to decorate the Christmas tree, and it's your fucking fault. I'm sitting here with thousands of dollars. My clients expect something. You pay me for my wasted time or find me somebody else who wants to sell."

The room was held in silence. At the pinball machine, the players paused. A squeak of a dry towel on glass sounded loud behind the bar. Svoray looked up. One of the pinball players coughed. The other turned and pumped a ball into the chute.

Müller stared at him. The other two men relaxed. Svoray pulled a packet of three hundred and fifty marks from his sock and slapped it on the table next to the two hundred.

"What is this for?" Müller asked.

"Find me someone else. You promised me. That's a fucking contract."

Müller fingered the money. He stood up and said, "Let's talk outside."

They left the others drinking at the table and walked into the street. Above the low roofs, the lights of Frankfurt's office towers were visible across the river. They were closer than Svoray had thought. He kept waiting for the door of the pub to open and Müller's friends to come after them.

"Schulz was scared after he met you," Müller said. "He didn't believe your story."

"So what? Forget him," said Svoray. "Look, I want to make some money here. I told you, I'm dealing with collectors."

Müller walked a few steps away and turned around. "I don't know," he said.

He looked at Müller in the light of a street lamp. The ridges of his eyebrows cast his eyes in shadow; Svoray couldn't see them but knew what they were doing, flitting like moths. He wanted to beat Müller bloody. He thought about the girl in the movie and Hitler tagged onto the end and he wanted to punish Müller for his arrogance. He hoped the skinhead would give him an excuse after he bought the soldier-book. He started pulling wads of money from his pockets.

"Look, I'm serious. If you can do something, you know where I am. If I don't hear from you, I'm going home tomorrow night. I want to get home for Christmas."

A cab was approaching. He put the money away and stepped into the street.

"Wait a minute," Müller said. "It's Schulz, really. I believe you."

"I don't care," Svoray called back to him. "Find me another guy. You know where I am."

He got into the cab and spoke to the driver, who headed toward the lights across the river.

Sixteen

H E WAS STILL IN BED the next morning when the phone rang. It was Christmas Eve.

"Don't leave," Müller said. "I'm working on it."

Svoray ordered breakfast and packed his suitcases. He went out to a phone and called Johannes to ask what to do with the equipment. In the end the concealed camera and recorder hadn't been that useful, because Svoray had never figured out what he would say if he were caught using them. He'd preferred playing the enthusiastic right-wing journalist, sticking a microphone in people's faces and asking them if he could take their pictures, as if they were some kind of heroes to him. He learned to his surprise that with an hour's notice, he could drop the stuff with someone who would meet him at the Frankfurt airport. From the phone he found a bank and withdrew all but a hundred Deutschemarks in cash, then returned to the room.

Noon came with no results. He paced constantly, changing television channels with the remote control. On the porno channels, people were writhing on the floor. A sports channel showed motorcycle riders soaring off the tops of bumpy hills. CNN was covering last-minute Christmas shopping and the Bush-to-Clinton transition in Washington. German television said that groups in Berlin and Wuppertal, near Bonn, were organizing Christmas Day demonstrations against violence and racism. Two-thirty came, and no call.

"Enough," Svoray said to himself. He could do without the soldier-book. He called the cashier to ask that his bill be totaled, he was checking out. When the phone rang at three, he answered expecting the desk to say a bellhop was coming for his bags.

It was Müller. "Schulz will sell," he said.

"I was ready to give up on you," Svoray said. "How much?"

"Ten thousand dollars."

"Come on, Charlie."

"That's how much he wants. He's still very nervous. I had to talk to him a long time."

"It's too much and you know it," Svoray protested. "I know we're both in it for the money, but give me a break. I've got to have a little profit, too. Maybe he means ten thousand marks."

"I don't know. I'll see."

He called back in five minutes to say it was a deal. Svoray wondered if Schulz had any idea of the price Müller was asking; probably not. Indeed, he wondered if Schulz was really Schulz. Svoray could have stomached him better if he'd been motivated by ideology instead of profit; at least Heinz Reisz believed in something.

"Do you know the Frankfurt opera house?" Müller asked.

"I can find it."

"Park your car at the end of the parking lot, and when we think it's safe we will come."

"I'll be there," Svoray said. "Look for a white Fiat."

The concierge expressed his hope that Svoray would be back again. The hotel staff murmured "Merry Christmas" and bowed like marionettes as he departed.

The reconstructed Alte Oper stood in a plaza at a convergence of main streets, near the modern skyscrapers of the West End and the pedestrian shopping zone that extended to the Zeil. He was early, a good habit for watching and waiting. He parked, left the car doors unlocked, and walked into the shadows on the portico of the pillared opera house.

At ten minutes to four, a Ford sedan with faded red paint cruised slowly down the street beside the opera. As Svoray watched from his hiding place, the Ford stopped beside the Fiat.

Müller got out, looked around and approached the Fiat carefully, stooped, and looked inside. He held one hand close to his body, and Svoray thought he was carrying a weapon. He reached down, ripped the tape from around his ankle and put his knife in his coat pocket, then emerged from the shadows and ran down the opera steps.

Müller looked up, startled to see Svoray approaching from behind him. What he was holding in his hand was not a weapon, but a set of keys attached to a large medallion.

"What is all this cloak-and-dagger shit?" Svoray demanded.

"Schulz." Müller shrugged.

"Oh, that's right. I'm with the Verfassungsschutz. Or the Israeli Mossad, I can't remember which."

Müller laughed nervously. "Follow me," he said.

Müller had watched too many spy movies. He led Svoray through illegal U-turns, mad charges across traffic at changing lights, wrong-way dashes down residential streets, pointless switchbacks. Svoray quickly grew impatient. They weren't being followed, and in any case the greater danger was being stopped for reckless driving. Darkness fell. Street lamps and Christmas lights blinked on. Müller persisted.

The city gradually changed character, from the glitter of the skyscrapers and shops to tree-lined residential districts, to a poorer class of houses interspersed with taverns and repair shops, and finally a mix of warehouses, industry, and truck yards. Finally, Müller pulled into a gas station near an entrance to an elevated highway. Lights above a guardrail illuminated signs pointing to Darmstadt and the Frankfurt airport. Müller followed a drive beside the station to the back, where a sign indicated a café.

A phone booth stood at the edge of the station lot away from the gas pumps and service bays and office. Svoray parked close to it and walked along the flanking drive. Concealed behind the station building—the base of its T—a dingy restaurant stretched lengthwise toward the back of the lot. It was one of those way stations where weary motorists stopped for sandwiches and coffee. The Ford was parked diagonally near the door. A motorcycle, two cars, and a van were the only other vehicles. Müller was standing by the door, next to a Santa Claus cutout taped to the glass.

"I don't think we were followed. Do you?" he asked.

"Only a drunk could have followed us," Svoray said. "I barely followed you myself."

Müller took that as a compliment and entered the restaurant, Svoray following. It was a typical roadside diner, with a floor of linoleum tiles in a checkerboard pattern, a counter with stools across the back and a few tables between the counter and windows looking onto the parking lot. Two men huddled over coffee at a far table. They looked familiar, like the skinheads with Müller when they first met.

"Friends of yours?" He jerked his head in their direction.

Müller shrugged.

Schulz sat at a table in the middle of the room. A waitress behind the counter glanced at the clock on the wall as they walked in. Presents wrapped in children's paper were stacked on the shelf of the coatrack. Svoray wondered if they were hers, waiting to be taken home when her shift ended. She moved slowly, then looked toward the door.

Svoray turned to see a young man with stubble for hair wearing a black watch cap, its brim tightly rolled so that it sat like a bowl on top of his shaved skull. The sleeves of his black turtleneck sweater were pushed up to reveal tattoos. He went to the counter, ordered a cup of coffee, and took it to a table near the door. When he sat, he turned so he could look into the restaurant. The other two men scraped their chairs and gave no sign of recognition.

Two empty beer steins sat in front of Schulz. He ordered a third as Svoray and Müller sat down on either side of him. Müller ordered, too, but Svoray shook his head. Schulz was nervous; his hands were trembling and when he took the fresh beer to his lips drops of moisture fell from the glass onto his white shirt front and the lapels of his worn suit jacket. He wore no tie. He held a cigarette cupped in his left hand, as if concealing its glow. When he raised his hand to smoke, he pinched the cigarette delicately between his thumb and forefinger. The hands were what Svoray remembered. They were long and fine-boned, out of place protruding from the old man's shabby sleeves.

Svoray faced Müller across the table. "Where is the document?"

Müller spoke to Schulz, who reached inside his jacket and

slowly drew out a bundle, about the size of a passport, wrapped in plastic. He unwrapped the covering to reveal a small book covered in olive brown cardboard with a fabric binding. It was embossed with the Nazi eagle surmounting a swastika and the word *Soldbuch*. Schulz had printed his name over the eagle with a young man's flourishes: serifs on the *S* and a long tail on the *h*. As he handed the treasure to Svoray, his hands lingered on it briefly.

Svoray opened the book. A young man's picture was stapled inside the cover. Rust from the staples had bled onto the picture. It had been taken outdoors; there were trees and what looked like a lake in the background. His dark hair was neatly combed and parted. His expression was both proud and serious. There were no marks of rank on his epaulets; one point of his collar contained the lightning bolt SS and the other the insignia of an SS Sturmmann, a private first class.

"Is it you?" he asked Schulz, pointing back and forth between the old man and the picture.

Schulz nodded. *"Ja, ja,"* he said. Then he flicked a glance at Müller. Svoray's suspicion grew that this was not the man whose service document he held.

"Can you prove it?"

Müller spoke to Schulz in German. Schulz dug into an inner pocket and produced a wallet, from which he took a rumpled card, apparently a driver's license, with the name Schulz. There was no picture. The old man snatched it back before Svoray could find a date. "That is all," said Müller.

Svoray leafed through the book. It was amazingly detailed, containing in addition to the picture, name, and rank—the soldier, Schulz or otherwise, had been promoted to SS Rottenführer, or corporal, and SS Unterscharführer, or sergeant, eight months apart in January of 1942—such information as the number of gas masks he'd been assigned, his immunizations, and all the weapons and tools he'd been assigned. And, of course, it listed his pay and all his postings.

"Buchenwald?" asked Svoray.

Schulz took back the book and turned its pages. When he stopped, a thin finger pointed to the words *Weimar-Buchenwald* and *SS Totenkopfsturmbann,* one of the Death's Head battalions.

"You son of a bitch," Svoray whispered to himself. He snapped the book shut, rewrapped it in the plastic, and shoved it in a pocket of his coat. Schulz gave a little sigh of resignation. He lifted his beer and drained it. Svoray brought an envelope from an inside pocket and handed it to Müller. Müller opened it and riffled through the banded notes. He handed it to Schulz, nodding. The old man wet a finger with his tongue. Hunching over to conceal what he was doing from the restaurant's other customers, he unbanded the bills and counted the money with a practiced speed, as if he had worked in a bank or at a betting window.

"What will he do with the money?" Svoray asked, although he no longer cared.

"We need many things for our movement," Müller said. "I have more of these if you have buyers."

Svoray decided to keep up the pretense. "Not from Buchenwald. From Auschwitz."

"I'll see."

"Good. I know how to find you. Don't be so hard to reach next time." Svoray rose. The two men who shared a table turned toward him. So did the youth near the door. The waitress behind the counter paused in her chores to watch.

Svoray remembered the knife in his coat pocket. He pulled it out and flipped open the blade. The boy stared. The men stayed where they were. The waitress said something in German. Müller said, *"Nein."* Svoray headed for the door, knocking a chair over in his rush, then pushed through into the parking lot.

He resisted the urge to run. He walked steadily, holding the knife inside his pocket, not looking back, waiting for the sound or shift of light that would tell him someone had come out of the restaurant behind him. His rasping breath plumed in the cold air. The car came into view. It seemed a long way off, down the dark drive toward the front of the station and the passing cars. His head hummed so loudly with adrenaline that he couldn't tell if the footsteps he heard on the gritty pavement were someone else's, or his own.

He reached the car. No one was behind him.

Frankfurt's airport glowed in the night like the heart of some fantastic engine. Svoray entered the sphere of lights and idled by the curb while he checked the rearview mirror. When he was satisfied he hadn't been followed from the diner, he parked and found a phone.

"Ah, my Israeli friend," Johannes said when he came on the line. Svoray was shocked, until he remembered giving the arms purveyor his Bank Hapoalim credit card. "How did things work out?"

"Taking pictures from the belly button is harder than I thought. But I got what I wanted."

"That's good. Go to the lost and found bureau at the airport. Someone will meet you there. Give it an hour."

He located the bureau, went away, and returned in an hour. As he waited, a man materialized beside him. He was nondescript, middle-aged, dressed in a rumpled blazer, slacks, and parka. Svoray handed him the green bag. Clucking his disapproval, the man referred to notes he'd scribbled on a luggage ticket, then extracted the camera and lens from the bag. He opened the recorder that resembled a datebook, looked inside, then at Svoray. "The jacket," he said in heavily accented English. When he had severed the button with a pocketknife, he handed Svoray another button and a sewing kit the size of a matchbook, the kind hotels leave for their guests. Then he took the gear and hurried away, disappearing through an unmarked door.

Svoray looked at the button. A mismatch. There were no flights that would get him to Israel tonight, he knew, yet as in September he had the compulsion to act, to move. He patted his coat pocket to reassure himself the soldier-book was there. In the parking lot, he loitered a distance from his car and rechecked for signs of surveillance. Müller and Schulz were still counting their money, he decided. Moments later, he was on the E42 headed west.

He drove through the night to Paris, listening to his Israeli music tapes, stopping only for gas and to go to the bathroom. When he returned the car at Charles de Gaulle Airport after retrieving his travel documents from the spare tire well, the clerk directed him to a hotel of sorts in the bowels of the terminal. It was a hotel of cubicles, a place for travelers to grab a quick nap and refresh, with a bed, a shower stall, and a rack to hang clothes. A TV was suspended at the juncture of wall and ceiling, as in a hospital room. He took a few minutes to saw out the heart of a French guidebook he'd bought, place Schulz's plastic-wrapped book in the cavity, and glue the pages shut. Then he slept until a porter awakened him in time to catch TWA's flight to Tel Aviv.

His family was waiting outside the customs gate. Ellie and Enosh, dressed in blue and white, held a sign written in Hebrew that said, "Welcome, Dad." Ohad toddled toward him calling, "*Abba!*" Michal stood behind them with a luggage trolley. They clustered together, hugging, while the streams of passengers parted around them. It was five P.M. on the sixth day of Hanukkah, and also Christmas Day.

They left the airport in a cloud of smoke. They had no car of their own; Michal had borrowed their friend Avrmik's broken-down station wagon, but it didn't interfere with the laughter of their reunion as they drove. Goulash, the large mutt they'd rescued from a roadside, was waiting on the porch of the house in Ganne Tiqwa. When they got inside they lit the Hanukkah candles and said in Hebrew the brief prayer that accompanies each day's lighting.

Later, the children asleep, Svoray and Michal sat at the dining table in what was part of one long room extending from the kitchen to the living room.

"It was a complete success," he said. "I accomplished everything I set out to do. The rabbis have the information they wanted and I have the soldier-book for them."

"I'm proud of you," Michal said. Her face shone in the candlelight.

"You would not believe the people I met," he said.

"You told me."

"Yes. All terrible. Except Heinz. He would be a good guy if he could get past the Jewish thing. I asked him if he knew any Jews, and he said Jews give him money. But I doubt it."

"You call him by his first name."

"I can't help it. I like him in spite of his beliefs. And he likes me. It's like we are brothers on different sides of a war. There's no explaining it. He has nothing. They live in this tiny apartment. He drives this old Mercedes. And yet he's very generous. He wanted to give me something and you know what he gave me? A book from before the war, all about the wonderful deeds of Hitler and the Nazis. With picture cards that people bought and pasted in. I'm sure it meant a great deal to him. Of course, now I won't see him again, but I would like to go back someday, sit and talk to him, change his mind about some things."

"His Hitler book." Michal shook her head. "What will you do now?" she said.

"Tie up the loose ends. I don't want to keep any of this stuff longer than I have to. I'm anxious for the rabbis to see the soldier-book, but I have to be careful how I send it. Mark Seal is supposed to be coming to Israel in a week's time. I'll talk to him and work out something."

"And then?"

"Then I can write the story and we will have some money. After that, I suppose I will have to think about getting a job."

"How terrible," she said, smiling.

This set them laughing, and before they went to bed they talked about how much they were looking forward to all the time they were about to have together.

January
1993

Seventeen

S VORAY SAT AT THE TABLE with a mound of receipts in front of him. Somehow he had to free himself from the onus of expense reports. Recording the nickels and dimes of toll charges was not what he was meant to do. That was only one of the things that frustrated him about working through the JTA. The other was that Mark Seal could not be reached.

He had been home for ten days. Seal had arrived in Israel and was at a resort in Tiberias, on the Sea of Galilee, attending a conference of Israelis and American Jews. Every time Svoray called, Seal was in a meeting. "He's very busy. He simply has no time," one of the conference organizers said importantly. Svoray waited for Seal to call back.

And as he waited, Svoray's sense of victory had begun to fade. The danger he had faced in Germany had been real, his accomplishments considerable; he wanted congratulations and praise, and instead he was being ignored. Michal often found him sitting by himself and brooding. What was worse, Tiberias was only two hours away.

"I'm going to rent a car," he told Michal.

She was clearing the breakfast dishes. Enosh was at school and Ellie at kindergarten. Ohad was still in his high chair. Outside, a light rain fell, and a mildew spot on the ceiling seemed to have grown. Michal dropped a stack of plates into the sink with a loud clatter. "You can't rent a car," she said.

"Michali, I don't think Avrmik's will make it to Tiberias, and I'd like to get back tonight."

"Yaron, no," she shouted, startling him. "We have no money. Just forget it."

"How can I forget it? I have to get in touch with Seal."

"Don't you understand? The guy's not interested." A handful of utensils followed the plates with a crash.

"What do you mean he's not interested?"

"He obviously has no understanding of what you've done."

"I've just risked my life. I've met some of the leading Nazis in Germany. One of them actually thinks I'm a friend of his. I've brought back the document. It's a great story. How can he not be interested?"

Michal dried her hands and pulled Svoray the length of the long room into the living area. She sat him down on the couch and held his hands and looked at him tenderly. "Yaron, don't be naive," she said.

"I'm not naive," he protested.

"In this specific case, you're showing an amazing amount of naiveté. The guy is just not interested. He should be, but he's not, so don't flatter him and waste time and money by going to Tiberias. You have to move on."

Svoray thought for a minute. In the kitchen, Ohad was starting to kick at the high chair. "Fine," he said. "I'll go to the Wiesenthal people."

"Who will pay for that?"

"They will."

"Why will they? If this Seal isn't interested, why do you think the Wiesenthal people will pay for it?"

"Because it has been their thing all along. The information I got I got for the rabbis. I got the document for them. They will not only pay for my trip, they will be happy to hear what I have to tell them. It has been a pain in the ass to have a middle man."

Michal looked toward the kitchen and the sounds of Ohad's kicking. He was starting to yell. Michal stood up, still holding Svoray by the hands, and tugged at him until they were standing together. "Well then, go," she said.

Svoray went to a photo shop he knew and had the photographs he'd taken at the solstice celebration developed. They turned out better than he had imagined. He swore the owner to secrecy and said he'd explain everything in a few days. After a final, unsuccessful try to contact Seal, Svoray boarded a plane to Los Angeles. He didn't bother to tell the rabbis he was coming. He was afraid they would tell him to stay home.

They just might have, he realized when he walked into the center. Phones were ringing in a nonstop chorus, and the staff members passing through the lobby seemed more hurried than usual. It was the beginning of the second week of January.

"When does the museum open?" he asked one of the receptionists, seeking the cause of the activity.

"Four weeks. Ha!" she said, adding her view of the possibilities. Then she turned to answer another of the ringing phones.

Abe Cooper looked up from his strewn desk to see Svoray, unshaven and bedraggled after seventeen hours in the air, standing in his doorway. His heart did not sink, but neither did it lift in exultation. Cooper still was struggling to bring the Museum of Tolerance's interactive research component on line. That was his first task, but not his only one. He also was helping the *International Jewish Gazette* deal with a slander suit filed by Pamyat, one of Russia's right-wing parties, complaining of being called anti-Semitic. He was himself bedraggled from working eighteen-hour days.

"How was Germany?" Cooper asked.

"Fantastic," said Svoray. "I got the document. I have it with me. I met people you would not believe, very big neo-Nazis. Have you listened to the tapes?"

Irritation showed on Cooper's face. Dark crescents underlined his eyes. "We haven't received any tapes in at least two weeks. Not that I could have listened to them anyway. Look, I have a meeting I can't miss. Things are crazy here. The museum's opening. The *International Jewish Gazette* could be shut down by a lawsuit in Russia. You say you have the document? Come with me."

Cooper had a smooth stride that made him seem to glide rather than walk. Svoray followed him down the hall and around the corner to the office that Aaron Breitbart and Rick Eaton shared. Cooper rapped on the door and went in without waiting. The heart-shaped red sign of Love's restaurant was on view through the window. Eaton was slouched in front of his computer screen, skinny jean-clad legs stretched under his desk. Breitbart turned to them with a look of inquiry.

Cooper said, "Aaron, you know Yaron Svoray. You and Rick briefed him before he went to Germany for us."

"Yes. You called about Michael Kuhnen. And you've been sending us some very interesting names."

"I've got meetings. He's got the document and some other information. Take a look and we can try to talk later." Cooper glided from the room.

Svoray had the wretched feeling that his trip had been wasted. The museum had to open on time, naturally. But the center had spent twenty thousand dollars sending him to Germany, and he could not imagine that the rabbis would not drop everything to hear what he had learned there. Being shunted to the researchers said that they viewed him with indifference. Miserably, he handed over to Breitbart the French guidebook that concealed the soldier-book. As he did, he noticed that Breitbart's hands were covered with white spots and there was a smudge of white on one of his eyebrows; his desk was littered with pages written in longhand, a newsletter layout, and a small jar of correction fluid used for dabbing over mistakes.

Breitbart noticed Svoray staring. "It's this," he said, holding up the jar. "Sometimes I'm covered in it. Rick tells me I should learn to use a computer."

Hearing this somehow made Svoray feel worse.

Bending over a corner of Breitbart's desk, Svoray used a letter opener to separate the glued pages of the guidebook. He pulled out the soldier-book wrapped in its plastic sheathing and handed it over. Breitbart unfolded the layers of plastic gingerly, until he lifted the final flap to reveal the nearly pristine book. Eaton wheeled his chair over to watch.

"*Soldbuch zugleich Personalausweis,*" Breitbart read from the cover. He read German fairly well, though not idiomatically. "His paybook and identity card at the same time." He opened the book carefully, as lovingly as Schulz had, as if he were handling butterfly wings.

As he turned the pages, with Svoray and Eaton looking on, Breitbart whistled under his breath and said over and over, "Amazing. This is amazing.

"Look at this. His blood type, you'd expect that. His immunizations. His eyes. He must have had twenty-twenty vision, there's nothing entered here. His teeth were good, it looks like. Here, times he was hospitalized, it's hard to read for what. This is incredible. It tells how many underpants he got, and when. And undershirts and shirts. The names of his relatives, so they could make sure he wasn't Jewish. His pay records, commendations, weapons—looks like a lot of weapons. Travel permits. They must have used these as some kind of internal passport."

"His posting at Buchenwald is near the front," Svoray said.

Breitbart turned to the page. "Weimar-Buchenwald," he read from the stamp. "A big series of camps, actually. Ninety thousand died there. Mostly Jews, but not all."

When he was finished perusing its nearly thirty pages, Breitbart closed the book. "Abe should see this. I'll be right back." He left the room carrying the book.

Svoray tried to make conversation with Eaton, but the lanky researcher withdrew to his desk, stretched out his long legs, and propped his cowboy boots against the wall. Before Svoray had time to wonder what was wrong, Breitbart returned trailing Cooper. The door had not closed before it swung open again and the kinetic figure of Marvin Hier followed them into the room.

"Okay," said Cooper, giving Svoray a weary smile. "You got our attention."

Breitbart handed the soldier-book to Hier. "Be careful, Rabbi. It's old."

"You don't have to tell me. I know." Hier sat at the corner of Breitbart's desk and opened the book. Within seconds he was lost in it, no longer the dean of an international organization with three hundred eighty thousand members and a fourteen-million-dollar budget, but the document reader he might have otherwise become. Breitbart translated the German. "Such detail," Hier mused, turning the pages. "You met this man?" he asked Svoray.

"I think so. It was hard to tell. The guy I met said he was this guy."

"So he's still alive. Unfortunately, it doesn't say how many people he killed. Proving he's a war criminal would be hard."

After several minutes Hier closed the book. Brushing his hand through his hair so it stood up like a wave against the rim of his yarmulke, he said, "I have to tell you, the reports we've been getting, we didn't know what to expect, but not much, some names. From what we were told, you were not successful at all. Now you come back with this. That's something. That's the real thing, that document. They were very sketchy reports, by the way."

"We really had no idea what was going on," Cooper added.

Svoray realized with a start that the rabbis had expected the mission to go sour. "I met the leading neo-Nazis," he said. "I reported all that to Mark Seal. I sent tapes. I don't understand why you didn't get them."

"I don't either," said Cooper.

The phone rang. Breitbart answered it and handed it to Cooper. The rabbi listened. Shortly, he said, "I can't talk now. I'll call him back. Listen, hold my calls. I'm going to be tied up for a while." He looked at Svoray. "I think you should bring us up-to-date."

For nearly two hours, Svoray recounted the events of his trip: meeting Reisz, their apparent friendship, Reisz's invitation to the solstice celebration, the trip to Mainz, and the gathering of neo-Nazis and skinheads. He told of meeting Bernd Thrun, Curt Müller, Friedhelm Büsse, and Wilhelm Köberich, the Fighting Cock. He spoke of Reisz's wide contacts in the neo-Nazi movement, his claim that there were more of them than the police admitted, and his offer to introduce Svoray to more figures in the movement. He showed his photographs of the goods Thrun had collected for the skinheads in Croatia; of Reisz, Svoray, and Büsse at Müller's Nazi shrine; of the toilet scrawled with the Jewish star dangling from a gallows.

When he was nearly finished, he remembered the book Reisz had given him. "Besides that, I got this." He dug in his bag and found the book of picture cards tracking the rise of Hitler and the Nazis. It was still in its wrapping, which Svoray had wadded back around the book and taped with duct tape. He pulled off the tape and handed it to Hier.

"What is this?"

"A gift from my friend Heinz."

The rabbi opened the book, leafed through it, and returned to the dedication page. "Is this to you? What does it say?"

"From a convinced German Nazi," Svoray said. "Under his name he wrote 'Nero.' That's his nickname. Also his dog's name."

The others looked through the book when Hier was finished. Eaton lifted a corner of one of the pasted-in cards and issued a sardonic laugh. "Like baseball cards," he said. "It's a wonder his mother didn't throw it out."

"I don't understand," Hier said finally. "Why weren't we getting this information?"

"A good question," Cooper said. "Another question: What do we do with all this?"

Hier and Cooper took the soldier-book, the book of picture cards, and Svoray's photographs and went away by themselves. Svoray, waiting in the office with Breitbart and Eaton, tried to imagine the reports the rabbis had received from Seal. He had assumed that the tapes and transcripts were getting to the rabbis quickly. That obviously was not the case. All they had gotten was Seal's interpretation, his disappointment in Svoray's narration. Not that it mattered now. He had proved himself to the rabbis. Now they would thank him and he could start his stories and put some money in the bank.

After a time the door opened. Cooper beckoned him into the hallway. Hier said, "We'd like to know if you'll go back again."

Eighteen

W HAT DO YOU MEAN you're going back?''
"Back to Germany. I was right, Hier and Cooper were
thrilled when they saw the soldier-book and heard my story. They
hadn't been getting full reports. They were thinking I'm some
schmuck who was in Germany wasting all their money. Now I'm
going to be dealing with them directly. Michali?''

The pause was one he recognized. Michal was reconciling wish
with fact, desire with reality, as she had had to do throughout
their life together. Svoray listened on the phone to the whisper
of electrons and, for all he knew of the transmission of signals
through space, the gust of comets. It was morning in Los Angeles, night in Israel, the time when resolve was weakest. He wondered if the children had been good that day. But he knew that
no matter what she thought of the unwelcome news, she would
understand his need to do it. She expected him to go his way, as
he did her.

"I suppose it is important," he heard her say, the tumbled
consonants of Hebrew breaking his reverie.

"Michali, yes. It's a chance to strike a real blow against these
bastards.''

"I have the feeling this means there is not going to be any
story.''

"This is going to be bigger than any story. The JTA is out,
anyway.''

"Well, Yaron, we are going to somehow have to keep eating and paying the rent."

"You know the center is not paying me, Michal. I don't want them to. It will be better in the long run. We can hold out a little longer."

"I don't know how."

"Michal, we can. We have to. Are you with me?"

There was another, shorter pause. "Yaron, you know we've talked about what is going on, how bad it is. I trust you that you will do the right thing."

"I'm going to be going straight from here."

"You would save the worst news for the last," she said. "How long will you be?"

"I don't know."

She sighed. "Not too long, I hope. But do whatever it takes to get it finished and out of your system."

Abe Cooper's cable to Mark Seal was terse and direct. It asked, in essence, "What happened to the tapes?"

Seal was in Jerusalem by then. The conference in Tiberias was over. He had tried several times to return Svoray's phone calls, but was never successful. He had sent Svoray's latest tapes for dubbing before leaving the United States, with instructions that sets be sent to him in Israel and Cooper in Los Angeles. He had hired a writer to clean up Svoray's prose before running the reports over the JTA wire.

Seal called his office. He learned that one set of tapes had been held up in Israeli customs. The other was still sitting on a desk at the JTA.

"Ship them," Seal screamed at an assistant, whom he would later fire.

When he returned to the United States, he tried to contact Cooper and Svoray. Neither man returned his calls. Seal would learn later, secondhand, the depth of Svoray's anger at his handling of the assignment. Svoray dropped all contact with Seal and the JTA, and the agency lost all connection to the project.

Shortly thereafter, Kevin Buckley, the editor of *Playboy*, received a letter from Svoray. He opened it and looked at the contents with amazement, for such things were rare in his experience. The letter contained Svoray's check for the amount of his expense advance and a note explaining that he could not proceed with the story. It offered no explanation.

Svoray had placed the annoying distractions of journalism aside. He was working strictly with the rabbis now.

Hier was at his desk, barricaded, it seemed, against the rapid approach of the museum opening. The office door was closed, the phones stilled. Svoray and Abe Cooper, along with the researchers Aaron Breitbart and Rick Eaton, sat across from Hier. They were mapping out plans for Svoray's return to Germany.

"It's like an octopus," Hier said. "There are so many directions we can go. The trick is choosing the right one." He corrected himself. "The right ones."

Hier still wanted Kohl to acknowledge the Nazi past. The chancellor had referred only to "extremist terror" in denouncing the Mölln firebombing deaths. He had not singled out right-wing extremists in his Jewish New Year's message the previous September, even after the Rostock riots and fires set at the former Sachsenhausen concentration camp, north of Berlin. Neo-Nazis and right-wing skinheads had murdered seventeen people in 1992. Seven of the dead were foreigners, eight Germans. All but the Mölln firebombing victims were male. They included a German gardener who was drinking in a bar when it was attacked by sixty neo-Nazis, and a Vietnamese who was stabbed on a neighborhood street in the eastern section of Berlin. Murder was only part of it. Police agencies had recorded over twenty-five hundred violent acts that could be considered right-wing hate crimes. The violence was aimed more at refugees and asylum seekers than Jews, who were fewer and less visible, although Jewish cemeteries and memorials were desecrated. Gays, the homeless, and the handicapped were also singled out for their "un-Germanic" character. Criminal violations of a right-wing nature, including so-called propaganda offenses such as graffiti, posters, flyers, and the Nazi salute, were up eighty-three percent over 1991.

The Office for the Protection of the Constitution counted eighty-two right-wing extremist organizations and groups. It reckoned the extreme right's numbers at forty-two thousand seven hundred, including two hundred unaffiliated neo-Nazis and six hundred more who were unaffiliated because their parties had been banned. The Republikaner party, in addition, had twenty-three thousand members. All these figures, too, were increases from the year before.

Hier wanted to uncover the existence of a master plan, if one existed, within this swirl of numbers. He knew his history well. The German Workers' party had six members when Adolf Hitler joined in 1920 and began its conversion to the Nazi party.

"Which of these octopus arms do you want me to follow?" Svoray asked. He had spent the last three days working to improve his cover, and he now felt confident of being able to tunnel deeper into the neo-Nazi scene.

The cover was an enhancement of Ron Furey's right-wing persona that had so appealed to Reisz. Breitbart and Eaton had briefed Svoray until he had a fanatic's knowledge of the extreme right in North America. Now he knew names like Willis Carto, the wealthy Californian who founded the Institute for Historical Review, dedicated to denying the Holocaust, the right-wing Liberty Lobby, and the racist and anti-Semitic output of the Noontide Press; Gary Rex Lauck of Lincoln, Nebraska, who called himself propaganda manager of the Nazi party's "overseas development organization" and was responsible for most of the neo-Nazi literature entering Germany; German native Ernst Zündel in Canada, whose posters and Holocaust denial tracts also were popular among German neo-Nazis.

Ron Furey also had a new employer. Svoray had decided that *News Time* magazine didn't have the necessary right-wing impact.

"What about *The Right Way?*" he had asked. He had been sitting with Breitbart and Eaton in their office at the time.

"It has a ring," Eaton admitted.

"Well, no one would do it if he was being serious, unless he was a neo-Nazi. Nobody would publish *The Fiery Cross* except a Klansman."

The Right Way's address and phone number had come from Eaton. He was the member of the center who monitored the right, attending the meetings and seminars of various white supremacist, anti-Semitic, and other hate groups. He rented a postal box where he received their mail and kept a phone in his desk for their phone solicitations. The phone only received incoming calls and offered a message appropriate for someone of the hate groups' ilk, with the sign-off "Have a white day." For *The Right*

Way, Svoray recorded a new message telling callers that Ron Furey was busy and would return their calls as soon as possible. The answer-phone went back inside Eaton's desk, where it couldn't be answered accidentally by unsuspecting Wiesenthal Center staffers.

To complete Ron Furey's cover, Breitbart and Eaton had produced gifts for Svoray to present to Reisz. Eaton's was a package of a dozen tapes made at the latest annual seminar of Carto's Institute for Historical Review. Eaton threw in a few Klan publications for good measure.

Breitbart's gift was even better. He had gotten from somewhere a pair of yellow baby booties embroidered with black swastikas. When he dug them from a desk drawer and held them up for inspection, Svoray had felt a wave of nausea.

"I don't believe it," he had said. "This is how they teach them, from babies." He knew Reisz would love them.

The earlier presumptions of his mission had been cast aside as he sat with Hier, Cooper, and the researchers. The soldier-book of Gerhard Schulz had been virtually forgotten. Hier had decided that even if Schulz was the man that Charlie Müller had presented, it would be too hard to locate witnesses and make a murder case for crimes at Buchenwald. Schulz was relegated to the archives. Charlie Müller's horrific movie was a footnote, Müller along with Wilhelm and the skinheads on the Zeil important only as part of the continuum leading to Heinz Reisz.

Reisz was a much different story.

"Work with this man Reisz, build on these contacts, just get into it a little further, see what's there," Hier said.

"See who's ambitious," Cooper added.

"They keep talking about a leader," Svoray said. "They're waiting for the movement to get stronger."

"To send the next Hitler from the beer hall to the Reichstag," Hier said sardonically. "So you can encourage them. See what happens when you start with the money."

This was the remaining component of Svoray's new cover. It was built on what he'd told Reisz earlier, that he was a pipeline for money to the German right. Ron Furey's employer, the publisher of *The Right Way,* was looking to invest in "viable" neo-Nazis as a kind of laboratory before launching a similar movement in the United States.

"What about Himmler's daughter?" Svoray asked. "She's an icon. It would be really embarrassing for them if I got close to her."

"A message of survival," Cooper mused.

"It would be good publicity," said Hier. "But it shouldn't be the main thing. This is about the neo-Nazis and what the Germans are doing as a government about them. Yaron has access to these people."

Cooper looked at his watch. "It's been lovely," he said with a wry smile. "Unfortunately, we have to get this museum open."

"I know," said Hier, rising as Cooper did in a signal that the meeting had ended. "The message slips are piling up. One thing, Yaron. Be careful. *Zie Gezunt,*" he added, using the all-purpose Yiddish term that meant "Be healthy."

Svoray laid over in New York and had a new batch of ID cards made. They identified him as a correspondent for *The Right Way*.

He found in shops around Times Square a number of other items a fascist warrior like Ron Furey would possess. He bought several copies of *Soldier of Fortune* magazine and books on knives, handguns, and tactical warfare. In a store not far from the Port Authority bus terminal—a place notorious for pimps, hustlers, addicts, and the down-and-out—he found a mimeographed sheet on the essentials of torture. He bought that, too.

As he packed, he went over each item of clothing and toiletries as he had before, checking for Israeli labels or laundry tags that could betray him. He found no laundry tags. And, he realized with slight embarrassment, everything he owned was thoroughly American.

After that, he deviated slightly from what he'd done before and took an overnight flight direct to Frankfurt, arriving on Saturday, January 16.

Nineteen

H E CALLED REISZ from the airport. Reisz was ecstatic to
hear his voice, and he excitedly summoned Renata, telling
her Ron was on the phone. She spoke a slow, simple German
Svoray could understand, and said, "Have you come back? We're
so glad. Heinz has been talking about you obsessively. You must
come see us straight from the airport."

Then Reisz took up the phone again. Compared to his wife he
spoke in a tumble of words, like water spilling over rocks, but
Svoray understood that they had made up a new code name for
him.

"What is it? *Was?*"

"Brünhilde," Reisz said, dissolving into a huge laugh. Svoray
recognized one of his own jokes turned back on him. He had
once amused Reisz by saying, in a leering reference to her phy-
sique, that Renata could fill the role of Brünhilde in a Wagnerian
opera.

"That's good, Heinz. That's very good," he said. "Listen, I just
arrived. I'm on my way to see you."

"Coming here?" Reisz said in German. "That's good."

Svoray rented a more expensive car this time, an Opel, and
reached Reisz's apartment within an hour. Despite the January
cold Reisz was outside, pacing briskly with Nero on a leash. When
he saw Svoray he broke into exclamations of "Ron! Ron!" and,
when Svoray approached, enveloped him in a smothering hug.

When they were inside, back in the presence of the Hitler portrait, and Renata had hugged him and planted several wet kisses on his cheeks, Reisz proudly introduced their son and daughter-in-law. Svoray heard his name as Marcel. Marcel, who spoke a little English, said he had been released from prison at the end of the year and had been looking forward to meeting him, since his father talked all the time about his new friend. The daughter-in-law spoke better English.

First he handed Reisz the set of cassettes. "You'll have to learn English for these," he said. "This is what some Americans think about the Holocaust."

"Propaganda," said Reisz.

The daughter-in-law shook her head.

Svoray dug out the Klan magazines and then showed Reisz one of his new ID cards. "I didn't tell you the whole truth before," he said, letting the daughter-in-law translate. "This is who I really work for. *The Right Way.* I couldn't say so before. I had to make sure I had the right person. I brought these, too."

He brought the yellow booties from his pockets where he'd rolled them and stuffed them, so he could ditch them in case he was searched and the illegal swastika discovered. He unrolled them and held them up for Reisz. A smile of wonder broke slowly over Reisz's expressive face. He took the tiny socks as if they were fragile. He shook his head, overcome with Svoray's generosity. Svoray actually saw tears come into his eyes.

"He says he can't thank you enough," said the daughter-in-law. Her tone implied that she didn't share Reisz's Nazi views.

Svoray then explained his mission and Reisz's role in it, the story he'd refined and practiced since his meeting with the rabbis.

"You have some friends you don't know in America. They are interested in the neo-Nazi movement here because of what it means to them. But your public relations are awful. The image of skinhead thugs beating up Turks is awful. If the right in Germany is going to rise again, you have to get away from this image."

"He agrees they have an image problem," the daughter-in-law translated. Svoray was beginning to like her. In another world they would have joked together about the neo-Nazis with their stupid strutting and *"Heil Hitler"* salutes.

"The reason I'm telling you this," Svoray continued, "is because I'm a believer and my friends are believers and I was sent here to see what can be done to help the right improve its image. Europe is the focal point. We believe the next century belongs not to Russia or America, but to Europe, and Germany is the center, the core of Europe. The way Germany will go is the way Europe will go, and the way Europe will go is the way America will go and the world will go. Refugees, this is the problem. Your laws encourage them, plus the war in Yugoslavia. How many did you have last year, half a million maybe? But it's a problem in America, too, and in my home country of Australia. These all used to be nice countries. Now with all the wetbacks and the blacks, you can't get into a taxi in New York and have the driver understand you. In Melbourne, where my parents live, the streets are full of Pakistanis."

"Ja. Ja." Reisz was in complete agreement.

"It's a bitch, you know what I mean? I am an intelligent man. I empathize with your problems here in Germany, because we have the same problems. My people are wealthy. They are willing to invest heavily. It is my job to come back with recommendations about who, and how much. Because if they can help create a solution to these problems here in Germany, it will be like throwing a stone into the water. Its ripples will spread throughout the world."

Reisz nodded with comic gravity. He seemed to be impressed with the importance Svoray was attaching to him and the movement. Svoray's naked flattery was working. If he could just get the daughter-in-law to stop rolling her eyes.

"So here is what we will do," Svoray said. He laid out a plan. Reisz would call contacts he thought would be helpful and arrange for Svoray to meet them. Then they would drive together to the meetings. He didn't want to meet only known neo-Nazis, but the *Mitteldeutschen,* the middle Germans, the doctors and lawyers and other professionals who were the movement's silent support. Viable, respectable people who could be counted on to use a backer's money wisely.

"Heinz, today is Saturday. Tomorrow, make your calls and I will be in touch with you. And then, I hope, we will go on a trip."

"Jawohl, Herr Kommandant." Reisz clamped a fist to his heart, saying he couldn't make the *"Heil Hitler"* salute because it was illegal.

Svoray shot his arm into the air. "You mean it is illegal to say *'Heil Hitler'?"*

He left a few minutes later. As he drove into Frankfurt he said a prayer asking for forgiveness.

The staff of the Parkhotel was glad to see him back. They remembered a big tipper. As Svoray slid a hundred-Deutschemark greeting across his counter, the concierge assured him smoothly that he had only to make his wishes known. The information on his registration card was immaterial; the hotel would know him by whatever name he chose. And Mr. Ron would be an acknowledged guest or not, as he required.

He spent the next day getting to know Frankfurt again. Little had changed. Christmas decorations had come down in all but a few shop windows, and these were dark because it was Sunday. The few pedestrians strolled instead of rushing. He gave a wide berth to the cluster of drinkers at the U-bahn entrance in Hauptwache Square; Wilhelm and his skinhead friends were of no more use to him. A thin sun glimmered off the glass towers of the West End, stuttering neon blinked among the strip clubs, whorehouses, and porn shops of the red-light district. Svoray passed through it quickly, not wanting to encounter Charlie Müller either. He thought of calling Stefan, but Stefan knew who he was and renewing the relationship seemed dangerous. Better just to let it drop. What he did instead was walk along the Main and across the Iron Bridge to Sachsenhausen, where he roamed the streets until he came upon a field where young men were playing soccer, and watched the game until the sun dropped low.

That night, Reisz told him when he called that they would begin their trip on Tuesday. In the meantime, Bernd Thrun in Mainz had someone he wanted Ron Furey to meet. The whiff of Yankee dollars was already on the wind, he told Abe Cooper when he woke the rabbi from a Sunday morning sleep.

Svoray emerged from Reisz's car coughing and waving the air in front of his face. "Too much smoking, Heinz. You're killing me," he said. Reisz and Renata emerged just behind him, laughing at his antics.

The slight, paunchy figure of Thrun, a caricature with his over-

Yaron Svoray and Heinz Reisz.

Weapons and Nazi memorabilia on display at a skinhead meeting place in Porz, Germany, outside Cologne. The pistols on the wall are illegal.

Neo-Nazis Detlev Wölk and Jaschka, at the meeting place, make the "Heil Hitler" salute.

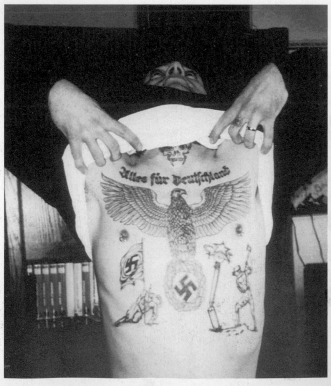

Jaschka displays his tattoos.

Hitler birthday poster displayed by Detlev Wölk. Poster was printed in Toronto, a source for much neo-Nazi material.

Left to right: Roy (Armstrong) Godenau, Heinz Reisz, Yaron Svoray, Wolfgang Juchem, Wilhelm Köberich ("the Fighting Cock").

Left to right: Yaron Svoray, Heinz Reisz, and Friedhelm Büsse pose in front of a shrine to Nazism on the grounds of the home of Curt and Ursula Müller, near Mainz, Germany, during the Winter Solstice celebration, a Nazi holiday. Public display of the swastika is illegal in Germany.

Young neo-Nazi at the Müllers' Winter Solstice celebration.

Young neo-Nazis in paramilitary garb, with Heinz Reisz.

Shrine composed of Nazi artifacts inside the Müllers' home.

Es soll'n die Lauten wie die Leisen
voll Inbrunst und mit Leidenschaft
und unverhüllter Leibes Kraft
—hier— auf die Sterne Judas scheißen!
U☆S   ☆   SA☆U

Sign on the outhouse on the grounds of the Müllers' home. It reads, in part, "Here is where we defecate on the Judas star."

The toilet inside the outhouse.

Hitler's valet, Karl Wilhelm Krause, with Simon Wiesenthal Center
researcher Richard Eaton, masquerading as "Millionaire Rick."

Karl Wilhelm Krause, right, with Hitler, c. 1942.

Yaron Svoray with Meinolf Schönborn, head of the banned Nationalist Front.

Bernd Thrun with packages of clothing he collected for German skinheads fighting on the side of Croatian militants against Serbs and Muslims in Bosnia-Herzegovina.

sized glasses and a thick mustache, greeted them at the front door. "Have you been to Croatia yet?" Svoray asked.

Thrun looked puzzled, until Svoray mimicked the action of steering a car and pointed to the garage where Thrun had shown off the clothing, food, and tools he'd assembled for the skinheads fighting there. Then he brightened. *"Noch nicht,"* he said. Not yet.

They went inside, where Thrun bobbed and nodded with apologies. He had invited Harald Neubauer, a right-wing member of the European Parliament from Munich, to meet his reporter friend. Thrun waved a fax in which Neubauer declined, as he was busy in Strasbourg, one of the cities where the twelve-nation body met to debate issues. But the fax contained Neubauer's invitation to meet with Thrun's friend in Strasbourg. Then Thrun introduced a heavyset man with a goatee.

Ernst Marliani was loud and self-important. He was a teacher, but made more of his service in the German army reserves, where he said he was a major and had worked with French and American security officers. "In the next months I will be a lieutenant colonel," he said in passable English. He seemed defensive about his Italian name, stressing that his family had been in Germany since the fifth century. He also worked as a financial adviser, and quickly offered to launder Ron Furey's contributions to the neo-Nazis.

"I am regularly abroad," he said, "and can get bank accounts in Switzerland or Luxembourg. Listen up. These accounts would be only receiving accounts, and they would only have numbers on them. At regular intervals I go there to pick up funds. And then I distribute the funds accordingly."

Over several hours, the discussion turned to uniting Germany's radical right. Yaron taped it openly, explaining that his publisher-boss would have the tapes translated and assess for himself the potential for right-wing unity as he decided where to put his money. Marliani and Thrun both were opposed to the Republikaner leader, Schönhuber, who like Neubauer served in the European Parliament from Munich. They were among those who believed the party was not sufficiently right-wing.

"Schönhuber has got to go," said Thrun.

Marliani fancied himself as the replacement, the instrument to expand the party. "We have very many conservative or right-wing people," he said.

"How many?" asked Svoray.

"I would say ten percent of Germans. But they are divided into groups that have too few able leaders. They fight against each other for survival."

Reisz started to interrupt, but Marliani shouted rudely, "Shut your mouth for a minute. We are trying now to set up a person who can be accepted by all political groups and who above all will be accepted by the people. We have to agree on someone whose outward appearance is acceptable to the normal conservative expectations. I declare myself to be available for this."

"You believe you have the chance to run the party?" Svoray asked. He could hardly believe the man's pomposity.

"Yes."

"Have you got problems?"

"I think that I haven't any problems, but the others think I do."

"What are they? What do the others say your problems are?" When Marliani hesitated, Svoray pressed. "No, no, you tell me. You're a politician. Don't be embarrassed. Are you a horse that is worth putting my money on?"

Marliani demurred. "The others should decide this."

"Don't let anyone else answer for you," Svoray insisted. "What are the problems that they say? Are you a homosexual? Do you have sex with little babies?"

"It was said about me that I had contact with right extremists and cannot be of use to the Republikaner party."

"Why don't you just stand up and say, 'Anyone who wants to, come to my side, and the other ones go home'? And you'll see what the majority is."

"That's exactly what I'm doing," Marliani said. "Last Saturday, the whole Kreisverband, the district council, of Mainz was unanimously on my side. Next Saturday, I want the state assembly to be on my side. I want to take over the organization."

When the Republikaners were his, Marliani would set about uniting all the right-wing parties behind a single, radical vision. "I don't like the word, but we need a new kind of führer, someone who is able to get the motivation of all the people."

As they were driving back to Langen, Svoray started to ask

Reisz if Marliani was the unifying leader he had talked about. But before he finished the question, Reisz was already shaking his head no.

There was no end of potential new führers.

The next day they left Langen in a two-car motorcade, Svoray in the rented Opel following Reisz and Renata in their Mercedes. Svoray had insisted on driving alone, saying Reisz's cigarettes were too much for him. It was a gray day with a white sky, the countryside bleak in winter. They drove north and east for about a hundred and fifty kilometers before leaving the autobahn at Bad Hersfeld and heading north toward Eschwege, a few miles from the old East–West German border. The roads seemed narrower and, as evening fell, less well lit. Unlike Frankfurt and Langen, with their bustle and modernity and the comforting presence of the airport, Svoray felt as if he was descending into a part of Germany that was closed and inescapable.

Eschwege heightened the feeling. It was a small city with cobbled streets and an air of rural neglect that gave a sense of foreboding, the kind of place where a scream would go unheard. They passed shabby half-timbered houses with dirt yards and weathered, broken roof tiles. Reisz stopped to ask for directions. Eventually they reached a two-story apartment building attractively set amid evergreen landscaping. Door lamps lit a small group of people around one of the entrances. A police van was parked at the end of the street. Svoray wondered how long it would take to run the license plate on the Opel and discover it had been rented to Yaron Svoray and not Ron Furey.

A small, wiry man was at the center of the group. Svoray recognized Wilhelm Köberich, the Fighting Cock, whose nickname in German was Kampfhahn and to whom he'd been introduced by Renata at the solstice celebration. He seemed as ubiquitous as Reisz among the neo-Nazis. Köberich's eyes sparkled with the same bright, cold intelligence. He introduced his niece, whom he had invited to help translate in case his rusty Hitler School English proved inadequate. "I'm very much against what my uncle stands for," she whispered. Svoray wondered if she was there to draw out his secret sympathies. There were several other men and women. They all went inside to a table laid with cups and saucers, long-stemmed glasses, liqueurs, platters of sausages and meats, black bread cut into thick slabs, and a homemade fruit-cake. Two fat red candles, one decorated with a swastika in a white circle, the other with a photograph of Hitler, formed a centerpiece.

"Let me take your coats," said Köberich. He handed them to his wife, a mirror image of Köberich with steel-gray hair and a birdlike alertness.

Köberich sat at the head of the table, motioning Svoray to sit at his right. "We had no time to talk the last time," he said after some small talk about the Hitler School.

"I have two agendas," Svoray said, taking out his tape recorder. His lie was beginning to come easily, growing in credence the more he told it. "I believe that the story of the right should be told correctly. Skinheads burning people out and shouting *'Heil Hitler!'* is a bad image. I want to portray the good parts. That's number one. Number two, a good, strong right-wing movement, an intelligent movement, that's the way to go. Some of my friends have got money, and they think it's a great idea to put the money here because we want to see what will happen. If good things happen, we will follow your example in America." He said his sympathies grew from problems at home in Australia.

"How old are you?" Köberich asked suddenly.

Svoray said he was thirty-eight.

"And you have a wife and . . ."

"I have a wife and three children."

"You like Germany?"

"I was talking about Australia."

"Yes, but do you like Germany?"

"I like Germany a lot," Svoray said, feeling the chill of Köberich's inquiry. "But in Australia—I'm from Australia but I live in America—it was a good country. Suddenly it's flooded by Chinese, Indians, Pakistanis. I believe people should stay where they are, Turkish in Turkey, Greeks in Greece . . ."

"Chinamen in China," added Köberich. "We want white people in Germany." The others nodded.

"You want white people? What about Jews? You want Jews?"

"Too much Jews," Köberich said, before he changed direction suddenly again. "What is your organization in America?"

"I've got no organization," Svoray said. "I know people who

have lots of money." He noticed the others were watching him carefully. There were murmurings in German.

"Ku Klux Klan?"

"Natürlich, KKK," Reisz interjected, coming to Svoray's defense.

"Presents. Tell the presents," Svoray said in an approximation of German.

Reisz lit up, but he spoke with authority as well. "After Christmas, he came from the U.S. and gave me, first, little socks with the swastika. From the KKK. He gave me tapes. He brought me historical books, drawings from the KKK, three pieces from the KKK. I thought, when he comes with swastikas, he is a very excellent man. I never asked. I see it in his eyes."

Svoray threw in the names of Willis Carto and Ernst Zündel, the Canadian publisher of anti-Semitic and Holocaust denial literature, to solidify his credentials. The group around the table nodded. There had been a pause. Now they began to pass the plates of food again and refill their glasses. Svoray, relieved, pressed forward.

"You had Michael Kuhnen for a while, who was good-looking, intelligent . . ."

"In one hour, you will learn the man," said the wizened Köberich, pale eyes watering as he took a deep draft of his liqueur. "The man is coming to us. He's the best man from the right in Germany. He's coming to us."

The man arrived as promised, six feet tall, well dressed, with silvery hair and a mustache set in a jowly, affable face. He came in rubbing his hands to warm them, shrugged off his coat, and hung it on a coat tree just inside the door. There was an aura of health and energy about him. Köberich had said he had spent twelve years in the German tank corps and another eighteen in military intelligence along the border. He had retired at a rank equivalent to captain. Now he traveled around Germany giving lectures.

Svoray began to talk to him as Köberich excused himself. But after only a few moments, he felt the cold steel barrel of a pistol laid against his cheek.

Twenty

SVORAY DIDN'T MOVE. He heard a clock ticking in the sudden silence. The people around the table stared, their mouths open. Reisz started to rise, then sank back into his chair, a cigarette hanging slackly from the corner of his mouth.

The Fighting Cock's reedy voice came from behind him. "I hope you are not a Verfassungsschutz agent."

Svoray jerked his head away and saw the gun, a nine-millimeter Beretta. The old Nazi had cocked it, exposing the chamber. Svoray grabbed his hand and twisted it backward. The gun swung toward the other guests and they scrambled to get out of the way. Dishes clattered and glasses spilled onto the table. Svoray took the gun with his left hand and pushed Köberich with the other. "Get away from me," he screamed.

Köberich stumbled, falling backward against the retired captain. It was then that Svoray realized the Fighting Cock was drunk. The captain propped him up and guided him into a chair. "I think you were playing a little joke there, weren't you, Kampfhahn?" he said in German.

Svoray eased the chamber closed and flicked the safety on, then laid the pistol on the table. The captain studied him. Some of the group started to laugh nervously.

"You see? Just a joke," the captain said. "He says it was just a joke," the niece translated. Svoray saw that she had bitten a knuckle almost bloody.

"A bad joke," Svoray said. He shrugged Reisz's hand from his shoulder and stalked to the door. His control crumbled under the flood of fear in his mouth and a sudden, bitter hatred. "A very fucking bad joke. No wonder people think you're only like the skinheads." He walked out of the apartment into the street.

As he stood in the cold, staring at the police van still parked down the street and wondering what to do next, his rationality returned. He could turn the confrontation to his advantage if he played it right.

Reisz appeared in the light of the doorway, followed by Köberich's niece. "I'm so sorry," she said. "He likes you. That's the only reason that he drank too much. He felt comfortable with you." Reisz urged him to come back inside.

"It's what I've been saying all along," he said to Reisz as the woman translated. "Too crude. Too much violence. You're like kids trying to do something it takes adults to do. I've come all this way to meet serious people. This is just a waste of time."

Reisz protested. "No, Ron. This man you just met is serious. He came a long way to meet you. Kampfhahn asked him. It's important you know him. Don't overreact. Come back inside."

One of the other men and two women came down the steps into the street and urged Svoray to return. "Kampfhahn is crazy sometimes," Reisz said. "He does things the old way. He was trying . . ." Reisz stopped to light a cigarette, and took a deep drag before continuing. "You want to support the movement, this is a way."

The old man came gingerly down the walk then. He was shaking his head and looking at Svoray tenderly, as if he were a child who had thrown a tantrum. He opened his arms as if to embrace Svoray, but Svoray backed away, shaking his head.

"No," he said. "You pulled a gun on me."

Köberich recoiled in embarrassment. He turned and retreated to the house. Reisz huddled with Renata and Köberich's wife. After a moment he came back to Svoray and said, with the help of Köberich's niece, "Ron, it is not right what he did, but you are too angry about it. You should have let Kampfhahn apologize. We will take you to a hotel and in the morning you will feel better. Renata is bringing your coat. Kampfhahn is a good man. He is important to us, and so are you, so that is the best thing. We will continue our journey tomorrow. I will arrange for you to meet this new man another time."

"Yes, Heinz, I think you are right."

Reisz, with Köberich's wife along to give directions, led Svoray to a hotel at the edge of the city. It was a provincial place, timbered and stuccoed, with paned windows. Reisz accompanied him inside, to a lobby full of dark wood and heavy furniture. They banged at a bell on the desk before a clerk appeared from a back room where he had been watching television. Svoray paid cash for the night and followed the clerk up a stairway with carved banisters to a room at the front of the hotel. As soon as he was sure Reisz had driven away, he came down again. The clerk had returned to his television program. Svoray slipped out the door and got in his car.

The streets near the hotel were deserted, or virtually so. Svoray drove to an intersection two blocks away, made a U-turn on the side street, and parked in the shadow of a building. There he settled down to watch the hotel entrance, half-expecting the police van, half-believing he was being paranoid. His watch showed eleven o'clock. He slipped one of his tapes into the cassette player. Bach gave way to Shlomo-Artzi, and Svoray smiled. The music wrapped him in a cocoon of nostalgia, lifted him out of the realm of neo-Nazis, and carried him to Israel. Odd, he thought, that the tapes that so easily could damn him provided a safe haven in his mind. A pair of headlights moved toward the hotel, and he sat up. They passed, and he settled down again. For long moments, nothing moved. Svoray fought an overwhelming drowsiness, but before long he was nodding.

He woke up with a start, cold, the music silent, struggling to remember where he was. He looked at his watch: one o'clock. Down the street past the corner of the building, yellow post lamps glowed at the hotel entrance. His mouth was dry and his clothes bore the smell of cigarettes. On the street, nothing was moving.

He started the car and sat for a minute more, watching. Then he nosed out of the side street and drove past the hotel, seeing no evidence of the police van, nor of any suspicious-looking cars. Continuing on, he cruised until he found a pay phone.

Michal answered groggily, irritation in her voice, without even a *Shalom.* "Yes, Yaron, what is it?"

"You knew it would be me?"

"Who else?"

"I hadn't called. I thought you would be worried."

"No, I wasn't worried. I was asleep."

"Go back to sleep. I'll call tomorrow."

"Now I'm awake. Where are you?"

"Eschwege. Near the old East–West border. I've had a very eventful day."

"That's nice. Here it is raining. I have buckets on the floor. And . . ." He heard a grunt, then a sharp intake of breath. "Oh, damn, I can't reach the light."

"What's wrong?"

"Nothing, just a catch in my back." She paused again, and this time he heard her sneeze. "Yaron, I must sleep," she said abruptly.

"I'll let you go," he said.

"Thank you," she said almost curtly, and hung up the phone.

She hadn't sounded well, he thought as he drove back to the hotel. Again he paused before making his approach, but there was still no sign that anyone was watching, and he parked and went inside. The television droned from the back room behind the desk. Svoray passed quietly and tiptoed up the stairs.

He seemed to have been asleep for only a few minutes before a pounding on the door woke him. His watch showed six-thirty, the window curtains admitted the beginnings of a chalky light. Reisz's voice boomed through the door. "Ron, Ron, *aufwachen,*" he called.

Svoray struggled to the door in his underwear. Reisz and Renata stood in the hall.

"Ron, what's wrong? You look as if you've been at a tavern. Or a whorehouse," Reisz said cheerfully in German as Renata craned around him and stole a glance at Svoray's baggy boxer shorts. "Listen, I have good news. With your permission, Kampfhahn will join us for breakfast. He is embarrassed by last night, and prefers to be on good terms. He has given me the name of a comrade in Dresden."

"Give me half an hour," Svoray said. *"Halbe Stunde."*

The hotel restaurant was full of men in work clothes, many obviously farmers. They were eating hearty breakfasts. Steam rose from thick mugs of coffee, and some of the men were drinking amber-colored beer. Svoray understood snatches of the conversation. It was talk heard in any farm belt—the American Midwest or Australia's Murray River basin, north of Melbourne where his parents lived—about weather, crops, animals, and the shortcomings of government. Reisz was at home in such a crowd. He and Renata had taken a large round table near the restaurant's public entrance.

Köberich arrived with his wife and niece a few minutes later. The Fighting Cock stood out among the robust, thick-limbed farmers. The old man wore a wool suit where work clothes were the rule and, with it, more sharp edges than a knife fight: blade-thin shoulders, pointy cheekbones that left carved-out hollows for his cheeks, eyes like flint. He inclined his head at Svoray. "I am sorry you misunderstood my little joke last night," he said. "I was too much . . ." He mimicked tipping a glass to his lips, then waited for a response. He was not a man to make abject apologies.

Svoray tried to figure out Köberich. Like Reisz, he seemed to be a gadfly among the hard-core neo-Nazis. Like Ernst Marliani, he apparently saw the right-wing Republikaner party as a vehicle to power. His candidate to unseat Franz Schönhuber was the silver-haired ex–army man and intelligence captain from last night. The man intrigued Svoray. So, too, did this old man, defined by Hitler, eager to ride out from the shadows on the shoulders of the young.

"I'm sorry I reacted too strongly," Svoray said, extending his hand. "Please, sit down." All three of them took their places at the table. "It's the image. Violence, guns, skinheads, firebombings, anything like that, my people don't want to be involved. They're looking for a viable movement. Do you understand viable?"

Köberich sat and signaled for coffee. His niece translated, and he nodded.

"How many Germans believe as you do?" Svoray asked.

"What do you think, Heinz? Thirty thousand?" Köberich spoke in German.

"Significantly more," Reisz answered. "Ten percent, at least."

"Why don't they get together?" asked Svoray. "Everyone is fighting for his own little patch. But they all want basically the same thing. Why not unify the movement?" Köberich's niece translated.

"No money," said Köberich. "The movement has no money."

"The problem is the money," Reisz added.

"What would you do with it? Buy Porsches? Drink beer? Tell me, Heinz, would you be buying cigarettes?"

"Marlboros," Reisz said, laughing as he lit another. "No, no, no. Postage, fax machines. To write one thousand letters, you must have one thousand marks. We have only three hundred marks, we can write only three hundred letters."

"So the money would go to improve the propaganda," Svoray said. He paused as a waiter approached with an insulated pitcher of hot coffee. "But you would still have the problem of everybody fighting one another. There has to be a central figure."

"You met him last night," Köberich said. "He is a serious man, and the right man."

"His name again? I don't remember it."

"Juchem. Wolfgang Juchem." The niece spelled it.

"He is also an impartial figure," said Reisz. "He's not affiliated with any of the parties. He has a clean slate."

"What is his agenda?"

"To unify us," Reisz answered through Köberich's niece. "To pour oil on the fighting waters and make our little voices powerful."

"How will he do that?"

"With your help," said Köberich.

Reisz pushed up from the table and clasped Svoray's shoulder with rough affection as he spoke. "He says they will do with your help what they have not been able to do alone," said Köberich's niece. "And now he is going to sample the breakfast."

The buffet was heavy with rich country food—sausages, meat, eggs, several kinds of bread, hot cereal. "No losing weight, here, eh?" Reisz said happily. When they were all seated again, facing their plates of food, Reisz said, "You know what I would like to see? Kampfhahn may agree with me. A central place, a kind of meeting place where . . ."

"A Nazi hall of fame," Svoray interrupted, loudly enough that two men at the next table turned toward them, shaking their heads sternly.

Köberich nodded at the men. "More quietly, please," he said, turning back to the table. "It's not good to attract attention."

Svoray lowered his voice. "What's the difference, if they agree with you? And if they don't . . ." He clamped a hand into the crook of his other arm and made a gesture.

"They may agree, but not want it known. Until the right time."

"Well, then, let's talk about this center for German studies. Where should it be? Heinz, let me have that road map you obviously never use, since you are always getting lost." When Reisz handed Svoray the map of Germany, Svoray spread it out and jabbed a finger toward the middle. It landed on a place called Eisenach, quite close to Eschwege, where they were, but on the other side of the old border. "Put it there," he said. "In the heart of Germany."

Köberich's head bobbed with approval. "He says you are a shrewd buyer," his niece said. "You chose the east. Property is cheaper there."

As they talked over the idea, it became a Germanic center that would mask a far-right propaganda center. Ron Furey was sure his friends in America would find it brilliant. It was after ten o'clock when Renata interrupted Reisz and pointed to her watch.

"Yes, my dear, you're right," he said. "We should get started."

Following Reisz and Renata as they drove east, Svoray tried to see himself as the neo-Nazis saw him. He recorded his impressions:

"I've turned from a journalist to a camp follower and now, in fact, I'm nearly anointed as their next organizer. They think that my eyes do not lie and that I am a genuine person. And that I do somehow have connections with the right people who are willing to give money to see the movement flourish. They are taking it totally at face value, and they are already calculating what should be done. They've built huge castles in the air."

In the process, he added, "I've become somewhat of a celebrity. But I'm not dumb enough to think that it's just because they love me that I'm given such treatment. They think I have connections to the media and can influence the masses."

It was another pale winter day, the sun hidden behind an even gauze of white cloud, color absent from the countryside. Presently Reisz signaled a turn into a gasoline station, and Svoray followed him. They had filled their tanks and Svoray was inside paying the attendant when a sleek dark gray Mercedes-Benz glided to a stop beside the pumps.

The driver was a man Svoray took to be in his mid-thirties, balding, wearing a sport jacket and tie. As he got out of his car he caught Reisz's eye. The men stared at each other as if in mutual recognition, but Reisz bristled. "What are you looking at? What do you want?" he demanded.

"Nichts," the man replied. "I just wondered if you are Heinz Reisz." Svoray paused to listen.

"So what?" Anger crackled in Reisz's voice. Renata twisted in her seat to see what was going on. The two men were behind her.

The stranger's response was enthusiastic. "Don't get excited. I just wanted to say I love what you are doing. Keep on doing it." The man stuck his hand in his pocket, pulled out a two-hundred-Deutschemark note and pressed it into Reisz's hand.

Reisz gaped. The gift caught him without words.

Svoray, too, was amazed. He rushed up to the man and introduced himself. The man switched easily to English. He dismissed his approach to Reisz, saying it was not unusual. "Many Germans feel as I do," he said. To Reisz, he added, in German again, "I basically have no time, but if I can help in any way please get in touch with me." He handed Reisz a business card indicating he was a business manager from Bad Driburg, between Dortmund and Hannover in western Germany.

Reisz watched him drive away, then turned to Renata and held up the bill. She clapped her hands. Reisz turned to Svoray with a grin. "You see? I'm fifty-three years old. All my life I've been a Nazi and I will continue being a Nazi. I am strong-headed. I go straight ahead. I'm not like these politicians. I'm different, and I know it. They call me 'crazy Heinz,' but that's me."

While Svoray understood some of what he heard, Reisz's happiness needed no translation.

When they were back on the road, peeling away the distance on the A4, Svoray found himself dispirited by the stranger and his gift. "I am totally bummed out," he told the recorder. "It's beginning to look more and more as though a lot of people, more people than I anticipated, are followers or at least believers in what these guys are doing. What would happen if they did get better publicity and people were less threatened by them? How dangerous would they be then?"

Twenty-one

I T WAS EARLY AFTERNOON when they reached Dresden, where Reisz had arranged a meeting with another neo-Nazi leader. If anything could have been grayer than the sky, it was the city, the buildings shabby and unpainted, the streets cobbled and full of boxy Ladas and smoke-spewing East German Trabants that skittered around like cockroaches on wheels.

Dresden was a tragedy. In February 1945, the same month that Sam Jacobs was burying his diamonds in the wall of his foxhole in Sarreguemines, German troops streamed through Dresden almost daily on their way to the beleaguered Eastern Front. But in more than five years of war, the city with its fifteenth-century roots, its Rococo and Baroque buildings, its great Protestant Frauenkirche, its Semper Opera House, was unscarred. Then, in thirty-six hours between February 13 and 15, Dresden was bombed into oblivion. Bombs and firestorms killed more than one hundred thousand people and destroyed much of the city's architectural splendor. Germans remembered the destruction of Dresden with bitterness. But to the inmates of nearby slave labor camps, the thud of the bombs and the flames over the city were harbingers of salvation.

Almost fifty years later, only the heart of the old city along the Elbe had been restored. But that sector, captured in paintings by Canaletto, was not on the route Reisz followed to an outlying railway station. They passed acres of bleak, boxlike apartment houses and evidence of westernization: ads for pantyhose and shampoo, a billboard for *The Last of the Mohicans.*

The station was a stone hulk that needed a good scrubbing. They found a table in the coffee shop off the waiting room, where a large board announced departures and arrivals in a riffling of letters and numbers that sounded like cards being shuffled. Constantin Mayer arrived five minutes later.

As Mayer lowered himself into the fourth chair, Svoray thought that here at last was a neo-Nazi who lived up to Hitler's physical ideal. The skinhead was tall, blond, and blue-eyed, with a finely chiseled, utterly straight nose. He wore glasses, a dark shirt with a tie, black pants stuffed into combat boots, and a black leather bomber jacket. He was the leader in Dresden of a banned party called the National Offensive. The ban was less than a month old, and the NO had appealed it to the courts along with two other recently banned groups, the Nationalistic Front and the German Alternative. Meanwhile, members were supposed to have suspended their activities.

"Are you paid by the party?" Svoray asked.

"No. I'm paid by the government because I'm unemployed." Mayer spoke excellent English.

They made small talk while they got to know each other. Svoray asked Mayer if he knew of skinheads in Croatia. He said he personally knew seven or eight, although as many as five hundred might be fighting there. "But these numbers you can't prove," he added. National Offensive membership, despite the ban, totaled about one hundred in Saxony and between five and seven hundred throughout Germany.

"I haven't met many women in the movement," Svoray said. "Why is that?"

Mayer grew very serious. "I think that women are mainly interested in winners," he said. "And the right wing, or the National Socialists, nowadays in Germany aren't winners. We are fighting and we are very underground, and we aren't winners at this stage. We will be winners in one or two years. Then the females will remember the real winners."

"To the winners," Svoray said, raising his glass of Fanta.

Mayer was denying the Holocaust and extolling Hitler when the people in a nearby booth started glancing at them pointedly.

Mayer dropped his voice and motioned for Svoray to drop his. "A little bit quieter," he said.

"You're not allowed to talk?"

"There are ears everywhere. There are a lot of people with those noses."

"What noses?"

"Those noses."

"The curved noses?" said Svoray.

"Right."

"Like the Jewish nose?"

"Yes."

Svoray hid his weariness. Every Jew knew how he was caricatured. The extravagantly hooked nose was a staple of anti-Semitic cartoons in prewar Germany. The cartoons were of a piece with Nazi doctors measuring the heads of Jews with calipers to identify a defining Jewish physiognomy. Mayer had said he was twenty-two years old and had spent his life in eastern Germany; Svoray doubted he had ever seen a Jew.

"Are there many Jews here in Dresden?" he asked.

"A good number, but the Jews who live in Dresden have a lot of power. Or perhaps there are only a few and you can't see them, but they have a lot of power and sit in good positions in the government and the economy." Mayer's tone led Svoray to his next question.

"And how would you get rid of them?"

"We can get rid of the Jews when we take back the power. Democratically. When we make laws which say all foreigners— and Jews are foreigners—aren't allowed to take good positions in the government and the economy and so on, then they haven't got the power and they will leave Germany because they are only interested in power." Mayer added that he preferred to see all the Jews in Israel, where they could be watched.

"Is this an idea that many people of your generation believe in?" Svoray wondered.

"Not many," Mayer confessed with some sadness. Only those who were hard and disciplined, today's equivalent of the dedicated troops of the SS. Even most of the skinheads, he said, "are only interested in fun, beer, sex, and so on." Mayer's single-minded voice might have issued from a Munich beer hall in 1920.

"Oh, ho. Look outside." Reisz directed their attention across the street, where a police van was parked, idling, with two uniformed officers inside. They had a clear view through the restaurant window.

"Are we ready to leave?" asked Svoray.

Mayer already had agreed to take Svoray to meet some of his comrades. They formed a caravan of three cars, Mayer leading in a light blue BMW, Reisz and Renata behind him, and Svoray following them. The police van and two police cars, one unmarked, fell in behind Svoray. They had been driving less than two minutes when the police pulled them all to the side of the road.

Uniformed officers moved quickly to each of the three cars, motioning its driver outside and demanding identification, keeping each apart from the others. Svoray produced his New York driver's license and the rental car papers from their hiding place in the car trunk.

"Pass," his policeman said.

Svoray dug out his Australian passport.

"Are you a Nazi?" the policeman asked in German.

"No, I am a journalist," Svoray replied in English. His lack of German was a problem, and for a time the police contingent discussed what to do with him. In the meantime, they waved Reisz and Mayer on their way. Svoray looked around. The road was well traveled, but desolate. A chain-link fence ran along the road, isolating railroad tracks that must have run to the station they had just left. Across the road was a series of gray industrial buildings. Darkness was falling.

Several minutes later, an English-speaking detective arrived. He looked over Svoray's documents. "Svoray. You are Australian? Or American?"

"Australian," Svoray said. "I live in America." He felt a familiar prick of fear, that the police could expose him to the neo-Nazis. He already had rehearsed his explanation: it was a middle European name; everyone in Australia was an immigrant; he used Ron Furey in his writing because his Zionist, leftist neighbors would attack him otherwise, insult his wife, and spit on his children.

As he answered the detective's questions, uniformed police

looked at his camera, his tape recorder, and his notebooks. They dug through his trunk. It was cluttered with luggage and debris. This was deliberate. Svoray had made a mess of the trunk on the theory that the sloppier it was the less likely it was to be searched effectively. From the corner of his eye he kept watching to see if they were going to take out the spare tire and get into the tool kit, where he had hidden his Israeli documents. The detective asked him to open his suitcase. The uniforms only poked at a pile of dirty underwear.

"Are you carrying any weapons?" the detective asked.

"Of course not," he said, discounting the switchblade he was carrying in the pocket of his jacket. "I told you, I'm a journalist doing a story on these guys."

"If I booked you," the detective said pleasantly, "I would say you were a wrestler, maybe."

Svoray laughed. "Well, if you're going to book me, I wish you would go ahead, because it's getting late and I'm getting hungry." The uniformed cops were still going through his trunk.

"Look," the man said. "I realize you're a foreigner and you might not understand who these people are you're with. They are heading in the wrong direction. Being with them is a dangerous thing. Very dangerous. It could kill you."

"You mean literally?"

"Oh, yes. These are very bad people." He caught the eye of the uniform who had been going through Svoray's trunk. The cop shrugged. "You can go," said the detective.

"Well, thank you. I'll be careful."

Reisz and Mayer were waiting a quarter mile ahead. Svoray slowed, blinked his lights, and waved them on. As the caravan continued, he thought he saw the unmarked police car several cars behind.

The building to which Mayer led them was in an office block amid a forest of construction cranes. All Dresden seemed to be under construction. He was borrowing the office from a comrade, Mayer said. The ten marks that National Offensive members paid monthly to defray expenses didn't cover office rent, and in any case the party was banned and therefore unable to rent an office legally.

As they were entering the building, Mayer stopped Svoray.

"You see the police are following. They would love a chance to raid us. When we get inside, we must all be careful what we say."

An old black-and-white photo of a gaunt-faced man hung on the wall. "Who's that?" asked Svoray.

"Otto Ernst Remer," Mayer said. "The man who destroyed the putsch against Hitler in July 1944."

Svoray recognized the name, and the background. Where had he heard it? At Köberich's, that was it. The man Köberich was touting as a leader had said that Remer was a friend of his. The capacity of the neo-Nazis for finding heroes in the past was amazing. Remer, a major in the Wehrmacht, was renowned for cutting short the military's plot to kill Hitler. The plotters ended badly; as many as five thousand people died, some close to the center of the plot hung on meat hooks and strangled with piano wire. Even after the war, when Hitler was repudiated, Remer called the officers traitors, for which he was briefly jailed. For that, and for founding the short-lived neo-Nazi Sozialistische Reichspartei, he became a symbol of Nazi loyalty.

Mayer said that Remer, eighty-one, was again in prison, this time for denying the Holocaust.

A young man showed up while they were talking. He was very blond and almost pretty, and was taken aback by Mayer's visitors. Mayer began to suggest that he go away and return later, but Svoray said, "No, no. I want to meet him."

Mayer served as the translator. The boy, who wore a striped red and white sweatshirt and conventional jeans, said he was seventeen. His father was unemployed and his mother worked as a nurse. He had dropped out of school to install carpets. He said he wanted to join the National Offensive. That it was banned made no difference—he knew it would reappear as something else.

"What do his parents think about his joining the party?" Svoray asked.

The young man said, "They don't support it because they worry that I'll get arrested. But they aren't against the thinking."

Mayer said that while most of the National Offensive's members were young, some were older, middle class, in jobs that prevented them from admitting their affiliation. When Svoray asked to meet them, Mayer declined. He said, "You can't say to them, 'Don't worry about it.' They won't believe you."

They continued talking, speaking in low voices to defy the listening devices Mayer thought might have been planted, while Reisz was on the telephone arranging the next stop on their schedule. The trip was free-form. Reisz was trying to reach a skinhead in Hamburg who had seen action in Croatia. If he failed, they would go somewhere else. As he called again, Svoray asked Mayer how Dresden's neo-Nazi cell would use an influx of cash.

"Two thousand marks a month would change a lot of things," Mayer said. "With more money we could build up a modern communication system, improve our office, where the people on the street could visit us and ask about our aims and so on. I think there could be one hundred thousand members."

He pledged to use the money for the cause. "I'm a National Socialist," he said. "The money will go to political work."

"What are your aims?"

"People say we need a multicultural society. I disagree. I want to preserve our German culture."

As the conversation wore down, Mayer revealed that he knew a number of American right wingers. He said he corresponded with a Houston, Texas, lawyer named Kirk Lyons. Lyons, head of an organization called the Patriots' Defense Foundation, had defended a variety of neo-Nazi sympathizers, including Fred Leuchter, a bogus engineer who used his false expertise to dispute the existence of death camp gas chambers, and white supremacist Tom Metzger of White Aryan Resistance. Mayer said he also knew an ex-GI named Kelner Williams, who had stayed in Germany at the end of his service and lived in Munich. Williams, Mayer said, helped funnel donations from the Ku Klux Klan to the German extreme right. Svoray fished for details of the pipeline, but while Mayer could not enlighten him, the young neo-Nazi had described an impressive web of contacts between American and German extremists.

They left Mayer after supper. Svoray had vowed not to eat with neo-Nazis, but this was one of those times when it was impossible to keep his vow, and each bite of his Wiener schnitzel had gone down like stones. The lump in his stomach remained as they began driving toward Stuttgart, Reisz having failed to reach his Hamburg contact. It was a long drive, five hundred and fifty kilometers, and Reisz's old Mercedes was not up to the speeds that would have put them there in three white-knuckled hours.

"It's funny," Svoray confided to his tape recorder, trying to concentrate on Reisz's taillights and keep his mind from wandering. "All you have to do is give him the right cue and he starts jumping and ranting and raving and talking about the Jews and the foreigners and about the glory of Hitler. And then you just switch off and he's nice and homey and deferential."

He turned off the recorder, but in a moment the dark road and the fan of light in which he traveled imposed their sense of melodrama. "I don't know," he continued. "I'm having terribly sad thoughts. All the poor Jews and unfortunates who traveled through these nights on the way from one camp to another, or from a ghetto to a camp. Germany is engulfing me. It's playing tricks on my brain. It's not the sense of imminent danger. It's the absolute horror of the fact that these men did what they did and continue to do what they do. They believe that what was done was right and that everyone else is to blame, and everyone else is a liar, and everyone else is at fault, and just given a chance they will do it again.

"Why did I think I could do this job?" he asked himself, still speaking into the recorder.

They stopped before midnight at a roadside hotel. The next morning—now it was Thursday, January 21—they rose and continued on to Stuttgart. A brighter day improved Svoray's mood, but he remained reflective and again reached for his tape recorder. "I can't help but be impressed by the lovely countryside," he said. "It's hilly. The fields are well tended and the ground seems brown and heavy. Every now and then you have a village with red roofs and white buildings and a church with a steeple. How could so much loveliness produce so much anger and hate?"

At such times Svoray remembered that he, too, was German, the child of a German father and grandfather. Its heritage was his, and it had been taken from him.

Frank Rennicke listened politely as a man named Klaus translated what Svoray was saying. Klaus, who had joined the Waffen SS when he was seventeen, fought in the Battle of the Bulge, and been captured on the Eastern Front, agreed wholeheartedly that the right needed unity, strong leadership, and money. He nodded enthusiastically at each leading suggestion of Svoray's. Rennicke was much younger, twenty-eight, and more reserved. He was a singer "on the right side, the national right side." His songs recalled past glories. He had what he called "a German attitude, a Fatherland attitude."

They were in a pub in Ehningen, a village a little west of Stuttgart. Rennicke had explained to Reisz when they arrived that his house, a tidy place of stone and wood with a gravel path leading through a garden to the door, was bursting with family. His wife was expecting their third child any minute, and her parents and his had come to lend support. The pub had frilled white curtains, the usual display of beer steins, and posters of Mercedes-Benz and Porsche racing cars. Stuttgart was a center of German auto manufacturing. The Mercedes star rose at one end of the main street. But Porsche sales were down and Mercedes was preparing to introduce a cheaper line, and Stuttgart's well-paid autoworkers were as restive as other Germans as they looked at the costs of reunification and the continuing flood of asylum seekers. They were worried about becoming Germany's Detroit.

Rennicke, an electrical engineer by profession, was an anomaly among German right-wing entertainers. The skinheads preferred heavy metal rock called Oi, performed by groups like Störkraft, whose name means "destructive force." Rennicke was a small operator by comparison. No record company would distribute him, so he recorded and duplicated his own tapes. These he sold by mail and at his fifty or so concert appearances a year. He accompanied himself on the guitar, and his songs were traditional. He was more like a Pete Seeger of the German right than Störkraft's lead singer, Jorg Petrisch, who screamed, "We fight shaved, our fists are hard as steel," in a song called "Strength for Germany." Instead of whipping an audience to rage with cries of *"Heil Hitler"* and fascist salutes, Rennicke extolled Germanic lore and military history and accomplishments. He recast old German marching songs. He milked the bitterness of Germany's past defeats as well as its dreams of a "greater Germany" that incorporated Austria and cut off Poland from the Baltic Sea. His cassettes, illustrated with pictures of old soldiers, bore titles like "My Comrade" and "On Germany!" The nationalism that he inspired was deeper and more enduring than Störkraft's, and arguably more dangerous.

Rennicke spoke cautiously. He already had been interviewed that day by a crew from the television branch of the German magazine *Der Spiegel*, and he was trying to counteract the image of the right as brutal skinheads. The skinheads have "no respect, no feeling," he said. "This doesn't correspond to our *Weltanschauung*, our philosophy of life. The feeling of homeland is a thing of the heart."

Svoray was impatient from the morning's drive and he urged Rennicke to speak more frankly. "Forget all that," he said. "I don't want to waste your time or my time on speeches. The question is, what do we do to get this movement stronger?"

"But I would talk differently to a friend than to a journalist," Rennicke protested. He was handsome in a long-faced way, and the Alpine sweater he wore, patterned with snowflakes, suited a troubadour of Germanic traditions. He looked frighteningly innocuous.

"I'm a friend of yours," said Svoray. "Tell me about the Viking Youth." Rennicke was a leader of a youth organization modeled after *Hitlerjugend*, and some of his tapes were aimed at connecting young people to Germanic tradition.

Hitler Youth and the League of German Girls had constituted the German youth movement. They were considered branches of the Nazi party, and in the mid-1930s sixty percent of young German men belonged to Hitler Youth. Its aim, in Hitler's words, was a "violently active, dominating, brutal youth" that would be "swift as the greyhound, tough as leather, and hard as Krupp steel." They camped, hiked, and played sports, for the Führer forbade intellectual training on the grounds that "knowledge is ruin to my young men." Eventually they were fed into the Storm Troopers and the Wehrmacht.

Pure Aryan blood was a prerequisite for Hitler Youth, and preferred in the resurrected version. "I relate to the natural blondness of a man," said Rennicke. "That's very usual in the Vikings."

Rennicke said that three hundred youngsters had attended a weekend camp the year before during Pfingsten, the German Christian holiday celebrated fifty days after Easter. They lived in tents, learned to build fires and find their way in the woods, and practiced sports like archery. The program was long on regimentation and military skills. They also did some singing; Rennicke had produced a cassette of the Viking Youth performing versions of old patriotic songs.

"Why not more campers? Why not eight hundred?" Svoray asked.

"There is a financial problem," Klaus translated for Rennicke. "But it is mainly the persecution. The pressure." Although the Viking Youth was legal and independent of any right-wing parties, parents who were against the indoctrination of their children opposed it. The young people who attended Viking Youth camps either had sympathetic parents or defined themselves as German nationalists in defiance of their elders. Rennicke, as a child, had been one of those. They were, as he put it, "the victims of a restless *Zeitgeist,*" the spirit of unsettled times.

They began talking about Hitler, the war, the Holocaust, and the Jews, Klaus participating as well as translating. He was saying that the Jews had not suffered unusually in the war when someone shushed them. When they got up to seek a more private place, the owner of the pub appeared. The man was a friend of Rennicke's, and sympathetic. He led them into a back room, showed them a button to push when they wanted drinks or food, and closed the door.

Klaus appeared relieved. "Big Brother is watching," he said.

Rennicke, too, said he had to be careful what he sang and what he told young people. "What I want to tell them has been forbidden to me. I could go to jail for this. I'm not allowed to say that there was never an Auschwitz. Viking Youth would have been long since forbidden if we hadn't followed this. Our enemies are watching me very closely. If they could file a complaint, they would. Then I'd be followed and punished."

In the safety of the back room, he expressed himself honestly. He agreed with Klaus that Hitler was the greatest man of the century. And, he said, "I think that if one is a Jew, he must go to Judea. And if a person is a German he must be in Germany. They don't work together, you see. They are black and white."

Twenty-two

THE REISZES AND SVORAY arrived in Starnberg on Friday morning to find Friedhelm Büsse pacing outside his apartment building. They were late because Reisz had gotten lost as usual, leading Svoray through the posh residential sections of the lakeside resort southwest of Munich before locating Büsse's more modest neighborhood. The mileage was beginning to wear on Svoray. They had stopped for the night a hundred kilometers from Stuttgart after leaving Rennicke at ten o'clock. Up early, they had driven toward Munich with the sun in their eyes until cutting south toward the lake. Büsse was traveling to Berlin in the afternoon, so they had only a short time. Nevertheless, the head of the FAP, the Free German Workers' party, insisted that they needed to evade surveillance. Renata moved to Svoray's car, Büsse climbed in with Reisz, and off they went.

They crossed Munich to the north side and the Olympic Park, site of the 1972 Olympic Games and an attack by Palestinian terrorists in which eleven Israeli athletes were killed. Svoray remembered the attack with bitterness. His parents had returned to Israel that year from their first sojourn in Australia. He had just turned eighteen and was headed for the army. The attack in Munich had been a jolting reminder of the hatreds aimed at Israel. It was timely, too, preceding the Yom Kippur War by little more than a year. By then he would be wearing the chevrons of a sergeant-major.

At the Olympic Park Reisz sped through a caution light and made a careening right turn. Svoray stayed behind him, cursing. Renata laughed.

They drove through a section of narrow streets and small cafés, interspersed among buildings of the University of Munich. Eventually Reisz signaled a left turn, darted across traffic with Svoray close behind, entered a confusing series of progressively smaller streets, and parked near what seemed to be the center of the old city. As far as Svoray could tell, no one had followed them.

Svoray had not spoken with Büsse when they picked him up. Now, as they got out of their cars together, Büsse strode aggressively toward him with his hand extended. His face was red and veined. A large cigar was clenched between his teeth. "I remember you," he said in German.

"Yes," said Svoray. "From Müller's. The solstice. I remember you, too. You are as big as me." He patted his belly and Büsse, though he understood little English, laughed.

They began walking. Büsse was a familiar figure on the streets of Munich. Some people they passed nodded to him cordially, others showed distaste, Büsse all the while talking and waving his cigar. Rounding a corner, they entered a bricked pedestrian zone that stretched past a large building adorned with neo-Gothic spires and turrets. It had the effect of an oversized, elaborate dollhouse. Büsse led them across the square to the entrance to the U-bahn complex underneath. They descended, moved through its wide and extensive corridors among a variety of shops, entered a department store, took a rising escalator several flights, and wound up in a restaurant overlooking the square.

The restaurant was between shifts, almost empty, and they took a table at the window. Büsse excused himself, and returned five minutes later with a girl wearing an overdress with the store's emblem. She was dark-haired and stoop-shouldered. She said that Herr Büsse had brought her to translate. She could take only a few minutes from her work. In a lower voice, as the burly Büsse nodded with approval, she added that she was a member of the party.

Büsse got straight to the point. "An encompassing propaganda depends upon financial means," he said. "One way is a good newspaper with a strong base, with ideals that are specific not only to the party but to the whole right. The radical right."

Büsse had both a small, struggling newspaper—"It's living hand to mouth," he said—and the FAP, which he said was the strongest right radical party in Germany, and the only one with a plan for the future.

"My opinion is that it's the only party looking at the world with the proper ideology. Take, for example, the Republicans and the NPD. They are right reactionary. They always look backward. They defend the Third Reich."

The NPD, the Nationaldemokratische Partei Deutschlands, was formed in the early 1960s to bring together several right-wing groups. Its platform predicted issues that still moved the right thirty years later: deportation of foreign workers; an end to the "lies" that Germany had started World War II and the "extortion" of German reparations; return to Germany of Austria and the parts of Poland it had occupied in 1939. The party reached its strength at the polls in the mid-sixties, electing some state and local candidates in former Nazi strongholds, and declined thereafter.

Svoray interrupted him. "Do you have contacts outside Germany?"

"Yes, yes, yes. The FAP has connections to foreign countries. France, Spain, Denmark, Switzerland, and we're also going to Poland and the Ukraine."

"America? The Klan?"

"Sorry to say, no." But Büsse had strong connections with Willis Carto's Institute for Historical Review. He had known Mark Weber, a key employee of the anti-Semitic organization, for years. He called Udo Walendy—another disavower of the Holocaust who served on the advisory board of the *Journal of Historical Review,* the institute's official publication—a good friend and a "man of vision relating to the guilt, the truth about Germany."

Büsse's own vision was startling and apocalyptic. Germany was central to any European radical right movement, he said. "The schooling, the spiritual base must be achieved because I can only bring about a structural change, here in Germany, when I have the appropriate people.

"My goal is to gather people around me who will be able to lead the masses at the given moment. Because right now, in the right camp, there is no base for the masses. To bring about change in a democracy, the masses must also bring their voices. I need professional revolutionaries. I must have the strategists and tacticians, the leaders. And a mass or a team, an army that is motivated by discipline, bravery, and obedience. I say, 'Fight,' and they say, 'Yes, sir.' "

"Herr Büsse thinks he is god," Reisz said good-naturedly.

"But if I want to carry on a revolutionary political stand, I may not only destroy," Büsse continued. "I must also be able to build anew after the destruction. I must have completely concrete pictures of how the state should be. What should my state look like? My state, my picture of a state, is based on five fundamentals: Race. Land. State. Honor. Work."

"How many men do you have?" Svoray asked.

Büsse sucked in smoke from his cigar and blew it out in the direction of the ceiling. Reisz and Renata also were smoking. The air over their table was blue. Svoray rubbed his watering eyes and waited for the answer.

"Nine hundred eighty registered. But that is this minute. I mean, I have such a pile of applications. When I finish them on Sunday, I estimate I will have about twelve hundred." He grinned and winked. "I know for a fact the Verfassungsschutz believes I have about one hundred fifty."

Svoray looked past Büsse out the window, where he saw a puppeteer performing for a group of four or five, and found himself thinking about Wolfgang Juchem. Juchem was the retired captain he'd met at Köberich's who had served in the tank corps and in intelligence. Büsse was all Nazi, no apologies, like Mayer, like Rennicke, like Reisz, and like Köberich, the Fighting Cock. Juchem had been different: subtler, harder to pin down than the full-blown Nazis. He had kept to the sidelines, was free of such baggage as Büsse's five-year prison term, was not identified with any of the radical right parties. He could mold himself to what the voters wanted and align with the party whose chances suited his ambitions. The possibilities were ominous.

Svoray wrenched his thoughts back to the translator's singsong voice. Büsse had started talking about skinheads. He knew one who had been returning from Croatia to Munich when he was killed in an automobile accident two days before Christmas, and another who was traveling to Croatia now. He had cells of skinheads in Cologne and in the industrial cities of Duisburg,

Dortmund, and Essen to the north. He would be happy to make an introduction.

The conversation ambled. The translator looked at her watch. Svoray asked if Büsse knew Himmler's daughter. Reisz had tried to dissuade him from pursuing her, saying she was unimportant to the movement. Büsse agreed.

"Now I must also say," he added. "I don't think much of Heinrich Himmler."

Svoray raised his eyebrows in surprise.

"I reject Himmler because the man couldn't laugh right," Büsse said. "He just looked so pinched. And a person who can't laugh and who looks a certain way only through his glasses . . ."

When they returned to Büsse's house the street was suddenly filled with police cars, and men with walkie-talkies were following them toward the building. Büsse shouted at a policewoman who was holding a German shepherd straining on a leash. The neighbors were peering out their windows. But for all the police presence no one stopped them, and they went inside.

Büsse had put the name Follmer on his doorbell. He led them through the apartment's modestly furnished living room into a bedroom that served as a work space and a library. It was obsessively neat, books lined up in wall shelves and magazines and papers stacked without protruding edges. The pictures on the walls hung straight.

"Oh, I see Frederick the Great," said Svoray.

"I painted it myself. As a child," said Büsse, with obvious pride.

"And is that a guillotine?"

"Yes." Büsse explained that the photograph was of the guillotine used to behead the leaders of the anti-Nazi White Rose movement at the University of Munich in 1943. These exchanges were in the mixture of English and German Svoray employed when a translator wasn't present.

Büsse had a collection of prewar documents that despite their Nazi emphasis would have interested Marvin Hier. Büsse shared with Hier a passion for old documents. He spoke proudly of his first German edition of a Bolshevik tract by Leon Trotsky and his copy of Henry Ford's infamous *The International Jew*. His library included the works of Ezra Pound, the expatriate American poet whose fascist broadcasts from Italy during the war led to his trial for treason and confinement in a mental institution. "It was a pure shame how this man was treated," Büsse said. "The greatest American lyricist next to Walt Whitman." Surprisingly, Büsse enjoyed some of what he called Zionist literature. He had a copy of Leon Uris's *Exodus* on his shelves and had seen the movie three or four times. His vocabulary included a small store of Yiddish expressions.

"I am *meshugah,*" he said. "You know, crazy."

More surprising was the greeting he used when he called Detlev Wölk, one of the skinheads in Cologne, to tell him to expect a visit from Ron Furey.

"*Shalom,* Detlev," he said into the phone. "Here's Friedhelm. Greetings."

"He said '*Shalom*'?" Svoray could hardly believe what he had heard. Reisz laughed at his amazement.

"Can you organize something by tomorrow or Sunday?" Büsse asked. "If you can get four or five good people together, he says he will do a story. A positive story. Furey. Ron Furey is his name. Prima. It's extremely important that he get to know you."

As a last gesture, Büsse unscrewed the leg of a table under the picture of the guillotine and pulled out a rolled-up sheaf of papers. He unrolled them to show Svoray a list of names. "My members," he said. "Nine hundred eighty. One hundred fifty more, kaput." He said he had tossed them out because of drunkenness. Then there were the new applicants.

As the neo-Nazi rolled up the papers and returned them to their hiding place, Svoray congratulated himself that Büsse, too, was convinced of his connections.

"So, Ron, until the beginning of the week."

The police had mysteriously disappeared from Büsse's street. Suburban quietude ruled the apartment buildings, parked cars, and the couple at the end of the block walking a weimaraner. Reisz and Renata were preparing to head back to Langen, where Reisz was assembling another meeting with the Fighting Cock and Wolfgang Juchem. Juchem seemed eager to resume the conversation with Ron Furey which Köberich had interrupted by laying the gun on Svoray's cheek.

"Until next week," Svoray said, submitting to hugs from Reisz and Renata. Svoray was staying in Munich overnight. He needed time alone, to ship tapes to the Wiesenthal Center, to talk with Hier and Cooper about what he'd learned so far, to call Michal. Then, before he left for the meeting Büsse had arranged with the skinheads, he planned to visit Himmler's daughter.

Reisz had told him it was out of the question. Büsse also had discouraged an attempt to meet the woman, although he had pointed out the number listed in her husband's name in the Munich phone book. He said the husband, once a member of the NPD, forbade neo-Nazi contacts. Gudrun herself, while not repudiating her father or her past, preferred a quiet life out of the spotlight, free of the passions that engulfed men like Reisz, Büsse, and Ron Furey. So, for that matter, did the children of Hermann Göring, Reinhard Heydrich, and Rudolf Hess.

Svoray drove into Munich and took a room in one of the small hotels near the main train station. The Munich Hauptbahnhof had none of the architectural ambition of Frankfurt's, but it provided the same concentration of services. He found a shop where he bought sealing tape and several thickly padded mailing envelopes. Three doors away, a photo developer promised to have his three rolls of film ready by four o'clock. He withdrew a thousand Deutschemarks from his bank account to replenish his cash supply and located a post office where he spent fifty marks to buy a phone card. While he was waiting for the photographs, he returned to the Hauptbahnhof and called Michal.

The receptionist at his hotel was a tall, reedy Scotsman. He walked long fingers through a phone book, made a call, and then gave Svoray directions to a Federal Express office that was located outside of Munich in the direction of the airport.

Svoray shipped the tapes of his conversations, beginning with Thrun and Marliani and ending with Büsse, more than a dozen minicassettes in all, and one set of the photographs of the people with whom he'd spoken, keeping a second set and the negatives. Being free of the tapes made him feel better, for he had confided thoughts that could have raised suspicions. Homeward-bound commuters, people with normal lives, streamed past in the evening darkness as he drove back to the city center. When he had parked the car, using the lot at the train station, it was after six o'clock, nine in the morning in Los Angeles. He returned to the bank of card phones in the station and called Abe Cooper.

The Wiesenthal Center's Museum of Tolerance was now two weeks from opening and the rabbi's frenetic pace had, if anything, increased. But Cooper and Hier had promised Svoray when they sent him back to Germany that they would be available. More, they sensed in Svoray a volatility and a need for contact. And because they both savored the chutzpah of what Svoray was doing and were concerned for his safety, they made time for conversation when he called.

"What's up?" Cooper said.

"I've just sent a shipment of tapes and pictures. They should reach you by the first of the week."

"Who have you got?" The rabbi turned his full attention to Svoray. They had not talked since Svoray had told him of the pending trip with Reisz.

"All sorts of Jew-hating scum. The Fighting Cock. Büsse. A skinhead in Dresden named Constantin Mayer, from the National Offensive, which is banned. Frank Rennicke, who sings old German songs and trains little Nazis at Viking Youth, which is like Hitler Youth. Do you know the Fighting Cock pulled a gun on me? He said he hoped I was not with the Verfassungsschutz."

"Did he suspect you?"

"No. He was drunk."

"Are you sure?"

"Yes. Just before that, I think he went through my coat. But there was nothing to find."

"Just the same," Cooper said, "if you suspect for a minute that they're on to you, get out, okay? Was there anything new?"

"The most interesting thing was a guy I met just before Köberich pulled the gun." Svoray began describing Wolfgang Juchem.

"Wait a minute," said Cooper. "Let me get Rabbi Hier on the line." There was a pause while Hier was patched into the conversation. Then Svoray heard the dean's gravelly voice. "Who is this guy?"

"A career army officer. Not an officer, apparently. Then worked in military intelligence and retired as a captain, or whatever the equivalent is. Thirty years in the service altogether, I was told."

"Why is he interesting?"

"He's got a clean background, a record of service to his country. He's got no ties to any particular party. He's staying out of the fray, which I think is a very smart game. He could be in a position to try to unite the various factions."

"What makes you think he wants to?"

"He sounded ambitious, like he's ready to start taking some chances. He was interested in the money."

"Any support?"

"He's got connections. Heinz knows him, of course, but Heinz knows everybody. Köberich. Apparently he's friends with this old general, Remer, who was a good friend of Hitler's."

"Otto Ernst Remer. Go on." Svoray pictured Hier at his desk, fidgeting in his big chair. In the parking lot outside the window, yeshiva students would be playing basketball. His own surroundings had a slightly forlorn look, with a scattering of passengers for night trains to places like Prague, Vienna, and Berlin, a few slowly moving baggage handlers, and—a universal sight—groups of teenagers hanging around the terminal's fast food shops.

"Well, Remer's one of these icons. All these guys consider him a man of great distinction and a good symbol of the movement. So whoever is a friend of Remer's is good for the movement."

"You say he's retired from the military?" It was Cooper this time. "What's he doing now? What's his name again?"

"J-u-c-h-e-m, pronounced 'Yukem,' first name Wolfgang. He goes around making speeches about the right course for Germany. I heaven't heard his speech, but I gather it's about making Germany cleaner, more German. Anytime he can get three people together, he talks to them."

"What else?" It was Hier again. "Himmler's daughter?"

"She's a housewife. Heinz says I shouldn't bother. He says she's nothing to the movement. Same with Edda Göring. Büsse knows them both. But I have her address. I'm going to knock on her door tomorrow morning."

"It sounds like you should skip it," Hier said.

"Then I have a meeting with some skinheads in Cologne. Büsse's troops. Nobody who's been to Croatia, though."

"Where do they train?" Cooper broke in. "If they go fight in Croatia, they must train somewhere. Is there a place?"

"I'll try to find out," said Svoray.

"That's a good idea. You should keep your irons in the fire.

But I think I would follow this man Juchem. Yaron, I think your instincts are correct. He has to be looked at very carefully.''

"I'm going to be needing some money,'' Svoray said.

Hier rang off, saying that was Cooper's department. Cooper promised a wire transfer into Svoray's account in Germany, made through a third party so the center's name wouldn't be attached to the deposit.

Twenty-three

THINGS MOVED QUICKLY after Svoray's conversation with the rabbis.

His weekend began outside Himmler's daughter's house and touched the former concentration camp at Dachau before he drove nearly six hundred kilometers to Cologne to meet Büsse's skinheads in the safe house where they kept their weapons. It ended with a drive back to Frankfurt in a snowstorm.

The house of Himmler's daughter had surprised him, or, rather, disappointed his sense of melodrama. He had thought to knock on her door and show her the SS ring with the tiny leering skull he'd persuaded Bernd Thrun to lend him. But as he sat outside screwing up his nerve, he decided that if she or her husband called the police it could harm his chance to learn more about Wolfgang Juchem. It was the neighborhood he noticed as he drove away, an ordinary neighborhood of bland modern houses, white with roofs of red tile, bordered by hedges and sections of fence and side yards that contained small gardens and driveways where ordinary cars were parked. He somehow had expected to find road signs, or historical markers.

These he did find at Dachau as he drove into the ancient town on the outskirts of Munich that was the site of Hitler's first concentration camp. Signs in all the European languages proclaimed the Dachau Concentration Camp Memorial. Again, though, he expected more attention to be paid. The horseback riding parties out on the cool Saturday morning, the soccer games, the evidence of industry and commerce in the form of billboards, auto dealerships, and restaurants—all the signs of life continuing seemed to diminish the enormity of what had happened there.

Dachau's was the first in a system that eventually included dozens of concentration camps and subcamps. It was built in 1933 on the site of a gunpowder factory. Its first prisoners were such enemies of the Third Reich as Communists, Social Democrats, and journalists. Other camps, principally Sachsenhausen and Buchenwald, were built on its model. After Kristallnacht in 1938, they were expanded to accommodate thousands of new Jewish prisoners. Later, Dachau's SS doctors used inmates as human guinea pigs, performing surgery on healthy prisoners, infecting others with malaria, and immersing still others in cold water to study the effects. American troops who liberated the camp discovered thirty coal cars filled with corpses, more bodies piled like twisted logs awaiting the cremation ovens, and in an orgy of disgust machine-gunned five hundred Nazi guards. Some two hundred thousand people died at Dachau. After the war, Nazi war criminals were tried there. Later it housed prisoners of war and displaced persons, including many children orphaned by the war.

It haunted Svoray throughout his tour of the camp and its museum that a German could look out his second-floor window into the camp site, could hang her washing in sight of the walls. But as he left the gates, he attributed his feelings to a week of neo-Nazi rhetoric and Holocaust denial.

"Life does go on," he told himself. He made a point of signing the visitors' book in Hebrew.

The drive to Cologne had taken six hours, with stops. The first person he met, after a night's sleep in a forgettable hotel, was a pale young man named Jaschka who had come to pick him up for his meeting with the skinheads. Jaschka was bright, spoke English well, and had a bizarre horned skull tattooed below his Adam's apple, the horns fanning out and back to embrace his neck like pincers. It was only the most visible of his collection. When Svoray remarked on it, Jaschka lifted his shirt. A German eagle spread its wings from armpit to armpit, clutching a swastika at the solar plexus. Below one pierced nipple, a dying German soldier held a swastika aloft; below the other, a soldier chopped away at a pole that held a Communist hammer and sickle and a star. Above the eagle appeared the exhortation *Alles für Deutschland*, in Gothic lettering.

Svoray asked him how long it took.

"About one hundred painful hours," Jaschka said proudly. "And cost two thousand German marks."

"You've got balls," said Svoray.

They were in the town of Porz, a suburb of Cologne, where the young members of Büsse's FAP kept an apartment in an anonymous eight-story building with trees in front and bicycles in a rack outside the door. It served as a kind of safe house. Inside the neat third-floor apartment, swords and pistols, swastikas, and Nazi documents, photographs, and posters provided the decorations, neo-Nazi literature the opportunities for reading. Other skinheads were arriving, ten in all. They seemed to be disciplined and organized. Svoray conducted an informal poll: they said that between them they could bring a hundred or more demonstrators into the streets within hours.

They preferred not to be called skinheads.

"There are different skinheads," said Detlev Wölk, the man Büsse had called to organize the meeting. He was a factory worker in his thirties, the oldest of the Germans at the gathering. He'd received the bump on the bridge of his nose in a street fight, and his short-sleeved gray T-shirt revealed tattooed forearms. "There are left-wing skinheads. There are skinheads that are not political. We are National Socialists."

"We are for our country, so we are called fascists," another complained.

With financing, they believed they could be more organized still. Norbert Weidner, twenty, tall, with his head shaved except for a short tuft at the front, ran the FAP office in Bonn. "The forces that fight us are relentless," he said. "Like the Jews. The capitalists. The foreigners. There are now new groups, like the gays. They are getting stronger. We still fight. We try to fight. But we need basic things before we try to start fighting. Like copying machines. We have no copying machines."

Copying machines meant more leaflets; more leaflets meant

more news of neo-Nazi rallies; more news meant bigger crowds to hear their message.

"We want a free Europe. A white Europe," said one.

"What's a white Europe?" asked Svoray.

"Where other races are sent back, to their roots. Some persons with big noses back to . . ."

"Who are the ones with the big noses? The Jews?"

"Yes, the Jews. I'm looking at your nose. I'm not sure about you." This stopped the conversation. The speaker was one of the contingent from Cologne, a blond young man with cold eyes who had brought his girlfriend. "Has anyone looked at his credentials?" He stared from face to face around the room.

Svoray jumped to his feet. "Are you saying I have a Jewish nose? Those are fighting words, my friend."

Laughter defused the moment, to Svoray's relief. His nerves were wearing thin.

There was more of the same, more of Jews with their money and power, more of Holocaust lies, more of an expanded Greater Germany taking chunks of Poland, Austria, and France, more of the need to cleanse the country of foreigners who didn't work and sat around and watched TV while German women cleaned their rooms. "We say they get sugar blown up their asses," Jaschka said. Svoray was finding it all tiresome by now.

Jaschka was racist in his soul. As he drove Svoray back to his hotel when the meeting ended, they passed a billboard Svoray presumed was aimed at convincing Germans to accept foreigners. In that it was a big mistake. The billboard showed a handsome black man with his head shaved and an earring, with the legend "Wouldn't he make a nice brother-in-law?" Jaschka began screaming at the sight of it, "Niggers, jungle bunnies, *Schwarze,* spades." Spittle collected at the corners of his mouth and he looked mad.

When he calmed down he told Svoray he was an only child. His parents were middle class. They did not approve of anything he did, but they especially did not approve of his tattoos. He had a very bad relationship with them. Svoray almost felt pity for him; his burden of alienation, loneliness, and hatred was enough for several young men to carry.

He dropped Svoray off and said, "I'll pick you up later with some friends. We'll go Paki-bashing."

"Paki-bashing" was another of the terms the skinhead right of western Europe used in talking about assaulting foreigners. It was more British than German. German rightists usually talked of "slamming Turks" or "slamming Chinks." While men like Friedhelm Büsse and Wolfgang Juchem plotted to gain political power, the war in the streets continued. Refugees were flooding into Germany in even greater numbers in the new year. Now they were spurred not only by war or poverty at home, but by a door that was slowly swinging closed. Germany's leaders were pressing to change Europe's most liberal asylum policy to one of its most restrictive. Housing and processing asylum seekers cost eight billion Deutschemarks in 1992. The voters were angry. Two-thirds of Germans polled the previous October were in favor of a tighter policy. Refugees were trying to get in before it was too late. The skinheads were unmoved by such niceties as laws.

They found no Pakistanis, but they did find some Greek Cypriots that night when they went out. Svoray joined Jaschka and four local skinheads in a VW Kombi van painted the same olive green the skinheads favored in their bomber jackets. Cologne, an ancient city that was settled by the Romans nearly two millennia before, was built along the Rhine. Its skyline was ruled by the twin cathedral spires of the Gothic Kölner Dom. Farther west, the university section with its selection of leftists and foreign students offered the skinheads opportunities. Still, they wandered the district for two hours, Jaschka pointing out sites of fights, stone throwings, and a corner where he had handed out neo-Nazi leaflets, before they found what they were looking for.

Snow began falling as they stood across from a Greek restaurant. In its warmly lit window, a huge round of meat turned on a vertical spit.

"What's the deal?" Svoray said crossly. One of Jaschka's friends, who looked like a bald Jack Nicholson, had insisted that he leave his camera and tape recorder behind. Svoray had agreed but then, instead of taking his word that he had done so, the skinhead insisted on patting down his pockets.

"Inside they have games and slot machines, and some guys from Cyprus hang out there," Jaschka said.

"So what's the big deal about that?"

"One of those Cypriot guys threw a stone at one of our guys recently and we want to make a payback." Jaschka was bouncing on the balls of his feet, feeling the anticipation.

"You're kidding," Svoray said.

Jaschka looked at him. "I thought you wanted to see what we do."

"Yes, but this is ridiculous."

"You think so? You think this is a joke?" Agitated, Jaschka pulled from inside his jacket a long boxlike instrument that Svoray at first thought was an electric phaser used by police in riot control. But he opened it to show Svoray a small bullet-shaped canister of gas. The gas was designed to be disabling, but at close range the canister itself was deadly. "You can blow someone with this," he said. He meant kill someone.

"Forget it. I'll see you guys later." Svoray turned to walk away.

"Nein," said the Jack Nicholson look-alike. He spoke to Jaschka in German. "He thinks you must stay," Jaschka said. "You asked to come with us."

Svoray shrugged. He felt in his pocket for his switchblade, but he was thinking of a French film he had seen as a student. *The War of the Buttons* was about a dispute between two towns, in which the children of each stole the buttons from the clothing of the other until everyone, in desperation, left their clothes at home. It spoke to the senselessness of war. In the peaceful night, people were passing on the street, snow was falling, light from the restaurant window cast a glow onto the whitening sidewalk. Suddenly two young men popped out of the restaurant door. They stared across the street at the skinheads, then disappeared inside again. Svoray sought neutral territory next to a parked car.

Seconds later the door flew open and a band of young men ran out, shouting as they charged across the street. The skinheads fell back uncertainly, startled by the abruptness of the charge. They were also outnumbered two to one. The Cypriots came punching and kicking. Jaschka tried to aim the gas gun, but an arcing kick knocked it from his hands. Jaschka cursed wildly and swung his fists. Svoray saw the fight as if in slow motion, balletic in the falling snow. Scuffling boots cut haiku in the coating on the ground. It was over quickly. The Cypriots ran back to the restaurant shouting, and disappeared inside.

The damage was minor on the skinhead side. Jaschka had a scratch on his cheek, the bald Nicholson a bloody nose, one of the others a torn jacket. Jaschka found his weapon between two parked cars. As they dusted themselves off, people passed on the street as if nothing had happened. No sirens wailed, no police cars converged on the scene. One of the Cypriots burst from the door of the restaurant, called out *"Faschisten!,"* and threw up his middle finger.

"There were more of them," Jaschka said. He and his friends talked among themselves. "Come," he said. "We are going to get something to drink and call some friends."

They were headed to one of the few pubs that would admit them, Jaschka explained as they piled back into the Kombi. They would drink a few beers and gather reinforcements. Then the foreigners had better case their balls in steel. Svoray begged off. Fighting would be harder to refuse this time. Tomorrow he was supposed to meet again with Wolfgang Juchem at Reisz's apartment in Langen. He couldn't be there if he was in jail for fighting in Cologne.

"Journalisten." The skinhead who had patted him down made a disgusted noise as they dropped him at his hotel.

Svoray ignored him. "Fight well, my friends," he said.

Jaschka gave a stiff-armed farewell salute.

Svoray went to his car to find a map. The key felt funny in the lock, and it seemed to him that someone had been at it. He opened the trunk. It was impossible to tell, in the dim light and intentional clutter, if anything had been disturbed. He rummaged in the mess until he was sure the documents he'd stowed were safe.

No one had been in his room. His suitcase showed no sign of it in any case. But the suspicion of tampering was enough to make him gather his things and check out. It was midnight and still snowing as he headed south toward Frankfurt.

Twenty-four

DESPITE HIS two A.M. arrival, by the time he arose for a late breakfast word was around the Parkhotel staff that Mr. Ron was back. The concierge greeted him effusively. The bellmen were all smiles. The man at the door tipped his hat when Svoray handed him twenty marks for bringing up his car. He was in Langen fifteen minutes later, driving through gray sheets of rain.

Five men were crowded into Reisz's tiny living room, in which a pall from his cigarettes already hung. It was only the men; Renata was at work. One of the men was Wolfgang Juchem, dapper in a gray herringbone sport jacket, dark slacks, and a red tie with blue polka dots. He looked relaxed and confident, with the air of a college professor. Svoray saw his appeal as that of a magnetic teacher, capable of conveying his beliefs and converting his students. The others were Reisz, of course; Bernd Thrun; Köberich, the Fighting Cock; and a man Svoray had never seen before. He was a head taller than Svoray, imposing, with a wide, straight nose and ice blue eyes. Although he wasn't old, he had a thick shock of straight gray hair. He had a German name: Roy Godenau.

"You say you're from the States?" he asked.

The accent, or lack of it, made Svoray's heart stop. The man was clearly an American.

"One second." Svoray went down the short hall and tossed his coat on the bed with the others. Köberich wouldn't go through it this time, he was certain, but he had greater worries. This was the first time his Israeli accent had been exposed to a native English speaker, and he hadn't expected it. "I'm from Australia," he said to Godenau when he returned. "My parents were immigrants. But the paper I work for is in the United States. California. Do you know Willis Carto?"

Godenau raised his eyebrows. "Oh, yes. I know him personally."

Svoray squirmed silently. Carto's was a name Svoray often threw out to establish his right-wing credentials, but it had been a mistake to mention it to Godenau.

"I was at his home when he lived in Redondo Beach," Godenau continued. "That was a long time ago. I heard from him about a month ago. He called me up and talked with me for a while. He didn't mention you."

It was worse than Svoray thought. "I didn't say I was from Carto. I'm in L.A., not Orange County. He's just someone we all admire."

"He must know your work," Godenau said.

"I doubt it. I've come there just recently. And it's a new paper. *The Right Way.*"

"*The Right Way.* Great name." Godenau took a tiny notebook from an inside pocket of his suit.

"Here. I've got a card. And you?" Svoray changed the subject quickly. "Born in America and one day decided 'Enough,' and came here?"

"Oh, no," said Godenau. The name was pronounced "goad-uh-now," emphasis on *goad.* His unaccented voice was smooth, rich, and persuasive. "I volunteered during the Vietnam War to go to Germany. I married a German girl."

"And you can't go back?" Godenau had the attitude of a permanent expatriate.

"I can go back. But I might be tried for espionage."

Svoray laughed. He felt suddenly confident that his accent was not an issue with Godenau. "One thing I've noticed, in the right everybody likes to talk about conspiracies . . ."

"No, it's not a joke," Godenau interrupted. He wore a crisp blue suit, white shirt, and striped red tie, clipped to his shirt. Svoray noticed the tie clip because few men wore them anymore. "The German federal prosecutor accused me of spying for Iraq in the Gulf War. The CIA intercepted all dispatches to the Iraqi embassy. And I had sent them some information. I put some leaflets out against the war. So I'm an Iraqi agent."

"You're an Iraqi agent?"

"According to them."

"What were you accused of?" An American expat, moving with German neo-Nazis, working for Saddam Hussein; Svoray wanted to know more.

"Sending information to the Iraqi consulate that German tanks would be stationed at the Turkish border with Iraq. Whereupon Hussein sent twenty divisions to the border. It was in all the newspapers. The government then didn't send the tanks, but they threw out almost the entire Iraqi embassy."

"Because of you?"

"I don't know." Godenau shrugged, and fiddled with his tie clip. "Other people could have sent the information. They had me arrested for interrogation and I refused to make any statement and then they took me home again. When I had an attorney look at the proceedings, they stopped the proceedings."

"America didn't try to extradite you?"

"No." But he said the German authorities kept close tabs on his right-wing activities. "I've been unemployed for ten years. No chance at getting a job. Three house searchings. Numerous charges. Jailed." He had been tried for distributing a Willis Carto book disputing the Holocaust, a case he won with a court-appointed lawyer. "If you're poor enough, the government is forced to pay. I've cost them quite a lot of money, actually," he said. He seemed to believe, as Reisz did, that having many enemies increased his honor.

"Do you belong to a party?" asked Svoray.

"I was a member of the Republicans."

"Are you a National Socialist?"

"Well, I believe in the principles of nationalism, the principles of socialism. But to call me a Nazi? That refers to the thirties. It was a different time."

His contacts included old Nazis, however, as he said when he expanded his fascinating résumé. "I operate a publishing company for one of our retired German intelligence officers in South America. He was in the outfit in the second war. He goes by the name of Maler, Juan Maler, but his real name is Reinhard Kops."

Svoray made a mental note of the name.

Maler's publications attacked Zionism and Freemasonry, Godenau said. Conspiracy theorists often linked the two, calling the worldwide men's fraternal order both a secret society and a religion. Godenau's version went like this: "Zionists set up the world government, and Freemasonry is used to support it."

"But the Freemasons are not Jews," Svoray said.

"In key positions there are several Jews that are not recognized as Jewish. B'nai B'rith, probably. That's the Jewish Freemason-like organization. It's like a brotherhood. The sons of the covenant. And the mark of the covenant is circumcision."

"But in America, everyone is circumcised. It's no big deal."

"Not anymore," Godenau argued. "It's going out of style. It costs too much money. It's not necessary, trust me."

And so it went. Godenau's belief in the Zionist-Freemason conspiracy took him throughout the Arab world, where he peddled Maler's literature. One of his customers, he said, was Muammar Khaddafi.

Godenau was Juchem's man. Or perhaps it was the other way around, but Svoray sensed that Juchem had asked Godenau along both to translate and to scrutinize Ron Furey and his offer of patronage. He, Juchem, and the stringy Köberich formed a triumvirate, all three in coats and ties compared with the casual attire worn by Reisz and Thrun. They were there as businessmen, tempted by a risky deal, but uncommitted. It was Svoray's job to draw them along, learn Juchem's plans and the extent of his support. It was already clear that he had laid his groundwork carefully.

"Let me explain where I'm coming from." Svoray went through his speech, pausing from time to time for Godenau to translate. "So a mirror organization is what my friends are looking for," he concluded. "The way you handle it, the way your white Germany handles the return to a different set of values, would be an example. That's why they believe money spent on the right wing in Germany is a good investment."

"If you have the right people to utilize it," Godenau said. "How many leaders have you talked to from the various groups? You mentioned Büsse."

"I think I met everyone," Svoray said.

"Schönhuber? Deckert? Dr. Frey?" The man was a catalogue of right-wing figures.

"Schönhuber, no. I'm supposed to meet Deckert. Everybody told me, don't waste your time with Frey." Günter Deckert was a longtime neo-Nazi, a former head of the National Democratic Party of Germany, the NPD, and founder of the German List and at least one other "camouflage" party. He had been convicted the year before of inciting race hatred by importing Fred Leuchter, the U.S. Holocaust denier and self-styled gas chamber expert, for a speech that Deckert later marketed in a German translation and as a videotape. Gerhard Frey, a wealthy Munich publisher, was head of the German People's Union, known by its German initials, DVU. It was a growing far-right party that challenged Franz Schönhuber's Republicans for votes. His nationalistic weekly newspapers, which reached eighty-five thousand Germans, implied praise for the Third Reich and questioned Nazi war crimes. He also bought and sold Nazi memorabilia.

"Unfortunately, there is no führer," Svoray continued. "Only two people I've met resemble future leaders. One is Büsse. He is the other." He pointed to Juchem, who immediately brightened and gave a small nod. "He impresses me for two reasons. He's got a clean record, a great record for Germany. Plus he's never been arrested and he's not considered a threat."

The others—Köberich, Thrun, and Reisz—had been listening and sometimes talking among themselves. Godenau was briefly translating his exchanges with Svoray, particularly for Juchem's benefit. Now Reisz broke in. "This is the man. He is acceptable to all parties. He is neutral. Men must come with charisma, that's this man."

"You agree with him?" Svoray asked Godenau.

"Yeah. He's clean. He has contacts throughout the right, cordial relations with all of them. People know him because he has speaking engagements all over Germany. He brings a lot of different people together. He's an integrating figure."

"Does he believe that in a year and a half he can lead the party?" Svoray asked. "The Republicans, if they're unhappy with Schönhuber, can he do that?"

"No, that's unrealistic." Godenau translated Juchem's response.

Juchem stood up and walked to the window. Raindrops were

pinging off Reisz's aluminum shutter installations. He stood
there, looking out through the sheer curtains, hands clasped behind his back. When he turned, he said, "Do we intend to develop a new party?"

"He's talking about a new party. A bigger party. He believes it
may be too late to do that," Godenau continued in translation.
To perform a political blitzkrieg, Juchem preferred to encourage
a draft by the strongest of the existing parties. "The Republicans,
you have to force the leadership," he said. "Put them under
pressure."

"An amount of money that will help you to start. What are you
looking at? Two hundred, three hundred thousand dollars?"

Juchem said he had never seen that much money.

"There are few people that can be trusted with large sums of
money," Godenau said. "Some people go crazy. But yes, half a
million marks would probably work. Would you send someone to
look at your investment?"

"No," said Svoray. "It would be ridiculous."

"Trust is good, control is better," Godenau warned.

"Yes, but worrying about control defeats the purpose. We want
to give you the means to get your act together and see what
happens. We don't want to get involved in German politics. You
have to figure out a way to get money into the country."

Godenau was concerned that the money would be traceable.
Juchem wanted it delivered in cash. The money talk had made
him nervous. He sat on the edge of the sofa. The healthy flush of
his face was mottled, and his hands played about his face. The
money now was almost palpable, and it seemed to attract and
repel him at the same time. He said, "It should go to a person
that has never drawn attention. Where no one would think he
could have anything to do with this theme."

"You will tell me how," Svoray said. "You give me the route,
how you want it, and I trust that you are not stupid enough to
screw me or screw yourselves. In a suitcase? Where and when? I
would suggest that you guys go out, have a walk, decide, write it
for me on a sheet of paper. Finished. I used to be a policeman.
The most complicated things are simple."

They decided to establish a propaganda center in the middle
of Germany, at Ron Furey's chosen site of Eisenach. Letters
would go out to the members of the rightist parties urging them

to push their chairmen toward unity. Juchem would be promoted in advertising media, principally urban kiosks, building his recognition until he could announce his alignment with a party. In the meantime, they would develop a cadre of leaders. Juchem would conceal his radical ties until he was in office.

"Will his life be in danger?" Svoray asked. "If he becomes the overall leader, would the long knives be out for him?"

When he heard the translation, Juchem struck a dramatic pose with his hand under his jacket lapel. "There's nothing more beautiful than to die for Germany."

Juchem seemed to treat the question lightly, and Svoray pressed Godenau. "The truth. Is there any danger?"

"At present there is some danger. Because of the hysteria."

"And in a year and a half, as a candidate?"

"He thinks there would be danger then, too," Godenau translated. "For anybody that's in the public eye, there's always a danger."

"More so because he's from the right?"

"Certainly," Godenau said. "Because he's young, he's more dynamic, has a clean record. He has a better human personality than Schönhuber. He would be regarded as a more dangerous man."

"If all this works out," mused Svoray, "then we can sit and wonder if this small amount of money made a difference."

"We could," agreed Godenau. "The straw that broke the kosher camel's back."

"For us the world has changed overnight," Reisz said happily. Svoray had lingered when the others left. They had agreed to meet once more before Svoray returned to America to work out the details of delivering the money. Renata had come home from work, and the three of them were talking in the half-understood way their language barriers allowed.

"Look at you, Heinz," Svoray said, as Reisz lit another cigarette. He felt relaxed and successful. Juchem had revealed his ambitions, Godenau the machinations of conspiracy that lay behind them, and it was all on tape. Bantering with Reisz was a necessary outlet. It made the danger that gnawed at him into a game, and softened the grotesque racism and anti-Semitism Reisz expressed at every opportunity. "Juchem will have to be careful with this money. If you get hold of it, you'll spend a hundred dollars every month for cigarettes.''

Reisz understood this well enough to laugh. "Better to have one hundred marks for cigarettes than a good word for a dirty pack of Jews," he said. "With this center, we'll blow up the Jewish Republic.''

Svoray's mind was on Juchem and Roy Godenau as he walked toward his car later. Juchem was dangerous, but in many ways Godenau was the more fascinating character. His extensive contacts were apparently worldwide, from the ex-Nazi publisher in South America he'd mentioned, to Leon Degrelle, whom he said he was planning to visit in Madrid. In his eighties, Degrelle was a Belgian fascist and admirer of Hitler who had started a Nazi-like movement in Belgium. When he fled to Franco's Spain at the end of the war, he avoided a death sentence imposed by a Belgian court for treason. Degrelle's was one of a handful of names —Willis Carto's was another—recognized by right-wing fanatics and anti-Semites the world over.

Lost in thought and hurrying in the rain, Svoray turned into the side street where he had parked. His rented Opel was under a street lamp in front of an apartment building, facing back to the main road. A number of other cars were parked alongside and facing the jumble of apartments and houses on the street. Svoray took the car key from his pocket and inserted it in the lock.

As he turned the key he sensed rather than saw the movement to his right. He jerked his head to see a dark-colored car bearing down on him, its headlights off. Svoray flung himself over the hood of his car as the other car zoomed by within inches of the Opel, its tires splashing sheets of water. The car reached the corner, its brake lights flashed, and it turned and roared out of sight.

Svoray sagged against the bumper, his heart pounding. His green bag had slipped from his shoulder in his wild dive. He retrieved it and, crouching by a fender, felt through its contents until he was sure his camera, recorder, and the precious tapes he had made of Juchem and Godenau were safe. Then, staying low, he crept from cover until he could see both ends of the street. He saw no suspicious movement, although he wasn't sure he'd recognize the car anyway. The driver had been the flash of a pale face behind the rain-streaked windshield, nothing he'd be able to identify.

The key wasn't in the lock. He cursed silently, but then saw the large plastic Avis tag glistening in a patch of water on the street ten feet away. He entered the car quickly and started the engine. At the end of the street, he paused for a long moment before entering traffic, but saw nothing he could say was suspicious.

Nonetheless, he circled past the airport before he headed back to Frankfurt, checking the rearview mirrors constantly.

Twenty-five

"THERE'S AN AMERICAN."

"What do you mean, an American?" Abe Cooper had put an Apple Computer technician on hold to take Svoray's call. The museum was scheduled to open in two weeks, and the final components were being wired into place.

Svoray described Roy Godenau. "Heinz said he'd never seen him before. He came with Juchem. Obviously he's a part of his plan. This guy knows everybody in the movement. He's a friend of Willis Carto's. I almost stuck my foot in it when I mentioned his name."

Cooper told the Apple technician he would call him back. "Does he suspect you?"

"I don't think so."

"Where is he from?"

"I don't know. He lives in Germany now. He was here in the army during Vietnam and married a German woman." All around Svoray, the cavernous expanse of Frankfurt's Hauptbahnhof echoed with the random noises of late-night cleaning crews and straggling knots of travelers. The noises kept him scanning the terminal for signs that anyone was watching him.

"What about Juchem?" Cooper asked.

"He wants to subvert one of the far-right parties. The Republicans, most likely, so it would draw members from all across the right. Tonight this Godenau said Juchem was a perfect unifier. He's not part of any faction. He's a sleeper. They're willing to take the money, too.''

"You've got them saying that?"

"I think so. I'm going to send more tapes tomorrow."

"So why don't you get out of there?"

"I'm supposed to meet with them again to make plans for delivering the money."

"Watch your back," Cooper said.

Svoray was teaching Reisz to drive a stick shift. They were headed in the rented Opel to meet Juchem and Godenau in Giessen. It was a forty-minute drive from Frankfurt at anything like a decent speed, but Reisz was reluctant to drive in fifth gear and Svoray, impatient, kept urging him to drive faster. Between instructions, Svoray tried to learn more from Reisz about the would-be führer. Their talk had its usual language gaps.

Juchem, Reisz said, was definitely a fascist.

"A Nazi?"

Reisz nodded, looked at the speedometer, decided against shifting. He said, "Juchem is a Nazi." Cars were whizzing past them. "Juchem is a differentiated Nazi, an intelligent Nazi. Juchem is a National Socialist fascist. He loves Adolf Hitler. Hitler is a big man for Juchem."

"And Juchem is the biggest man in the right?"

"He's the best man in the right."

"More than Frey, more than . . . ?"

"All kaput. Frey is kaput since ten years ago."

"Althans?" Here Svoray referred to high-living Ewald Althans, a well-known and articulate neo-Nazi who was criticized within the movement for an extravagant lifestyle. His critics also alleged that he was homosexual.

"Althans you can't smoke in a pipe," Reisz said. The expression meant that Svoray could forget about Althans.

"Deckert?"

"Deckert is used up. Deckert is finished."

"Who else? Büsse?"

"Büsse is a wonderful man but Büsse is very much to the right. We need a man who is also outwardly presentable. Camouflage, that's Juchem."

Reisz patted his pocket for a cigarette, then groped for the lighter. The car wandered on the road. "Two hands on the wheel. You're crazy," Svoray yelled.

Reisz recounted the disgrace of being a neo-Nazi. He said he had few friends. His grandson had been ridiculed in kindergarten and changed his name from Reisz to Koch. Some friends, however, occupied high places. Or at least places high enough to warn him of impending police raids.

"Five in the morning, the telephone rings," Reisz said. 'Heinz, watch out,' someone says. 'The police are coming today. Get out of there.' And I say, 'Thank you very much. What's your name?'

" 'No problem,' the voice says. 'A good friend.'

"One hour later, the militia are at the door, saying, 'Open up, police.' "

"How many times?" Svoray asked. He had managed to extract most of the meaning from the German. This confirmed what Reisz had told him all along, that the police ranks were riddled with neo-Nazi sympathizers who coddled skinheads, took an indulgent view of violence toward foreigners, and subverted efforts to crack down on the right.

"It's been three times already. And always a different voice."

Beyond the verges of the autobahn, the neatly parceled countryside gave way to towns at frequent intervals. The road to Giessen was Germany at its most densely populated. Reisz became suddenly pensive.

"My feelings say yes," he said to Svoray. "My feelings say Ron, this good fat man, is an ambassador and brings money for our political fights. But my head says no."

"No, Heinz," Svoray protested.

Reisz looked at him, sadness combined with affection, and took a hand from the wheel to place on his shoulder. "My head says no. And then everybody will say, 'Goddamn Heinz.' "

In the next moment, he launched a bizarre soliloquy on World War II. "It's just a shame in this fight that two noble peoples, because the British are a noble people, and the Germans, too, and the Americans, that there were more whites bloodied than blacks. Adolf Hitler always said the biggest lies came from the Americans. You were fighting for democracy. We looked, and the black apes were coming. In America, they didn't have equal rights. All the battles, there was much white blood flowing. And that's a shame. Good American blood. Good German blood. Good English blood. And that's the craziness, that honest white blood flowed. Today it's only bandits. We don't have any good people anymore. In America the best fell, in England the best fell, in Germany the best fell. Look around today. Fifty years after Adolf Hitler, the world is starving. The air is unbreathable, the people are afraid, no one has a homeland. Murder, killings, hate, drugs. Nationalism has got to come. Only National Socialism can free the world. With England, with France, with Germany, with the white race.''

Svoray understood this well enough. Nationalism was resurgent throughout Europe, from the ethnic cleansing in the form of rape and murder in Bosnia and Herzegovina, to the sentiment in every western European nation to restrict immigration and the flow of refugees. Voices like Reisz's won followers everywhere there were disaffected people. The dizzying power of hate made Svoray giddy. His friendship with Reisz was increasingly disturbing.

"The six million." Reisz was off on another tangent. "That is the biggest lie that has ever been told in human history. The six million is a bigger lie than the Thousand-Year Reich.

"You know who suffered the most. That was the Gypsies. The Gypsies, not the Goddamned Jews."

Svoray laughed, an involuntary bubbling of hysteria. It was the only reaction that made sense.

Reisz interrupted him by bursting into song. "The day of revenge is coming. One time we will be free. Sleeping Germany awake, break your chains in two. Load the blank weapons . . .''

Juchem and Godenau were waiting for them in a café attached to the train station in Giessen.

Besides planning the money drop, Svoray hoped to get from Juchem a copy of a tree diagram he had drawn of the various right-wing organizations. For Juchem, it was a planning document; for Svoray, valuable information. He also wanted to compromise Juchem by giving him a check. This was to be a sort of down payment, an advance on the much larger amount he would bring in cash in three weeks. The payment delivered at that time was to be the first in a regular series, as the center in Eisenach grew and Juchem made it the base for his campaign.

"Thank you very much, for five hundred dollars," Juchem said when Svoray handed him the check. Written on Svoray's bank account, the check was actually for five hundred marks.

The cash payment would be harder to deliver, for the plotters already had seen potential problems. "We want protection that this isn't some kind of a trap," Godenau said. "That we don't open the bag and 'Boom!' "

"You want me to do it?" Svoray asked. "I mean, what do you prefer? Why would I bring a bomb? What do you want?"

"It would be preferable that you do it," Godenau said.

"You've been elected," said Reisz to Svoray after hearing Godenau's translation. "Elected to go 'Boom!' "

"If I do the first shipment, I won't do the second or third," Svoray said. "I don't want to be in a situation where they can identify the courier. It should not be in the same place, either."

Godenau agreed. They left the time and place open. Svoray said he would be back in Germany to join Reisz for a big neo-Nazi rally he was planning in Langen for the second Saturday in February.

They were parting when Juchem reached inside his jacket and withdrew a thick brochure that he handed to Svoray. It had at a glance the earmarks of a Nazi document in its Germanic lettering reminiscent of the Third Reich and the red, white, and black of Imperial Germany. Juchem's name appeared in block letters at the top. "This is his presentation," Godenau said. "It's what he talks about."

"What does it say?" Svoray asked.

"Truth and Right Against Lies and Agitation. That's the title. Germany's fate from a German point of view. Maybe your publisher would bring it out in English. I could do the translation."

"That's a good idea," Svoray said as he pocketed the pamphlet.

The idea left his mind immediately, however, for as he drove back to Langen with Reisz, Svoray believed he had encountered all these men for the last time. He had identified Juchem as a leader poised to unite the right into a force strong enough to break into the Bundestag. He had Juchem accepting foreign money and talking about accepting more. And though Juchem had let Godenau speak for him much of the time, Svoray was confident that somewhere the would-be führer had revealed his

Nazi sympathies. The rabbis would hold a news conference and that would be the end of Juchem and his supporters.

Reisz betrayed no inkling. He was celebrating Ron Furey's promise to return for the Langen rally with a suitcase full of money. The manner of his celebration was to sing the festive Jewish song "H'ava-Nagila." The words mean "Let us be joyous."

"It's crazy, but the Jews have good females," he said. "Intelligent, good females, but otherwise nothing much."

He segued into the "Horst-Wessel Song," and ended with a resounding *"Sieg Heil."*

"You're happy," said Svoray, struggling for control. Reisz's merrymaking once again was pushing the edge of hysteria.

"Ja, ja. I'll tell you, dear Ron, and also your comrades who stand behind us, you won't recognize Germany. We will cause so much unrest in the German people. After we have the center, one year after, we will have two thousand people, but not only people. Fighters.

"Come back in one year. The shitty state will stop following us. We'll have property. No one can run us off. We can make propaganda. We will have young people, thousands and thousands of young people. From this seed, a tree will grow. We'll make trees all over the place. Adolf Hitler's ideas will live forever.

"There will be your statue there, your likeness, so everyone can come in and see you. But without your name, so you won't get into trouble. When you come with your friends, they will always know that you, as ambassador, as emissary, have helped us. We don't ever forget friends."

Reisz seemed to have forgotten what his head had told him earlier.

February
1993

Twenty-six

SVORAY LEFT REISZ in Langen. For the next ten days, he crisscrossed Germany and sought out skinhead groups. He made no recordings and took no photographs. Without these barriers, the men he met were brutal in their honesty. In Solingen, in the heart of the German Rhineland between Cologne and Düsseldorf, he sat in a bar and heard some right-wing skinheads say that last November's fatal firebombing in Mölln was nothing compared to what real skinheads could do. In the North Sea port of Hamburg, skinheads who had fought in Croatia showed him videotapes of rapes and murders. Svoray was never clear if the victims were Serbs or Muslims. Nor were the skinheads, to whom it didn't seem to matter; the Croatian militias for which the skinheads fought were at war with both groups, and the victims deserved their fate. It was in Hamburg during the first week in February that he was told if he wanted to see a skinhead training camp he should call someone named Alex. Alex lived near Frankfurt.

"But I don't know you," Alex protested when Svoray called the number he was given. He spoke English. His voice was young, and sullen.

"You can find out about me. Do you know Heinz Reisz? Or Wilhelm Köberich? Ask them. Ask Friedhelm Büsse. Ask Bernd Thrun in Mainz. He collects food and clothes for your comrades in Croatia."

Thrun's name nudged Alex toward a semblance of civility. "Maybe if he calls me," he said.

Svoray found Thrun at home in Mainz, but could not explain what he wanted in German. He was lucky to reach Renata, and after a roundabout series of calls, Alex was persuaded. He said he would pick Svoray up in Frankfurt.

"Meet me at the Marriott in the West End, near the university." Svoray did not want to expose his whereabouts to Alex.

He drove straight through to Frankfurt from Hamburg that night and checked into the Parkhotel. Half an hour in the sauna eased the stiffness of nearly six hundred kilometers on the autobahn, and he walked to the Hauptbahnhof to try to call Cooper. For the last week the rabbi, and even Breitbart and Eaton, had been hard to reach. Svoray failed to connect this unavailability with the museum's pending opening. When Susan, Cooper's secretary, said she couldn't find him, Svoray complained that the rabbi was trying to avoid him and walked back to the hotel muttering. He went to sleep without thinking of the next day.

The morning was cold and overcast. At eight-thirty, he caught the streetcar in front of the Hauptbahnhof. Ten minutes later, he got off at the Marriott and walked into the lobby. His leather jacket, rumpled slacks, and black Nikes stood out among the business suits that comprised the standard uniform. Coveys of people wearing name tags fluttered past, headed for the nearby exhibition center. Svoray bought a newspaper and sat pretending to read it, conscious of the weight of his knife against one ankle and the credit card and laminated photo he'd taped to the other. He had re-created the conditions of his trip with Stefan to Curt Müller's solstice celebration. It had been less than six weeks, but seemed like a century.

At nine o'clock, he looked up from the paper and saw a battered Audi pulling up outside. The driver parked by the curb and got out, said something to the uniformed attendant, and came into the lobby. His paramilitary look drew open stares; at the cashier's desk, two young women and a man stopped and turned their heads in unison, as if at a tennis match. Svoray got up quickly and met him.

"Alex?" he asked.

"Yes. You are Herr Furey?"

"That's me. Ready to rock and roll? I'm looking forward to seeing this place."

Alex was about twenty, and very pale. His cropped hair was a dirty shade of blond and his narrow, bony face contained a residue of teenage acne. He did not seem happy about his role as escort. They went to the car. A second man sat in the passenger seat, staring straight ahead; he was huge, with massive shoulders that could only have come from hours in a weight room. Alex opened a rear door and held it for Svoray.

"Oh, no," Svoray said. "I'm going to follow you."

Alex shook his head. "That is not possible."

"Why not?"

"No one knows where this is."

"I won't know either, I'm very bad at directions," said Svoray. "I'm telling you, I go places and have no idea how to get there. I get lost getting back."

Alex looked at him sideways and laughed, but he still held the door.

"No, no. I'm not joking. What, do you think I'm going to tell? Don't be an idiot. We are comrades. My car's right over here. I'll follow you."

Alex motioned for the second man to roll his window down. They talked quietly in German for a moment. Then Alex said, "Okay. Follow us."

They drove out of the Marriott and joined a road that took them west and onto an autobahn. Svoray saw signs to Wiesbaden and Mainz. Then they turned south and after a time, it seemed, back east again. The heavy clouds opened and it began to rain. Alex pulled off under a bridge. Svoray stopped behind him as both men got out of the Audi and came running back.

Alex leaned into his window. "As I said, no one knows this place and we cannot lead you there. We must blindfold you now. Then Dieter can drive you. Or we can forget it. It's the same to me."

"This is crazy," Svoray protested. "Didn't Bernd tell you you could trust me?"

"I don't even trust him."

"But he . . ."

Alex jerked his head at Dieter. They began to walk back to their car. Svoray quickly ran through the options. Juchem, the would-be führer, and the traitorous American Roy Godenau were the crowning discoveries of his mission. In that sense it was complete. But as the Jew in him sought the bottom of the well of hate to know how deep it was, the army veteran was curious. Was Büsse insane when he talked about a well-trained fighting force for his imagined cadre of leaders to command when they established the Fourth Reich? Neo-Nazi commandos storming the country was a nightmare dreamed by a lunatic. But history was not immune from lunatics. Svoray leaned out of the car and called, "Okay, blindfold me."

The blindfold was a strip of linen dish towel. At least it was clean. Svoray looked at his watch. Ten-thirty. Then the strip of cloth blackened his vision as Alex knotted it behind his head. He was in the Opel's backseat. Alex said, "You can sit up like you're being driven. But don't look. Then you will have to lie on the seat."

The muscle-bound Dieter grunted as he got into the driver's seat. He moved some levers and cursed, then the seat slid back abruptly, almost catching Svoray's foot. Svoray tilted his head forward and back until he saw a thin strip of daylight at the rag's lower edge. In the next instant he felt a thick hand pulling his head down. "Okay, okay," he said.

They continued in the same direction for what seemed a long time, though they may have swung to the right or left. The tires sizzled in the wet, and the wipers slapped from side to side. Svoray called to the front seat. "Hey, Dieter. Have you been to Croatia? Fight the Serbs? I hear you get land. Sounds like a good deal."

There was silence from the front. "You speak English, Dieter? *Sprechen Sie Englisch?* I'm sorry to say I don't speak German. My father did, but I never learned. I understand a little, though. You can talk to me." More silence. "What about girls? You get girls in Croatia? You get to rape them, I bet. Spoils of war?" The car wavered and a ringing blow caught Svoray on the side of the head. Dieter spoke at last. He said, "Shut up."

They slowed and joined a smaller road, or a series of smaller roads, that eventually and obviously turned into some kind of dirt lane. The car slewed through ruts, and he heard weeds brushing the sides. They stopped, he heard a gate swing open, they drove through, continued, then the car swung in a circle and stopped.

He lifted the blindfold and blinked at the sight of a forest shrouded in rain. The cars, along with two or three others, were parked facing a fence that joined the gate. Dieter got out of the car and ran toward a building behind them. Svoray's watch showed a few minutes after twelve. He got out of the car and followed his escort.

Twenty yards away sat a cabin on low posts, a concrete porch across its front under an overhang. Alex and Dieter were stomping the mud from their boots on the porch while three other men watched. These seemed almost to be derelicts; their field clothes were filthy and they'd gone several days without shaving. They warmed their hands over a fire built from wood scraps in an oil drum. Smoke from the fire had reddened their eyes and blackened the beams overhead. When Svoray reached the porch, he could see that all three were skinheads and were younger than they first appeared. One had a military rifle slung behind his shoulder. The others wore pistols in mud-spattered holsters on their belts.

They greeted Alex and Dieter casually and glanced at Svoray. Alex shrugged. "A journalist from America. Our supporters wanted him to see where we train," he said in German.

"I believe in what you're doing, guys," Svoray said. "I think my story will really help the movement."

Alex translated this. The three nodded, but Svoray could see they didn't care. They had no use for him at all. One spat into the fire.

Alex turned to Svoray and said in English, "These three are training for Croatia. They will be going soon."

"Is this it?"

"Oh, no. There are others here now, but they are just beginning. Some are going. Some are coming back. Many are in Croatia now."

"How many?" asked Svoray.

"It's hard to say. Some stay on and settle and we don't hear from them anymore. I think over a hundred. They go also from France and other countries."

Svoray was disappointed. The three skinheads looked as if they'd signed up for the pittance and the food. Food of which there was no evidence. But they followed as Alex led the way across a muddy, grass-patched field bordered by a row of ugly corrugated metal huts. White smoke drifted from tin chimney stacks. Alex said those were the barracks. They reached the far side of the field and Alex explained, "The training course is over here." Dieter trailed the group like a herder dog, ready to keep strays from bolting.

Looking back to the cabin and the squatty huts, Svoray thought the whole place resembled a rundown Poconos resort, down to an unidentifiable flag that drooped wetly from a pole. Paths of mud and haphazardly placed boards converged on a small building set apart from the others, and Svoray reasoned that this was the latrine.

His feet by now were soaked and muddy, and he gave up trying to find the dry spots as he walked. Alex, in his boots, ignored the wet. So did the three "soldiers," two walking close on his and Alex's flanks, the third behind them, so that Svoray felt like a prisoner being escorted. His baseball cap and the shoulders of his jacket were heavy with the rain.

A patch of small, bare trees marked the edge of the field. They entered the trees and beyond them came to a series of obstacles in a course laid out over the space of perhaps one hundred yards. It reminded Svoray of the place in Israel where he'd done his military training.

"*Freiwillig?*" Alex barked.

The skinhead with the rifle stepped forward. He was short, with a thick neck and heavy shoulders. A scar ran through one eyebrow, with stitch marks still visible.

"Good, Max," said Alex.

Max ran to the right, to the far side of a row of barbed wire coils. He took a bayonet from a sheath at his belt, fixed it on the rifle, and waited, red-rimmed eyes staring fixedly ahead. Alex took a pistol from beneath his jacket. Svoray had not realized he was armed. He pointed the gun in the air and pulled the trigger. Its sharp crack lifted a small colony of crows from hidden perches, squawking angrily. The bird noise and the pistol shot were quickly swallowed by the mist and dripping trees.

At the sound, Max ran toward the barbed wire and flung himself into the rutted mud under the coils. He wriggled through, ran thirty yards to an eight-foot wall of boards and posts sunk in the ground, leaped, and clambered over the wall. Alex, Svoray, and the two other youths ran parallel. When they could see him again beyond the wall, Max was running up a palisade of logs set diagonally against each other with the ends extending into an additional barrier. The next obstacle was a double row of tires. He unslung his rifle and held it as he high-stepped through the tires, left foot, right foot, left, slipping once as he landed in mud, pausing at the end to hoist his rifle back onto his shoulder. Then he ran to a bridge of metal pipe that arched over a pool of muddy water, grasped a pipe at the near side, and began to swing himself across. He slipped two-thirds of the way across and fell in water to his knees, near a rudely painted skull and crossbones tacked onto a post extending from the water. The skinhead set his face, slogged out of the water, and ran dripping to a knotted rope that dangled from an overhanging limb. This he shinnied up twenty feet or so, came down knot to knot, jumped, and landed in a crouch. Then he began to run and scream at the same time, holding the rifle in front of him, until he reached a waterlogged dummy that was leaking sawdust and plunged the bayonet into its midsection with a final, primal scream.

"Now he will go to the firing range," Alex told Svoray.

Max still was breathing heavily when they caught up with him. He had mud to his knees from his fall into the water. "When I was in the army we had to do that with a field pack," Svoray said to Alex. "Sixty pounds. Tell him."

Alex looked curiously at Svoray. He repeated what he'd said in German. The panting skinhead, trails of sweat cutting grimy runnels down his face, turned to Svoray with an expression of contempt. He grinned all of a sudden and thrust the rifle at Svoray, hard against his chest.

Svoray thought Max was going to come at him. Instead, he jerked his head at a row of paper targets set up on timbers backed by a bulldozed berm of earth forty yards away. The outlines of human forms were already pocked with bullet holes, and strips of paper were peeling away in the rain. Svoray, knowing he was foolish to do so, accepted the challenge. He fired from a standing position, aiming at the cleanest target. It was only as he squeezed off the first shot and felt the rifle jolt against his shoulder that he realized he was seeing something odd. Squinting through the rain, he saw a Star of David traced over the heart.

Equally bizarre, someone had drawn a bikini bottom on the target and filled it in with stars and stripes.

His first shot struck the target in the left shoulder. He was content to group the rest of his shots there. His hands and shoulder tingling from the concussions, he handed the rifle back. "Well," he said, the shots still loud in his ears, "this is just like Machne Shmonim."

As loud as the rifle's roar had been, the fields and woods around them now fell silent. There was a moment of uncertainty among the others in which Svoray repeated to himself what he had said, and then felt the racing of the heart that follows a disaster. "Machne Shmonim" was Hebrew for Camp Eighty, the camp for new recruits in Israel where he had trained.

"What?" said Alex sharply.

"Just like Camp Lejeune," Svoray said, using the first name he could think of.

"You did not say that. You said something else." Alex was close to him, in his face, while Max was shoving a fresh clip into the rifle's magazine.

"Camp Lejeune. All this looks like beautiful, glorious Camp Lejeune. It's the Marine base where I trained. Is this guy going to shoot, or what?"

Alex stared hard. Svoray didn't think it mattered if they believed him. They didn't seem to care. They would just as soon shoot him and leave him lying in the mud. The ground was soft; they could bury him in half an hour. He tried to think if anybody who cared knew where he was.

Max sent the fresh clip home, flopped onto the firing line, and aimed carefully. The clatter of fire echoed through the woods as the bullets stitched a pattern in the target. When the clip was empty he jumped up and glared a challenge at Svoray, letting the rifle swing in his direction.

Svoray glared back. "Good shooting, my friend. But point it somewhere else if you don't mind."

Alex spoke in German to Max, who lowered the rifle. They returned in the direction of the buildings. The residue of Svoray's mistake hung over them, charging the atmosphere with suspicion.

Svoray tried changing the subject. "How long do they stay?" he asked.

"Six weeks, more or less," Alex said. "Only enough time to teach them not to stand up to look for bullets."

"Do you teach them yourself?"

"What I can."

"Where did you learn?"

"From being outside. Viking Youth. I study the techniques of survival. And I believe in the fight that is coming. Here, we will go through one of the barracks."

They entered the end door of one of the huts. Svoray reached in his bag for his camera but Alex stopped him with a hand on his wrist. "No pictures," he said.

They stood at the end of a short row of unmade bunks, eight on each side of a central aisle that was muddy with boot prints. A steel locker stood beside each bed. As far as Svoray could tell, there was no running water. What heat there was came from a guttering firebox with a few damp pieces of wood stacked on one side and the remnants of magazines on the other. Most of the magazines appeared to be pornographic. More of these were scattered on some of the bunks, where half a dozen shaven young men lounged and played cards in the light of a bare overhead bulb. Svoray could hear the putt-putt of a generator outside. The men paid the visitors no attention.

"So these are the soldiers of the great revolution," Svoray said, unable to restrain his sarcasm.

"When they come back, they will know what killing is," Alex said.

They walked through the building and out the far end, onto a muddy path that passed the latrine and led back to the cabin. The barrel in front still sent up wisps of smoke, and one of the skinheads poked inside it with a stick in an effort to revive the fire. The rest of them went inside. Max sat on a wooden chair, removed the bayonet from the rifle barrel, and replaced it in the sheath on his belt. He wiped the rifle free of mud with a rag, stood it in an open gun rack, and tossed the rag into a corner. Alex opened a cabinet and took something from a shelf.

"Would you like to see some of our trophies?" he asked.

"Sure. Trophies from the war?"

Alex stepped toward Svoray holding out a jar. Svoray looked closely, then stepped back. The jar was full of severed penises, the organs withered and dark in their immersion. "Our pickle jar," said Alex. "Our jar of little pickles." Max and the other skinheads nudged each other, grinning. Max drew the bayonet from its sheath and pretended he was sharpening it, moving even the stolid Dieter to utter a cruel laugh. Alex replaced the jar and closed the cabinet door. "Now you will stay with us until we eat."

"Thank you, but no. Now I will go," said Svoray. "You spoke to Bernd. I have to go and meet him now." This was a lie, but Svoray had seen enough. The thought of eating with the skinheads turned his stomach.

"But we have extended you our hospitality. We will have something to drink first."

"You are not understanding me, my friend. Bernd is expecting me." Svoray swung his bag onto his shoulder, wishing his knife was inside it and not down on his ankle where it might as well have been in Frankfurt. The skinhead who had tended the fire came in the door, admitting a billow of wood smoke, and when he closed it Dieter moved beside the door and leaned back with his massive arms crossed. Max's bayonet was still unsheathed. Svoray turned back to Alex. "But he can wait a little while. Let's have a drink." He took his jacket off and threw it on the chair where Max had sat.

"Good." Alex spoke to the skinheads and they broke into smiles. Dieter relaxed. They moved through a doorless opening into a second room. "Our mess hall," Alex said.

A long wooden table with benches on each side stood roughly in the middle of the room. The lone window had one of its four panes replaced with tar paper. At the back, an old tin stove stood before a grimy splash plate. To its right, beyond a dingy sink and a span of plywood counter, an ancient refrigerator clattered and groaned. Max went to it and took out six of the large brown bottles of beer Svoray had first seen Wilhelm and his friends drinking on the Zeil. He placed them on the table and they all sat down.

Nothing was said for a moment. Then Svoray lifted a bottle and said, "To the good fight." When Alex repeated in German what he had said, the others raised their bottles and drank in long gurgling swallows. Svoray only pretended to drink. When his hosts had drunk their bottles down, he gathered his and theirs and took them to the counter, opened the refrigerator, and took out fresh ones. On one of the refrigerator shelves he saw their meal: a mass of sausages loosely wrapped in greasy paper, linked and winding back upon themselves like entrails. When he brought the bottles to the table, he purposely knocked his over. He snatched it up quickly, cursing, and ran to the sink where most of it foamed out, then returned with the depleted bottle. Dieter shook his head at Svoray's clumsiness. The others laughed without trying to conceal it. On the third round, he told Alex he was going outside to urinate.

"Yeah, you go pee-pee," Alex said. They hoisted their bottles all around and drank to Svoray's puny bladder.

He gathered his jacket and walked quickly to the car without looking back. He was climbing into the driver's seat when he realized he didn't have the keys, that Dieter had driven the car and the keys were probably in his pocket. With a groan of resignation he looked back at the cabin, then scanned the inside of the car in desperate hope. Miraculously, the keys were dangling from the ignition where Dieter had left them. Svoray slid behind the wheel.

The grinding of the starter seemed to fill the compound. The engine caught, and the tires slipped on the wet earth as he backed the car up. He glanced toward the cabin: no one on the porch yet. Then the door swung wildly and Dieter sprinted out, followed by Max, Alex, and the others. Svoray shifted into first. Dieter ran at the car. He caught up, making Svoray flinch as he pounded at the window. In the rearview mirror Svoray saw the two skinheads fumbling for their pistols.

He left Dieter at an open gate post that he missed by inches as he slithered onto a muddy forest road. He had not gone fifty yards before a closed gate loomed. Svoray's heart fell. But as he neared it he saw it was only closed, not locked, and it opened outward as he nosed the car against it. The tires slipped again as he accelerated, but then they caught and he was driving through thrashing weeds that he imagined obscured the sound of pistol fire.

The weedy track joined a two-lane country road. Muddy tire marks headed in one direction. Svoray followed them, reached an intersection, and turned arbitrarily. Ten minutes later, road signs told him he was approaching the town of Aschaffenburg. He entered the town, found a municipal parking lot, and parked where the cars were thickest. From here he lowered himself in the seat and watched. His heart had slowed by now. His feet and legs were wet and cold, his jacket waterlogged. By his watch it was midafternoon. He took off the suede-brimmed cap—also water-logged—and draped a towel over his head like a scarf. Then he moved to the passenger seat, thinking he would look like a farmer's wife waiting for her husband to complete the shopping.

He listened to one of his tapes and forced himself to think about what had just happened. He had slipped and used He-brew. But Alex hadn't recognized the language; he only heard something unfamiliar, and therefore suspicious. Could he re-create it in a way that someone, Büsse perhaps, with his smatter-ing of Yiddish phrases, might identify? He doubted it. Camp Lejeune made sense, barely.

Then he thought, What does it matter? He had given the rabbis what they wanted. In the process he was exhausted and half-mad from the constant drumming of hate upon his psyche. He could simply declare victory and head home.

Twenty-seven

THE WEEKEND leading to Monday, February 8, was an exhausting and fulfilling time at the Simon Wiesenthal Center. The center's Beit Hashoah–Museum of Tolerance was ready to open at last. West Pico Boulevard was awash in limousines delivering celebrities to the preliminary events. Simon Wiesenthal himself, now eighty-four, had come from Vienna for the opening. California Governor Pete Wilson, U.S. Senator Dianne Feinstein, local congressional representatives, and the director-general of UNESCO were there to show their support for the ideals to which the center had dedicated itself and its museum. Private dinners on Friday and Saturday nights and a Sunday night gala honoring Wiesenthal led to Monday's grand opening ceremonies, which were covered by "CBS This Morning" anchor Paula Zahn.

CBS, of course, was interested in the museum itself. It was impressive not only for its marble and glass architecture, but for the range of its concerns. It offered material on the American civil rights movement, Pol Pot's killing fields in Cambodia, and Turkish genocide against Armenians, as well as on the Holocaust. Visitors could feel the isolation of Jews in Nazi Germany; they also could confront their own prejudices in a series of questions and scenes from the previous summer's Los Angeles riots. The Multi-Media Learning Center, the second-floor complex that only weeks before had been without phones and air conditioning, was running smoothly.

Marvin Hier was voluble on this special day that meant so much to him. He mentioned to Zahn as they were chatting that the center was working on something that would interest her.

"I can't tell you about it now," he said. "But when I can, I'll call you."

The successful museum opening freed the rabbis to concentrate on the material from Svoray's investigation. The next day, for the first time, Hier and Abe Cooper sat down with Aaron Breitbart and Rick Eaton in the research office to review the material Svoray had sent. They had before them photographs, including Jaschka's startlingly illustrated torso, the guns and knives kept at the safe house of Büsse's FAP skinheads in Porz, and Svoray together with Reisz, the Fighting Cock, Wolfgang Juchem, and the American Roy Godenau. They had hundreds of pages of translated transcripts from Svoray's tapes scattered across desks and tables. The costs of transcription had run into thousands of dollars.

"An American," Hier said indignantly. "What kind of a lowlife is this guy, to betray his country?" They had just gone over the portion of the transcript in which Godenau had described passing information to the Iraqis during the Gulf War. "What the heck is an American doing there anyway?"

"You do wonder about that," Breitbart said blandly.

"Do we know anything about this guy?" Hier demanded.

"He's a new one. These are names we've never seen before," Breitbart replied with ponderous precision. "Juchem came from nowhere, too, remember. Godenau. The Fighting Cock." He rolled his eyes.

"Where are they going with this thing?"

"It's pretty plain where they want to go," Eaton said.

"But can they do it? Let's talk about this Juchem. Where has he been? Why didn't we hear of him before?" Hier's hands were flying through his hair, worrying his forelock.

Cooper raised a hand. He was able to think clearly for the first time in weeks. He said, "Let's speculate a minute. I think if you wanted to gain power, this is how you'd go about it. You'd build a following outside of politics, and when the politicians couldn't agree, you'd be available. Yaron is right. It's a very clever game.''

"What do you think they're going to do if we tell them about this?'' Hier asked, referring to the government of Helmut Kohl.

"I think they're going to ignore it if they can,'' Cooper said. "They're still pretending right-wing violence doesn't count. They still haven't put it on a par with violence from the left.''

"And as Aaron says, these guys aren't known quantities,'' Hier said. "So the government can say they're nothing, they don't count. Don't worry, we've got everything under control. They're also going to consider the source. An Israeli Jew. How can he know more about the neo-Nazis than they do?''

"What are you saying, Moish?'' Cooper was accustomed to Hier's leaps of mind.

"Wouldn't it be great if we had them dead to rights? On camera, talking about what they want to do? I mean, you listen to them and you hear how vicious and sick their anti-Semitism is and it has to be paid attention to. We can't afford to let this be ignored. I was talking to Paula Zahn when she was here for the museum opening. I'll bet they'd do a story.''

He placed the call that afternoon. At the same time, Cooper was passing on what he'd learned about Roy Godenau to his federal government contacts. Their titles were just vague enough to indicate they might be with the CIA.

By Thursday the story was arranged. Zahn had given it to a "CBS This Morning'' producer named Jim Murphy, an affable man with curly gray hair whose skinny body was all angles. Murphy saw the story as requiring an undercover camera, and hired a crack photographer from Texas who was an expert in the field. He planned to shoot the February 13 Langen rally and combine footage from the news event with undercover video he'd get with Svoray's help. Murphy put the story in the hands of a field producer from the CBS London bureau to save transportation costs. Svoray had been halted in New York, where he had stopped over on his way to Los Angeles to make his victory declaration. He had left Germany only the day before, flying from Frankfurt on the morning after he'd escaped the skinhead training camp. He wasn't looking forward to returning, but the prospect of a network story on his mission was irresistible.

"CBS is doing something. I'm feeling very good about it," he told Michal on the phone.

"What are you saying?"

"That I'm going back for just a couple of days. They're sending a camera crew."

"Yaron, I agree that it's important what you're doing. But there has to be an end to this sometime."

"I know, I know."

"I and the children are not the only thing. People are beginning to wonder what you're doing. There are rumors."

"What kind of rumors?"

"About a secret mission. Your friends at the papers have been after me with questions."

"Why don't you just tell them I have left you to go live with a gorgeous blond-haired German woman who sings the Wagnerian operas?"

She snorted. "I bet you wish I thought that was funny."

"You mean you don't?"

"No, I don't," she said. Michal laughed in spite of herself. But Svoray knew she was nearing the end of her patience, as surely as he was nearing the frayed end of his sanity.

Aaron Breitbart was alone in the office he shared with Eaton on the afternoon of Friday, February 12. The Wiesenthal Center, at the end of the week that opened the museum, was collectively welcoming the approach of the first normal weekend in some time. As sundown neared and with it the beginning of the sabbath, observant staff members began leading a rush home. Eaton already had left when the dead phone in his desk rang.

For some reason the answering machine did not click on. The muffled ringing of the phone continued. Breitbart got up and walked across the room, hoping to hear the answering machine engage. He opened the drawer thinking, quite specifically, "Don't say 'Wiesenthal Center.'"

He picked up the phone and said, *"The Right Way.* May I help you?"

"I'd like a copy of your magazine."

"Certainly. Let me have your name and address."

"This is Mark Weber." Breitbart knew the name well, but was astounded when he heard it. As an employee and a longtime associate of Willis Carto of the Institute for Historical Review, Weber's name had been in the center's files for a long time. He had been identified in 1978 as the news editor of a neo-Nazi publication called the *National Vanguard*. Weber gave a post office box number in Newport Beach.

Breitbart hurried down the hall, knocked on Abe Cooper's door, and opened it without waiting for an answer. He was grateful to find Cooper still at his desk, on the phone as usual.

Cooper knew when he saw Aaron standing in the door with a finger in the air that he had important news. "I'll call you back," he said into the phone.

"You're not going to believe this," Breitbart said breathlessly.

"Try me," Cooper said.

"Mark Weber just called the dead phone and asked for a copy of *The Right Way*."

"Aaron, that's incredible." The call was a stark answer to one of the first questions Cooper and Hier had raised when they sent Svoray to Germany: What links existed between German and American hate groups? If Godenau knew Willis Carto, he certainly knew Weber, and the dead phone's number could only have come from Godenau or the other German neo-Nazis. Svoray hadn't given it to anyone else.

"Gotcha," Cooper said.

He and Breitbart went to Hier's office to tell him the good news.

It was not until the weekend, as the euphoria of the museum opening and the dramatic and unexpected confirmation of the phone call dissipated, that Cooper realized Svoray might be in danger. Curiosity was by no means the only possible explanation for Weber's call. The more ominous one was that Godenau was suspicious about Ron Furey and his claims. There was no way to warn Svoray, since he had flown back to Germany on Friday night. Worse, there was no magazine to send to Weber. *The Right Way* existed only as a business card.

"We don't have a magazine, you know," Cooper reminded Breitbart on Monday morning.

"We can make one," Breitbart said.

They stopped short of that, but by Monday afternoon *The Right Way* had come into being as a subscription form devised by Breitbart with the help of the Wiesenthal Center's graphics department. It purported to show the magazine's January cover, complete with an American flag and the slogan "Know the True Way." In bold type, it promised articles such as "Uniting the Conservative Movement in Germany," "Middle East: The Double Standard," and "The Australian Right: Another Silent Majority." A twelve-month subscription was twenty-four dollars.

There were patches of snow on the ground when Svoray and the cameraman, Steve Jackson, got off the plane in Frankfurt on February 13.

They rented a car and drove into Langen. Traffic moved normally, and there was no police presence at the major intersections entering town. Svoray was surprised and uneasy. He had expected the big neo-Nazi rally to have brought out the police and clogged the streets. He reached Reisz's to learn that the rally had been shifted to Kassel, two hundred kilometers north.

He also learned, to his dismay, that Juchem was having second thoughts.

"He was warned, he got a call," Reisz said, Svoray filtering the essence of his meaning from the German. "Someone in the police. He told Juchem he is being watched. And that if he takes money from Americans, he will never be führer and will maybe be dead."

"Heinz, that's not important," Svoray said as Renata arrived to help with the translation. "I don't have the money with me anyway. But look who I've brought with me—CBS. They've agreed to do a story on the right, to tell the story my way. This is really what we want."

Reisz either accepted that Svoray had CBS at his command or was too polite to argue. Wearing a khaki brown shirt, a black tie, and a heavy cardigan sweater, he inserted the metal shields into his windows as the camera rolled. He kissed Nero the dog good-bye and they began driving, Svoray and Jackson following Reisz and Renata. A thin fog dispersed as they drove, revealing a sky of pale blue. Jackson had little to say; he was tired from the overnight flight, but Svoray was running on adrenaline. He had thought at first that they were going to Kassel for the rally, but that was not the case. They were headed for a little town called Philippsthal, astride the old border with the east. Soon they left the autobahn, wound through several small villages, and, at a point where a group of cars was clustered, left the pavement for a dirt road that entered a forest.

The road seemed to go on forever, although it could not have been much more than a kilometer. At one point it emerged on a hillside, the forest opening to give a view across the hills and hollows of the snowy countryside. Then it dipped back into the forest and approached the brick pillars of a gate. Beyond the gate, in an open field on a rising hillside, stood a chaletlike building. A sign said it was the Waldgasthof, the Forest Inn.

Young men in black uniforms, following German shepherds straining on their leashes, patrolled the verges of the entrance road. More young men, plus some girls in jeans and bomber jackets, milled in a parking area occupied by at least two dozen cars. This activity had not prevented a man who was apparently a policeman, wearing tan uniform pants and a jacket, from walking among the cars and taking license numbers. As he was parking, Svoray saw the substantial figure of Friedhelm Büsse entering the inn.

The Forest Inn apparently was a popular weekend luncheon spot, for its dining room of white stucco and heavy dark wood beams was filled. The only clue to what was going on in a back room was a pair of men in khaki shirts seated at a table against the wall. One of them wore a red armband emblazoned with a white circle, inside of which was the castellated circle symbol of Büsse's FAP. Another brownshirt barred the cameraman from the back room, but admitted Svoray.

Büsse, the swell of his gut making his tie seem comically short, stood at the head of a U-shaped group of tables. Around the tables sat perhaps sixty men and a few women, guarded by two uniformed brownshirts who stood against the wall. Several of the seated men also wore the khaki brown uniforms with armbands, and some wore belts, military-style, across the chest. Close-shaven skinheads with tattooed arms ignored the military look by wearing T-shirts. Everyone else—and this Svoray found frightening— looked normal, their clothing offering no clue to their neo-Nazi beliefs. Reisz had told him the meeting brought together Büsse's local leaders as well as neo-Nazis from France and Denmark. Red, white, and black FAP banners hung from standards around the room, contrasting with the ersatz cuteness of plastic flower baskets hanging from the walls and plastic ivy looped around a center post.

Büsse was talking about his vision of the FAP. "We are national, revolutionary, socialist," he said. "But not the pseudo-socialism of the Jews under the camouflage name of Karl Marx."

He said, to cries of "Bravo, Friedhelm," that he wasn't racist, he just didn't want the government choosing his friends. He said, "We are of the opinion that everyone who comes to us and remains here as a guest, he will leave again one day. I have nothing against it if a colored man studies medicine here with us and after seven years goes back again to Africa as a medicine man."

Here he was interrupted by laughter.

He said, "I see it as a cruel joke that the union with former East Germany is seen as the reunification of Germany. It can only be considered a German reunification when Königsberg becomes German again. When South Tirol is German again, then we can talk about a reunification of Germany.

"That point makes us different from the usual so-called National Socialists. Frey from the DVU, Deckert from the NDP, Schönhuber from the Republicans, what Germany do they want? You know German history. What do I want? My dear comrades, whoever claims he wants the borders of 1937 is of the same opinion as I. Treason, high treason if he freely renounces West Prussia or Austria."

Continuing over the applause, Büsse inveighed against the German justice system. "When one of us drunkenly runs over a Jew, and by coincidence is a member of the FAP, then we are charged with murder under the influence of alcohol and the Holocaust is brought back to life on the autobahn." He complained about antifascist laws. "An Adolf Hitler probably only comes along every two thousand years," he lamented. "We can't wait for a person to solve our problems. We have to bring the power ourselves."

Svoray began to grow impatient. He was afraid that without the neo-Nazi rally in Kassel, or Büsse's brownshirts and Nazi-like banners, CBS would lack dramatic footage and he would be responsible. And once again, he believed that he would not be returning to Germany. He went to the lobby, summoned Jackson, and reentered the room.

When Büsse paused, Svoray strode to the front of the room.

Jackson held the camera casually and recorded shots of brown-shirted storm troops in their armbands, the FAP's banners, the skinheads, and the rest of the audience around the tables. Svoray said, "I know some of you don't trust me. But I've met some of you before, and I've come today with one of the most important TV channels in America, because I believe that your propaganda is not good enough outside of Germany."

There was a swell of outraged protest. "Look," Svoray said, "if anyone doesn't want to be seen, just leave for two minutes."

Someone ran at the camera and raised a hand in front of the lens.

"Don't do that. Hey, leave him alone." Svoray rushed at the man who was pushing the cameraman toward the door. "Don't touch my guy. I'll kick your ass."

"Jew!" came a cry from the back. Others took up the chorus. Reisz and Renata, sitting together at one of the tables, looked mortified.

Svoray gave a bravado performance. "We came all this way," he shouted. "This is one of the problems you have. Everyone sees conspiracy everywhere. Everyone is paranoid. This is crazy. You want to get good propaganda and the guy's talking about Jews."

Büsse tried to calm things down. "People see behind every person an agent, a Jew, a devil." He said he didn't care who filmed him, what was important was that the FAP be seen. But the protests refused to die. A brown-shirted young man with dark hair shouted at Svoray.

"Have I met you?" Svoray demanded. "I'm trying to unite you, and everyone is screaming at me." He turned to a familiar face. "I arrived today and they're treating me like a Jew. It's paranoia."

"It is just that some of them don't know you," said Norbert Weidner, the tall skinhead from Bonn whom Svoray had met in Porz before the fight with the Cypriots. "The right wing has had many hard times with the media." He was interrupted by cries of *"Raus! Raus!"*

Jackson had continued shooting during Svoray's tirade. He gave a slight nod and they walked out with Svoray still cursing, threatening, and complaining, "I came from America today to be with you, and I'm treated like shit." Reisz and Renata followed moments later. Renata said that Reisz was unhappy at the uproar, but embarrassed by his comrades' lack of trust.

A phalanx of police stopped them as they drove away. The police, former East Germans who wore bomber jackets and green pants, recorded the information from their passports and waved them on.

Two nights later, Svoray paced outside the entrance of the Gravenbruch Kempinski, one of Frankfurt's fine hotels. It was located in its own preserve south of the city, and as he paced, expensive cars disgorged beautifully dressed people against a wooded backdrop. Svoray had chosen the Gravenbruch because it fit his image as the emissary of a rich man. It was a properly auspicious setting for a meeting at which Wolfgang Juchem and Friedhelm Büsse would agree to forge an illegal coalition. Just as important as those factors were the points from which concealed cameras could shoot into the cocktail lounge.

Svoray had told Reisz the day before that his cameraman had gone back to America. In reality, Jackson and the field producer, who had arrived too late for Saturday's confrontation, had taped Svoray's strolling interview with Reisz from inside a rented car. Reisz's daughter-in-law, Marcel's wife, unaware of the full nature of her role, had translated. Svoray had been wired with a hidden microphone.

For the Gravenbruch meeting, the producer had rented in Ron Furey's name a first-floor room from which the cameraman could shoot across a courtyard into the lounge. Then he had prowled for an hour before discovering a second shot in the lounge, looking down from a terrace of the hotel's atrium. Finally, he had concealed a small, remotely operated camera in a ceiling air vent of the room. Svoray was wired for a second time.

Reisz, Renata, and the daughter-in-law, whose name Svoray always struggled to remember, arrived first. Svoray steered them to the tables he'd reserved in the lounge. The daughter-in-law had long, straight auburn hair and wore a plunging off-the-shoulder top for the occasion. Marcel had stayed at home.

Büsse arrived accompanied by a man wearing a sporty jacket with the sleeves pushed up. Büsse introduced the man as a friend and a professional pilot, but Svoray took him to be a bodyguard. The same man had also been at Curt and Ursula Müller's solstice celebration the first time Svoray met Büsse. He looked out of place in the glittery elegance of the hotel.

Svoray questioned Büsse about the treatment he had received at the FAP meeting.

"Why did they scream at me when I came with the camera?" he asked. "I could have had the guy for three days. But after that, he left."

Büsse seemed to bear no ill will for Svoray's outburst. "Everybody has to agree to it," he said in German. "You can't photograph somebody against their will. People would have problems with their jobs if they were seen on television." He invited Svoray back in May for Pfingsten, the Whitsuntide weekend when the Viking Youth would gather. "Then you can bring your camera," he promised.

Ten minutes later, Juchem and Godenau arrived, resembling central casting heavies in their belted trench coats. Köberich accompanied them; small and spry, he looked like a child following his bigger brothers.

"Nothing goes out of these circles," Godenau cautioned as they got down to business. He was sitting in the glow of a brass lamp, with bow-tied waiters passing in the background. Köberich smoked a cigarette.

The meeting began in a promising fashion. Svoray took Juchem to the rented room and passed him some more money, confident the transaction was being recorded by the hidden camera. Back at the table in the lounge, Godenau said he would have no problems moving money despite being scrutinized by German authorities as an Iraqi agent. Juchem, with Godenau translating, explained that his disillusionment with Gerhard Frey had spawned his own ambitions. Frey, he said, had "no serious interest in uniting the right." But then Juchem rose and went off with Büsse and Reisz to discuss their plans in private. Svoray was left with Köberich, the pilot, the two women, and Godenau. The three men returned, but the remaining talk was bland.

Whatever else the cameras did, they livened Svoray's sense of melodrama. Convinced now that his mission was ending at last, he planned to produce his Israeli passport, show it to Reisz, Juchem, Godenau, Büsse, and the Fighting Cock, and tell them, in effect, that they'd been had. He knew it was juvenile, but he wanted to see their faces. He wanted to punish them for wanting to destroy his race and for hating him unreasonably, when all along they'd called him their friend. They would say, of course, that they knew it all along, that they had only pretended to enjoy his company. When the meeting broke up, he suggested they walk to the car together.

"He wants to tell us something," Godenau told the others.

"But I feel that this is not the right place." Svoray hesitated to complete his plan.

"Maybe we can go a little farther."

"No. This is okay. It is okay here." They were standing in a group just beyond the hotel entrance.

"So." He laughed. "I want to come in one year and see my statue."

Reisz explained. "I told him, 'A plaster statue of you will be placed at the entrance. When you come, you will see it.' "

"But plaster is no good," said Büsse, grinning and waving his cigar.

"All right, then, cement," said Reisz, and everyone laughed while Büsse clapped Svoray on the shoulder and said, *"Gip-sköpfel,"* which means "blockhead."

Juchem promised a sensational propaganda campaign within three months of receiving the money. "After all, these things do not happen overnight," he said.

Now Svoray asked if they thought he had been helpful. Reisz responded, "If everything that has been planned comes true, this is the most valuable thing to happen for the last thirty years in the Federal Republic."

"Thank you very much," Svoray said when he heard the translation. He wanted to know how Juchem and Büsse felt. "So ask them," he said to Godenau. "Am I the best thing that happened in thirty years? Am I the best thing that happened in Germany?"

They laughed uneasily, as if they were not sure the question was serious. After a pause, Büsse said, "No, but he can rest assured that now—and I have known the entire right-wing scene since 1946—for the first time the right people are being supported in the political fight."

"And you will march behind him"—Svoray indicated Juchem —"in fire and in water, even do illegal things?"

"We are ready to do anything."

Svoray drew the men into a close circle, as if they were school-

boy athletes at the beginning of a game. He made them lean in
toward one another, place their hands together and give a cheer
for victory.

As they stood back, he reached for his passport. Then he
paused, suddenly uncertain. One of the cameras captured him
withdrawing his hand from his green bag. Some instinct told him
to keep Ron Furey alive a little longer. Instead, he made a promise. "You'll all get a very big surprise in one month. Everyone will
be surprised."

Reisz opened his arms as they parted and gathered Svoray into
a pummeling, back-slapping embrace. "We will always be grateful
to you, Ron," he said.

Svoray was stiff in the embrace, shrinking instinctively as he
had at their first meeting, but Reisz did not appear to notice.

When he returned to the room, Svoray found the cameraman
and producer huddled together. They looked up grimly. The
hidden camera had failed to record Svoray's handoff of money to
Juchem. What should have been the redeeming moment had
been lost.

Twenty-eight

MARVIN HIER sat in his big chair and looked at the men seated in his office. Svoray was the loudest and the most insistent. The others—Abe Cooper, Aaron Breitbart, and Rick Eaton—listened quietly. Outside, yeshiva students played basketball near the trailer classrooms. Their shouts filtered through the office windows to the group inside. March in Los Angeles, a city of mild climatic change, had begun with a restlessness for closure. There was a sense in the room that the Wiesenthal Center might now be well satisfied with the outcome of Svoray's mission; in addition to luring Wolfgang Juchem from the shadows, it had revealed the face of neo-Nazi hatreds across Germany and given a context to the violence against foreigners. Hier wagged his head up and down and brushed a hand across his forehead as if trying to launch a thought in opposition. His face was creased in its deceptive look of mischief.

"We hit a triple," he said. "We didn't bring it home yet."

"I can't go back." Svoray had been saying this throughout the meeting. "I have been living since December with people who are spitting in my face every day with every word they speak. I'm going nuts. I feel like things are crawling on me. I told you I spoke Hebrew in front of them. They tried to run me over. Do you want to get me killed?"

The rabbi waited until Svoray's histrionics were exhausted. "Listen to this," he said. "Abe and I were talking. You're all along telling them about a millionaire, somebody with money who wants to contribute to their movement, is this right? Yes. So, why not go to them with the millionaire?"

"We've got a lot of information, Rabbi. Is it worth the risk?" Breitbart had sifted through the transcripts of tapes that had been translated and retranslated. One of their revelations was that Godenau's employer, the anti-Semitic publisher Juan Maler, once Reinhard Kops, lived and owned a hotel in San Carlos de Bariloche, Argentina.

"We've got information, but we don't have all the proof. This Juchem says he has military people, middle Germans. Who are these people who support him? We don't have a conclusion. We didn't bring it home yet. We hit a triple," Hier repeated. "They're desperate for money. If you bring them a millionaire who's going to invest money in their movement, they're going to roll out the gold carpet. If we bring in the millionaire, they'll melt. What do you think, Abe?"

"I think it's worth it." Cooper stroked his close gray beard and wondered where they were going to find a "millionaire." Los Angeles was a city of actors, but it wasn't that easy. They would have to find someone who knew the right-wing scene well enough to be convincing. Or a very fast learner. Cooper didn't place most actors in that category.

"Even when I'm going crazy?" Svoray got up from his chair and walked to the window. As he watched the boys feinting and shooting the basketball, he craved for himself their normal, uncomplicated lives.

"They aren't onto you," Hier said, fiddling with his hair and patting down his yarmulke. "They trust you. I don't think you'll be out of your league if you go back once more. One more shot, we can knock them out, hook, line, and sinker."

Cooper spoke. Sometimes he had trouble hiding his impatience, but he could be smooth and persuasive when the occasion required. "Yaron, we've gone right to the brink of showing that this is something to be concerned about. It would be a shame not to finish it."

"Who's supposed to be the millionaire?" Svoray demanded.

"That's a question," Hier admitted. "Maybe Abe has got it figured out."

"I thought we could hire an actor, Moish," Cooper said.

"Wait a minute," Eaton said sharply. "If you're sending anybody, you're sending me."

All eyes swung to Eaton. "Look," he said. "An actor won't know about the right. I do."

Cooper raised his eyebrows. "Rick's right. He knows the hate groups. He can talk the talk. We'll have to get you out of those jeans into a suit, though. And cut your hair. You wouldn't mind cutting your hair, would you?"

"Call the barber."

As Eaton thought about the prospect of going to Germany with Svoray as his assistant, a smile spread slowly over his lean face.

Svoray dreaded the phone call to Michal as much as he had ever dreaded anything. He couldn't count the number of times he had told her he was almost finished, and to expect him home. He consoled himself with the knowledge that from the very beginning they had agreed on the importance of his task, and also had been ready for the uncertainty of what lay ahead. In spite of that, he had agreed on this final trip only with mixed feelings. Trip upon trip—the mission transmuting from a quick survey and the purchase of Gerhard Schulz's soldier-book to what had become, with the discovery of Juchem, an elaborate sting designed to lure secret neo-Nazi sympathizers into the open, all of it started by his outrage at the pleasure of men in the death of a young girl in a film that must by the look of it have been thirty years old—he had never expected it to go on this long.

Nor had Michal. "Do you remember the last time you were at home? It was January. This is March." Her voice was rough with a cold. He remembered how the children seemed to sneeze each time he spoke with them. Not that he could have cured their colds, but he could have offered comfort or, better still, taken them to Eilat on the Gulf of Aqaba for a therapy of sunshine.

It was because he was so certain that this time he really was going on his final trip to Germany that he spoke to Michal more sharply than he intended. "I remember. But you remember that we said at the beginning we could not predict the course of this. It would take what it would take."

"That's fine, Yaron," she snapped. "Then you don't have to tell me every time you call that you will be home and then the next day call and say you won't. I'm tired of hearing it. I don't tell the children anymore, because I am tired of disappointing them."

"Michali, you are trying to make me feel guilty because this is taking longer than I thought."

"That's not what I am doing. I am asking you to tell the truth."

"I have always told you the truth. Things change."

"And what is the latest version of the truth?"

"Okay, the truth is this," he said, angry now because, in fact, he did feel guilty. "I am going to Germany once more as Rick Eaton's fucking butler. He is a researcher here who is going to be the millionaire who is supposed to give them money. We will talk to as many people as we can in a very few days."

"You're going as a butler?" This was hard for Michal to imagine, for she knew her husband's ego.

"Butler, chauffeur, employee."

"Well, Yaron," she said with mocking sternness, "make sure you do everything you're told."

He muttered an obscenity.

"And I can expect to see you in a proper uniform and cap, like when you drove Leona?" Hotel queen Leona Helmsley had been one of his limousine clients when they lived in New York.

"I'm glad you are so amused," he grumbled.

"What choice do I have?" she said. "But I tell you, Yaron, and I know we agreed that you would go your way without my crying, and I know this is important. But you can tell the rabbis that your patient wife is losing her patience very quickly."

Rick Eaton had transformed into Millionaire Rick. He wore a gray Giorgio Armani suit. His brown hair caressed the tops of his ears and curled up at the collar, his beard and mustache were neatly trimmed. He sat like a potentate in his suite at Frankfurt's Arabella Grand Hotel, near the Zeil, while Svoray ordered mineral water, orange juice, and sandwiches from room service. It was the first Saturday in March. Eaton, a Jew who had worked for the Wiesenthal Center for seven years, had never been in Germany before. Across from him on a splashy flowered sofa, wearing a cheap tan suit, a black shirt, and a white tie, sat Adolf Hitler's valet.

Karl Wilhelm Krause was a shadow of the man he had been when Hitler discovered him in the ranks of the SS. Then he was arrow-straight and tall, and had trained to run the eight hundred meters in the 1936 Olympics in Berlin. In 1937, when Krause was just eighteen, he began more than five years in Hitler's employ, shadowing Hitler everywhere, opening doors, holding his coat, acting as a bodyguard, even choosing the Führer's Christmas gifts to others. In 1943 he was returned to service in the navy. Now he bore the weight of age; his hair was white, his skin was creased, and his dark eyes looked as if they had seen too much. Roy Godenau had brought him to meet Ron Furey's millionaire employer. Wolfgang Juchem rounded out the group.

For a time Krause reminisced and passed around old photographs. Hitler, he said, with Godenau translating, was like a second father. That had not stopped him, however, from recently selling Hitler's bathrobe to supplement his pension. He thought much less of Himmler, calling the SS chief and Martin Bormann, Hitler's private secretary, "the gravediggers of the Third Reich." Hermann Göring, he said, was "a soldier and a braggart."

There was a knock at the door. Svoray went to open it, and Krause paused while a room service waiter wheeled a cart with food and drinks into the room. When the waiter left, they resumed the conversation.

"Did you know Eva Braun?" asked Eaton, speaking of Hitler's twelve-year mistress and eleventh-hour bride, who committed suicide with him as Berlin was falling in the last days of the war. "Did you like her?" Svoray added, unable to stay entirely in his supporting role.

"Actually, no," Krause said. "I didn't get along with her at all." He reached for a sandwich while Svoray poured the juice and water into glasses.

Krause told, as if by rote, some old stories that tended to excuse Hitler's role in the terror and death of the Third Reich. "He didn't know anything about this business of Kristallnacht, for example," Krause said. "When he heard about it, he said into the telephone, 'What have you done? I will have to pay the price for this later.' And he stood up from the dinner table and locked himself in seclusion. He didn't know about any of it."

Hitler often tried to distance himself from the excesses of his regime. In fact, the rampage against the Jews had been planned by the Nazi leadership and awaited only an excuse. This came in the assassination of a German diplomat in Paris by a Polish Jew on November 7, 1938. Two nights later, Nazis destroyed nearly two hundred synagogues and smashed thousands of Jewish businesses. Hans Bernd Gisevius, a Nazi diplomat who turned against Hitler and testified at Nuremberg, wrote in his memoirs that "the Führer himself inaugurated these frightful and portentous excesses" while the middle class "stared at the Nazi monster like a rabbit at a snake."

Later, the Nazis blamed the Jews for the whole affair, fined them a billion marks for the murder of the diplomat, banned them from public parks, and confiscated the insurance money paid in compensation for the damage.

Krause also said that Hitler didn't really know about the concentration camps. "He only heard about Dachau," he said. "He let these things be mostly handled by subordinates."

"Were you afraid of him?" Svoray asked.

"No."

"Could you say anything you wanted?"

"Yes. I once told Hitler his knowledge of human personality left something to be desired."

Moments later, Krause's reminiscences exhausted, Eaton thanked him and turned to Godenau and Juchem. "Let's talk about Germany today," he said. "I tell you honestly, and I don't mean to insult our guest, that while the remembrance and the spirit of the past are important, they will not help us achieve our goals."

"No, we don't think so either," said Godenau.

"In fact, these types of things, in public, can be very harmful."

"Yes, I agree."

"Tell me, do you think that there are other people looking for the type of leadership that was here during the thirties and the forties?"

"Yes," said Juchem, as soon as Godenau had translated. "But maybe not to the same degree."

"Ron has asked me to put out a great deal of money to support this movement," Eaton said. "He has been very enthusiastic about you, Mr. Juchem. He says you are the one most capable of achieving the goals we might be interested in. And I like what I see so far. I believe there is a future here. But Le Pen has gotten fourteen or fifteen percent of the national vote in France; Jörg Haider may one day be chancellor of Austria. Can we say the same here?"

"At the moment, we have a media dictatorship. It's very difficult to get our message across to the public." Juchem said he had done several television interviews that had been kept off the air. Godenau, who often did not wait for Juchem to finish speaking before he translated, making it difficult sometimes to separate their thoughts, said it was the fault of German networks that were connected to established political parties. "The head of one is even a Jew," he said.

"Because of this prejudice of the mass media," Juchem continued, "the nationalist side will first have to get representation in the Bundestag. Once that is done, we will be heard."

However, he said, the known right-wing parties in Germany were stigmatized. "There are five or six major groupings, but the mass of people would not go to a right-wing party meeting. The majority of them stay away. That's the reason I don't belong to any party. To get the masses of people, you have to have an organization that's structured as something other than a political party, a co-op or something."

Juchem's own organization, Aktion Freies Deutschland, Action for Free Germany, was structured as a club. Its innocuous symbol, an oak leaf, implied an ecological concern. Juchem always wore its pin on his lapel. By contrast, his real message was contained in the first sentence of the brochure he'd given Svoray at their January meeting: "The first half of this century was marked by the realization of devilish plans to destroy Germany." He spoke of a German renaissance in the same way Hitler had done.

"I don't want to lead a new party," Juchem said. "That would only split the right further. But one party will emerge as the strongest; then we will see."

Eaton said, "What I'm interested in is a political party, an organization, whatever it may be. But I want to know that the influx of money will create something that will reach the man that wears the hard hat and works in construction, the man that goes to his shop every day, the doctor, the attorney, the politician. I don't expect to reach everyone. But I want to know that when people see the light at the end of the tunnel, they will come together and join this movement. That's why this has to be something that's clean. No excess baggage, such as''—here he looked at Godenau—''your friend David Duke.''

Godenau had said he had known Duke, an open racist and former Ku Klux Klan leader who had almost won the Republican nomination for governor of Louisiana and before that had made a strong run for a U.S. Senate seat, since before Duke had been involved in politics. Eaton wondered if there was anybody in the extreme right wing Godenau didn't know.

''Excuse me.'' Svoray interrupted Eaton to act the part of his employee. ''Would you like both *The Wall Street Journal* and the *Financial Times* tomorrow morning?''

Eaton nodded and Svoray scurried off to order the papers. When he returned, Eaton excused himself to make some urgent business calls. For this he used the suite's bedroom at the top of a short flight of stairs. His voice floated down into the sitting room where Krause, Juchem, and Godenau waited with Svoray. The calls sounded very important.

When he came downstairs again, Eaton apologized. ''Publishing. I inherited the company, and it's all I can do to manage it.'' The rabbis had decided, together with Eaton, that he could never talk like an entrepreneur.

''Here's what I want,'' he said, resuming the discussion. ''If you can give me a day and a half and organize meetings for me to meet the people who support you—I want to know that there are people out there who represent the future of Germany.''

''I could try,'' said Juchem. ''I can assure you I have people from all stations in life, in all occupations. I have contacts with all the parties and organizations.''

''It will be worth your while. You will make it up a thousand times over.''

Juchem's face clouded. He showed an instinctive wariness, a resistance not to the scheme of the proffered money or the silent candidacy that it implied, but to the cares of leadership. ''I didn't ever want personal financing for myself,'' he demurred. ''I only heard about it from my friends, who thought I can use it most effectively. I am a worker for Germany.''

''That's fine,'' said Eaton. ''But one wants to know where one's investment goes.''

Twenty-nine

THE NEXT MORNING Svoray and Eaton picked up a black BMW, the biggest they could rent, and drove north to Gilserberg to pick up Godenau. The day was cool and clear. The autobahn took them to Giessen, but the planned connector to Kassel had an unfinished stretch, and they shunted off to smaller roads that led through the crazy-quilt countryside of fields, woods, and small towns. Gilserberg was one of these, a backwater without historic sites or castles or any particular attractions. Svoray stopped at the edge of town to let Eaton switch to the backseat.

Godenau was waiting outside a restaurant along the town's short shopping street when the BMW pulled up. It reeked of wealth beside Godenau's small, shabby car. Svoray opened the door for Eaton, and they went inside for coffee. Afterward, they followed Godenau to his modest farmhouse outside of town, where he dropped his car and got in the BMW's backseat with Eaton.

When they were on their way, angling east toward Bad Hersfeld, Eaton pressed him for an assessment of Juchem. Godenau said Juchem was a good speaker and a persuasive personality, but lacked organizational discipline. That could be handled by his people, though. "He's going to delegate authority," Godenau said. "A lot of these people want to handle everything themselves."

"Could he be drafted by one of the parties?" Eaton asked.

"I think so."

"We talked to some Republikaners who wanted to draft him," Svoray threw out from the front seat.

"Oh, I think Schönhuber is not going to be in the Republican party for that long," said Godenau. "He's an old man. I think he's shown some early signs of senility. His secretary, she may even have been Jewish. Maybe an agent of the Mossad."

"Does that happen often, infiltration?" Svoray asked innocently.

"It does happen," Godenau said.

"Back to Juchem," said Eaton, enjoying his role as Svoray's superior.

"He's biding his time. He wants to observe the ninety-four elections and see which party will emerge. There's always the chance that some other groupings will develop from elements of other parties. He could step into a situation."

Godenau said that Juchem made, on average, ten speeches a month. His audiences ranged from fifty or sixty people to as many as three hundred. His message had special appeal to ethnic Germans who had retreated to today's Germany from what Godenau called the eastern territories. "The real eastern Germany—Silesia, Pomerania, East Prussia," he said, naming areas of Poland that were inside the Germany of 1937. "He tells them that the treaties were unlawful, agreed to under protest."

"Two or three hundred. That's a big gathering," said Eaton.

Godenau said that Juchem attracted the public as well as Aktion Freies Deutschland members. His speeches were announced in local newspapers and in the pamphlets he tirelessly handed out. "Anybody can come and see us, which of course is sometimes a mistake," he said. Leftists had made bomb threats.

While Juchem shared Godenau's anti-Zionist, anti-Masonic views, he had learned to soft-peddle those views and stick to issues of public concern. "You can't give them all the truth at once," said Godenau. "Even Churchill said the truth is such a dangerous thing that you have to accompany it with a bodyguard of lies. I don't think it's lies, but Juchem puts information that is more in the public mind together with his nationalistic ideas."

He said that Juchem had been named as a racist and an anti-Semite in a recent book. "But he's not racist or anti-Semitic in the sense that the words are used. He's for the preservation of the biological character of the German people, but he doesn't want to export people on the basis of race.

"Juchem says that eighty percent of the people feel the same way he does. They have the same views on almost everything, but as soon as you put it in a political package, then they shy away."

"How do you get around that?" Svoray asked over his shoulder.

"I've made a suggestion that our party be called the German Middle Party. In German the Mittelstand, Middle Ground, or simply the German Middle, the Deutsche Mitte. That would be good because of the initials, DM, like the Deutschemark. Up to twenty percent of the people would vote for the right-wing parties now under the right circumstances."

"Which would be what?" It was Svoray again.

"Say you have refugees kill children or something right before the election. Here, Ron, take a left."

Their introduction to Juchem's Deutsche Mitte, his Silent Majority, began near Rotenburg not far from the old East–West border.

Kurt Müller, no relation to the Curt Müller who had hosted the solstice celebration, had known Juchem since 1959 when Juchem was an Oberfeldwebel, a master sergeant, in the tank corps. Müller had helped patrol the border when Juchem was a listener there in the intelligence service. Müller said that having seen the system on the other side, he could not understand how anyone could be leftist. He favored a one-party system on the right, and saw Juchem at its head.

Their short meeting with Müller formed the pattern for those to come, as they shuttled between towns in central Germany. On the way to Kassel they stopped to interview a man named Gabrielli. The oak leaf symbol of Action for Free Germany was displayed prominently on Gabrielli's mailbox. The retired forester said he had been drawn to one of Juchem's speeches by a newspaper ad, after which he had joined enthusiastically.

Dr. Friedrich Klaren lived in Kassel. He was a healthy-looking ninety, with a complexion that matched the pink silk flowers on the sideboard in his dining room. He was not a medical doctor, but a Ph.D. in business administration who managed a masons' cooperative before the war. Such skills were valuable in wartime,

since the Nazis worked quarries with slave labor at some of their
concentration camps; Klaren said he was sent to inspect the gran-
ite quarry at Mauthausen, near Linz, Austria, and was impressed
as a soldier for two days guarding prisoners. Those two days
haunted him in later life, hampering his career when he returned to private quarry operations.

"Fantastic," Klaren said of Juchem's lectures. "Well received."

He recalled that Juchem, in the tank corps, was disciplined for
posting a map of 1937 Germany, and was confident that Juchem
would win the support of veterans' organizations if he were a
candidate.

Their next appointments were near Minden, an hour by fast
car. The first, in Porta Westfalica, was with a technical school
professor who moonlighted as the leader of a series of weekend
seminars that preached "the dangers of over-foreignization" and
a clean environment.

"That's important because you can't have a healthy people
without a healthy earth," said W. G. Haverbeck. He threw up a
preemptive hand at Svoray, who was aiming his camera, and lec-
tured, "It's against the law to photograph people unless you ask
them personally."

Haverbeck said he had been the president of a group called
the World League for the Preservation of Life. He extolled
Juchem's leadership ability, saying he was an impressive and convincing speaker who inspired trust in people. He was also honest,
truthful, and clean.

Doris Walz, whose oversized glasses rested on an interesting
nose and who wore her brown hair in a short bob, was a pharma-
cist. She said she had to keep her allegiance to Juchem under
wraps because of her position. His network was largely underground, she said, not visible because it was not a political organization per se. Nevertheless, he had contacts across the political
spectrum and, as far as she was concerned, was absolutely a candidate to lead Germany.

Dark had now fallen. They were behind schedule to meet
Juchem back in Gilserberg, but they were only ten minutes from
Sigrid Schenk, and they decided to take the time.

The retired police inspector was a striking woman with blue-
tinted hair who said she was eleven years old when Hitler came to
power in 1933. "I didn't experience anything negative," she said.

She believed that reeducation since the war had brainwashed the German people, but her club of some five hundred members across Germany was presenting "an accurate view of history." This had earned her a place in the files of the Verfassungsschutz, she added proudly.

Schenk believed that the forces of the right had to organize underground and then spring suddenly. Juchem, she said, had the ability to do this.

"Who would you prefer as the new führer?" Svoray asked.

"Whoever has the best abilities for Germany," she said. "Someone who obligates himself for Germany and not his own bank account."

"Is Juchem such a man?"

"Certainly."

It was then, with the day closing, that Svoray and Eaton relaxed, talking to each other like the right-wing supporters and financiers they were supposed to be.

"You have all these people," Eaton told Svoray. "We have an organization. We need you to interview Juchem for *The Right Way* to tie it all together."

Perhaps Schenk understood more English than Eaton or Svoray suspected, and maybe she heard more than neo-Nazi enthusiasm in their remarks. In any case, her voice turned cold with suspicion. She looked carefully at the men from the Wiesenthal Center, and said to Godenau in German, "Whoever comes to help us, we have to be a little distrusting, because we don't know who's behind it. FBI, CIA, the Jewish Anti-Defamation League, all these evil groups, you never know which one is going to pop up."

Godenau translated what she'd said and, with Svoray and Eaton, also tried to reassure her.

Sigrid Schenk, with all the intuition of her seventy-one years, said, "It could be too late."

In the more than two hours back to Gilserberg, Godenau gave no indication that Schenk's warning had affected him. He continued to prove himself an encyclopedia of Holocaust denial. He said earnestly that Dr. Josef Mengele's medical experiments at Auschwitz were performed solely on volunteers who got special treatment—if they survived. He repeated the discredited statements of so-called engineer Fred Leuchter that the Auschwitz gas chambers could not have been used for killing, and argued that the Zyklon-B could not have killed the millions that it did because it worked too slowly and left too much residue. The Jews that died, he said, died of typhoid fever. And, of course, there were food shortages at the end of the war and the German people had to be fed.

"Were you never afraid for your life?" Svoray asked from the driver's seat, watching Godenau in the rearview mirror.

"You mean in the army?"

"No, lately. There are some people who must disagree with your views."

"Quite a lot of them. But everybody has to die sometime," said Godenau. "Dying probably hurts a little bit. But it is usually over quick." He sounded as if he was reading from a bad movie script.

The kilometers clicked past in darkness. Godenau said that his wife, whose father had served in the Hitler Youth division of the Waffen SS, was also "right-minded." She was running for the Kreistag, the county parliament, on the Republikaner ticket. Godenau was her name, not his; he had been born Roy Armstrong in Seattle.

Juchem had been waiting for two hours beside the byroad that led to Godenau's farmhouse when the black BMW whispered to a stop beside him. But he greeted them cordially. Godenau picked up his car outside the farmhouse, and they drove three cars in tandem to the restaurant where Svoray and Eaton had met Godenau that morning.

Over a late supper, they discussed exposing Juchem gradually, by placing his face and name on advertising kiosks. In the meantime, they would hire a Madison Avenue image consultant to consider a new haircut and mustache trim. Juchem reacted enthusiastically to the prospect of his makeover. When the last plates had been cleared, Svoray and Eaton began to wonder where to spend the night.

Juchem went to the adjoining bar and leafed through the phone book. Eaton could see him mentally calculating the sort of place a millionaire would stay. He came back and recommended a place near Bad Wildungen, a few kilometers away. The road map showed a castle and a golf course, and Juchem led them through the lamplit streets of the small town to the resort hotel. When they shook hands in farewell, Eaton sensed that Juchem believed power was within his grasp.

The final day of Svoray's mission in Germany began like those just previous, clear and cool. The cobbled streets of Bad Wildungen added a picturesque quality as he drove through them with Eaton on the way to pick up Godenau.

Manfred Röder was Godenau's first introduction of the day. A mild-looking man in his fifties whose brown sweater and slacks, steel-rimmed glasses, and neatly combed gray hair gave the appearance of a college professor, Röder proved the saw that things are often not as they appear. He had served nine and a half years in prison on charges related to the bombing of a refugee hostel in 1980 in which two people were killed.

"You don't look like a terrorist," Svoray said.

Röder turned on him. "Well, how do you know?" he said in English. "How should a terrorist look?"

He warmed as Svoray described his exposure to the neo-Nazis and criticized the divisions that kept the right from gaining power. Röder had a long history on the right, including membership in the Deutsche Bürgerinitiative, the German Citizens' Initiative, an extremist group dating to 1971. He envisioned an axis of German and Russian nationalists. He suggested that the Mölln firebombing was a plot against the right. While they disagreed on the approach—Röder favored a "political and social earthquake" to the elective process—he supported Juchem, who had visited and written to him in prison. However, he believed that German politics were controlled in New York by the B'nai B'rith and that candidates for office, from state's attorney up to chancellor, had to swear to support the Jewish quest for world power. Thus, Juchem would be killed if he gained power.

Meinolf Schönborn's style was more to Röder's liking. Schönborn headed the banned Nationalistic Front. After a call from Röder, Schönborn met Svoray, Eaton, and Godenau at his home in Detmold.

Schönborn, a big, easygoing man with wavy brown hair who appeared to be in his mid-thirties, ushered them into a room that had been his office. The place was bare. Scuff marks on the floor showed the positions of absent filing cabinets. He said the police had taken everything in a recent raid, the latest of many. Volunteers working in another room were stuffing envelopes by hand. Schönborn was unconcerned about the raid because his computer, which was taken along with his files, contained only phony names. "The real, important names of the party we keep somewhere else, in another building," he said with Godenau translating.

As for the ban against the Nationalistic Front, instituted the previous November, he simply ignored it. "This does not make any difference. We continue our work," he said.

Schönborn claimed seven thousand members and nearly nine thousand sympathizers. He said he had short-, medium-, and long-range plans for achieving power. "Not just power. We want to be in control, so we can determine the future course of history.

"We do not want to improve anything in this system. We want to abolish it. We want a new system. The Fourth Reich."

Svoray asked him what the Fourth Reich meant.

"The ideology, the Fourth Reich, is incredibly similar to the Third Reich," Schönborn said. "Get rid of all the racial aliens."

"Jews also?"

"Yes."

"How do you throw them out? They seem to be thriving."

"That can be changed," Schönborn said, to laughter from his volunteers.

His plan was to establish underground cells of unarmed supporters, aged fourteen to thirty-five. At those ages, he said, people were more susceptible to indoctrination and military training. They would be available at the right moment. Meanwhile, a leadership cadre would be trained at a center outside Germany, to avoid the surveillance of the Verfassungsschutz. After some prodding, he named Denmark as the site he preferred for his center, since neo-Nazi activities were not banned there.

"One could set up a think tank without being harassed. You could create a philosophy and prepare professional propaganda. People, nationalists who want to abolish this state and create a new one could work in peace without having to fear that at five in the morning there is a ring at the door that is not the milkman."

His view of Juchem, Schönborn said, was that he was not an organizer, but was a good populist speaker and a potential figurehead.

As they left, Schönborn promised to fax Eaton his million-dollar wish list and three-phase plan. A million would cover only Phase I, but with a headquarters and the communications, transportation, professional services, organizers, and propaganda that the money would buy, the banned Nationalistic Front could begin creating the Fourth Reich. Eaton gave Schönborn the fax number at his home in the San Fernando Valley, now encoded as connecting to *The Right Way.*

They drove west in falling darkness, skirting the urban-industrial sprawl of Dortmund, Essen, and Duisburg that was known collectively as the Ruhrgebiet, the Ruhr region.

Rich in coal fields and steelworks—the Krupps arms factories were at Essen—the Ruhr had been occupied by France and Belgium in 1923 to enforce French demands for reparations following World War I. The foreign troops were a sharp humiliation added to the costs and indignities of the Treaty of Versailles. German resistance took the form of sabotage and reduced production, but it cost the economy dearly and contributed to its collapse. The humiliation of the occupation also helped set the stage for Hitler's rabid nationalism, so that when Germany reoccupied the Rhineland in 1936 and resumed undisguised arms production in defiance of the treaty, these were regarded as the actions of a savior and a hero.

Toward the end of this fifty-kilometer band of congested speeding cars and lumbering trucks, the A3 angled off toward the northwest. Less than an hour later, they sped across the border into Holland.

Florrie Rost van Tonningen was Godenau's final offering, another icon of the neo-Nazi movement. She lived in a large white house outside of Arnhem and was proud of her nickname, the Black Widow. Her late husband, Meinoudt Rost van Tonningen, deputy leader of the Dutch Nazi party, had committed suicide in 1945 rather than face a trial for treason.

Now seventy-eight, Frau van Tonningen was a vain woman with a haglike countenance and threads of silver-blond hair falling about her face. She carried on the Nazi spirit. "It's the only way of life, you know," she said. She knew Wolfgang Juchem and supported him strongly, though of course she was not a German voter.

Her living room was a shrine to her husband and to Hitler. She twice had been convicted of distributing anti-Semitic and Holocaust denial literature, and the discovery that she used part of her state pension to help finance a neo-Nazi party in the Netherlands caused an outcry in 1986. She also knew Willis Carto, and had spoken at conventions of the Institute for Historical Review.

Svoray and Eaton were flying back to Los Angeles from Amsterdam, so they said goodbye to Godenau outside the van Tonningen house. Eaton proposed a U.S. lecture tour at which Godenau would receive money for Juchem in the form of an account at a bank Eaton owned. This would prevent the problems of transporting cash and allay suspicions of a bomb. At the end, Svoray pulled some money from his pocket.

"I don't want to take your money," Godenau said. "It's a pleasure to fight the common enemy."

"Take it," said Svoray. The amount was far more than the train fare Godenau would need to return to Gilserberg.

"You're sure?"

"Hey, it's small time," said Svoray.

"If you're sure," said Godenau, and pocketed the bills.

Thirty

RON FUREY existed for a few weeks longer. His name appeared on a fax transmission to Roy Godenau, suggesting topics for Godenau's upcoming lecture tour. Audiences would want to know about the "Future of the European Right" and the "True Agenda of the Marshall Plan," Svoray offered. The fax actually was sent by Eaton.

Svoray, meanwhile, went home to Israel.

When at last he emerged from immigration and customs into Ben-Gurion Airport's reception center, what pained him was the curiosity on the faces of his two older children. Their smiles were almost shy. Enosh and Ellie seemed to ask unspoken questions, as if wondering whether something they had done had kept him away. Only Ohad was untroubled; at sixteen months he was not old enough to ask himself those sorts of questions. Svoray knelt on the floor and gathered them all into his arms, embraced their stickiness, inhaled their smells of chewing gum and fruit, and said over and over, to convince them, "Daddy's home."

He rose after several moments and looked into Michal's steady, knowing eyes. She was containing her happiness of the reunion. What she showed was an aura of inner strength and confidence. Svoray, on the other hand, wore a grin as vast as his sense of his accomplishment. "Ah, Michali," he said. They held each other for a long time.

The roads out of Tel Aviv into the suburbs were typically

crowded. Michal drove Avrmik's station wagon. The borrowed car reminded Svoray that while his mission may have neared an end, his financial woes continued. But this could not diminish his enthusiasm. He wanted to drink his family in.

"So, how is everyone? Are my wife and children glad to see me?" A green car rode their bumper, then passed with its horn blaring. Tel Aviv drivers were aggressive; this, too, was a part of coming home.

"Yes, *Abba,*" came from the backseat.

"Tell me how much."

"As much as a lot," said Ellie.

"You recognized me. For that I can be grateful."

When they reached the house in Ganne Tiqwa, Goulash bounded from the porch in a shaggy orgy of welcome, placed two huge paws on Svoray's shoulders, and thrust a cold nose into his face. "Goulash missed you too," said Enosh.

Sleep eluded Svoray that night. Despite the long hours on the plane and the homecoming celebration that kept the children up beyond their bedtime, he lay restively awake. At some dark hour, he placed his hand on Michal's naked back and felt the rhythm of her breathing. He moved his hand to the swell of her breast, hoping she would wake up, and she did.

Afterward, he still found sleep impossible. Rising, he went into the children's rooms, each in turn, and listened to them breathe. He walked into the kitchen, peered through the dim light at the mildew splotches on the ceiling, and was glad that the winter rains had passed. When Michal joined him, he was standing in his robe in the open doorway, looking out into the night.

She closed the door because it was cold and drew him to the sofa. "You are thinking about Heinz," she said.

"He is right. The others are going to hate him."

"And you?"

"I don't hate him. He hates me and doesn't know it, so he likes me. At the moment."

Late in March, the German Interior Ministry used the coined word *Rechtsterrorismus,* "terror from the right." It was the first such official use, and it appeared in a request by the Verfassungsschutz, the Office for the Protection of the Constitution, for additional manpower to monitor right-wing extremist groups.

Its left-wing counterpart, *Linksterrorismus,* had been used for years.

This semantic construction was the Kohl government's tacit admission that right-wing violence was as great a threat to Germany as violence from the left.

The Verfassungsschutz also had begun to explore hints that neo-Nazi and skinhead groups were networking, sharing intelligence and information. *Interlacing* was the delicate word chosen to describe these contacts.

Lenient treatment in the courts remained a problem. *Rechtsterrorismus* still was considered largely the work of drunken adolescents. German justice had long been said to be "blind in the right eye."

Rick Eaton took off from Los Angeles on April 2 and traveled for twenty-four hours, flying first to Miami, then to Buenos Aires, and finally to San Carlos de Bariloche. He was still Millionaire Rick, the right-wing publisher, to Godenau, who had arranged a meeting with Juan Maler. The resort town sat at the dry western edge of the Argentine Pampas, in the shadow of the Andes on Lake Nahuel Huapí. On his taxi ride from the airport, the Bavarian flavor of the town, its steep roofs and overhanging eaves, its window boxes bright with fall flowers, impressed themselves on Eaton. It was almost as if he were back in Germany.

Juan Maler owned a small hotel called the Campana. It was closed in preparation for the winter skiing season. A clerk was on duty, however, and she sent the haggard Eaton to the Edelweiss.

Maler, or Reinhard Kops—Eaton didn't quite know how to think of him—proved to be a short, sturdy man who protected his bald head with a beret in the cool Andean fall. He took Eaton on a tour of the town, which seemed to occupy a peninsula between two branches of the lake, and the surrounding countryside, pointing out in serviceable English its lavish, European-style resort homes. To the west, the mountains were white-tipped with early snow. He swept out an arm. "All this has been made by Germans," he said. "All this."

Kops had joined Hitler Youth as a boy before the war, had gone to France with the occupying forces, and then had entered the Abwehr, the foreign and counterintelligence service of the German military. He was assigned to root out partisan resistance in Albania, Bulgaria, and Yugoslavia. Communist partisans were strong in the Balkans, and German reaction was particularly brutal. Villages were burned, villagers routinely shot. Interned at a British camp near Hamburg after the war, Kops told Eaton he simply walked away. He returned to Hamburg, his home, with the help of citizens who fed, clothed, and sheltered him. For a time he worked in Rome with the Vatican as a commissioner of refugees, feeding Germans into the "ratline" that spirited many war criminals out of Europe, before making his way to San Carlos de Bariloche in 1947. The town was a magnet for fleeing Nazis and collaborators. Kops had become Juan Maler, and had lived there ever since.

Eaton said he had heard of an old guy in Vienna who still pursued war criminals after nearly fifty years.

"Wiesenthal," said Kops/Maler. "I'm not worried about him." He still worried about the British, though.

As Eaton described his plan to supply money to Juchem and the German right wing through Godenau, Maler became agitated. He said that in the twenty years Godenau had worked for him, he had never kept a proper accounting. He urged Eaton to require controls, at least a monthly accounting of expenses, and offered the name of a contact in Luxembourg who could be trusted to funnel large sums of money to various neo-Nazi groups in Germany. "Of course, you will want to pay his costs," he said.

"Of course. You have to understand that my assistant, Ron Furey, whom I sent to Germany, gets very excited and tells people they're going to get this and that and there will be no accounting. I think like you, that there has to be a certain amount of control, especially since we're talking about half a million dollars."

Maler leaned forward and cocked his head. "How many?"

"About half a million."

"Half a million, yes," he said. "Get in control. Strict, strict, strict control." He sat down at a typewriter and typed a letter of introduction to his friend, a Mr. Puruckher.

As he was leaving the next day, Eaton had an odd exchange with Maler. He was admiring Maler's library when he saw a book on the Mossad, the Israeli counterintelligence service. "Know thine enemy," Eaton suggested.

"No, that's my collaborating brethren," Maler said.

Eaton's face revealed surprise.

"Yes, of course," Maler said without irony. "We will make a better world together."

Maler's surprising statement may have been a veiled admission. Reinhard Kops had been posted to Sofia, Bulgaria, in 1943. Sofia was the headquarters for the Soviet double agent operation called MAX, many of whose members worked for Allied intelligence services after the war.

Eaton left San Carlos de Bariloche on April 4 knowing more about Maler as an author and publisher of anti-Zionist and anti-Masonic tracts and books, but with other important questions still unanswered. He would have liked to know why the British had interned Reinhard Kops after the war, a treatment usually reserved for war criminals, and how he had managed to so casually escape. He wondered, too, how many other ex-Nazis lived in the small town, and what their histories would reveal.

Two days later, Ron Furey received an urgent fax from Germany at Eaton's San Fernando Valley number. By then Eaton and the Wiesenthal Center already had the Nationalistic Front's three-phase plan in hand.

Schönborn, in a document sent several days earlier, listed as phase one his need for computers, laser printers, scanners. He wanted a headquarters with video surveillance, vans and a car, portable telephones and radios, wiretap detectors, salaries for area administrators, funds for training and the development of propaganda, postage, and "a good political attorney." He estimated the cost at one and a half million marks.

A cover firm should be created to comply with legal requirements for bookkeeping and tax statements, he suggested, adding that Greenpeace was a good model for creating propaganda.

In phase two of the march toward the Fourth Reich, Schönborn foresaw the creation of "a secure and professionally conducted training center in the middle of Germany." Eisenach was one of the suggested sites. This would cost another two million marks.

As for the third phase, Schönborn's document said, "Attack is the best defense," adding that further explanations would have to be conveyed orally.

In the latest fax, Godenau appeared uneasy. He was beset with suspicions. Eaton had taken to Maler, to prove his publishing connections, three books brought out fifteen years earlier by Brookhouse, a company his family actually had owned but long since sold. Maler wanted more proof, Godenau said. Juchem, too, thought something was wrong.

"Unfortunately, our dear friend Juchem still has serious doubts about the whole arrangement," Godenau said. "Therefore, I believe it to be of great urgency to 'convince' him by having Richard deliver a significant sum as soon as he is again in Germany. I believe that US $5,000 would be enough to do the trick. Cash only! This amount is quite legal: no obligation to declare it. And it can be deducted from the *other* amount!

"Please understand our position. Extremist radical Zionists have threatened the lives of Rightist leaders in Germany. We do not yet know you well enough to be safely convinced that you have nothing to do with them."

He added the costs of renting kiosks to display Juchem's picture, however, along with the good news that his wife had been elected to the Kreistag as a Republikaner. He also said he needed seven hundred Deutschemarks for two new suits for his upcoming U.S. speaking tour, for which Furey had supplied five dates.

"Please send the money right away," he wrote, "since I am broke."

Another worried message followed a week later. Godenau apologized for the checking and cross-checking that was going on. "We want to be certain of the people we're dealing with. Most German rightist leaders have been 'skrewed over' [*sic*] so many times by the Media here that they automatically reject anyone connected with them. Also, taking photos and recording conversations are usually grounds for suspicion here."

Vaulting Juchem to leadership of a unified, militant right would be difficult at best, he said. "Nevertheless, in analyzing it, I personally believe it is indeed the right thing to do ('the right way')!"

He went on to say, "Any militant organization will bring about massive government interference and persecution . . . even if it is based in a neighboring country. Verfassungsschutz agents have massively infiltrated most of the present militant groups and funneling support to them might put the other options in jeopardy.

If undertaken, such action would have to be highly covert and narrowly channeled."

He closed with his signature line, "Ahoi, Roy."

Eaton responded with a fax in Furey's name. Furey thanked Godenau for arranging Eaton's visit with Juan Maler and reminded him that he and Eaton were returning to Germany the following Monday, April 19.

On April 19—the day preceding Hitler's birthday—Ron Furey and Millionaire Rick had different plans from those they'd given Godenau. They appeared with Rabbis Marvin Hier and Abraham Cooper at the Wiesenthal Center's news conference in New York announcing Svoray's penetration of the German neo-Nazi movement. "CBS This Morning," with its head start, began a two-part series on its morning broadcast the same day.

The news conference attracted a large turnout at New York's Grand Hyatt Hotel that morning. German, French, Israeli, Spanish, and English reporters and crews attended, in addition to representatives from the major U.S. newspapers and networks.

The FBI chose the same day to begin its tank and teargas assault on the besieged Branch Davidian compound of cult leader David Koresh in Waco, Texas, where four agents had died weeks earlier. The booby-trapped compound exploded in spectacular flames; Koresh and dozens of his followers died. The news dwarfed all other stories that day.

The CBS broadcast portrayed Heinz Reisz as a dedicated Nazi. It showed Svoray brazenly arguing with the brown-shirted members of the FAP at the meeting at the Forest Inn. It revealed the secret coalition forged between Wolfgang Juchem and Friedhelm Büsse at the meeting at the Gravenbruch Hotel.

Juchem's aims and portraits of the cross section of German neo-Nazis, skinheads, and middle class alike were among the Wiesenthal Center's revelations. Svoray's information included the wide discrepancies between membership figures given him by Büsse for the FAP and Schönborn for the Nationalistic Front and the much lower estimates of the Verfassungsschutz. No such comprehensive picture of the German neo-Nazi movement had been compiled since violence against foreigners began to rise in 1990.

The Wiesenthal Center had presented a summary of its findings and copies of Svoray's tapes in advance to the German embassy in Washington. The reaction of the German government to the transcripts and other materials submitted by the center, to the news conference, and to the CBS report was silence.

Six weeks later, on May 29, a fire set at a Turkish home in Solingen, Germany, killed two women and three girls. A nation already sobered by the Turkish deaths in Mölln the previous November was shocked by the latest violence. Turks reacted with angry demonstrations. Solingen's mayor offered a passionate apology.

Helmut Kohl, however, refused to attend the funerals and memorial services that were held for the dead in Solingen. The chancellor declined, as well, to attend their burials in Turkey. The Free Democratic party, the small liberal bloc of Kohl's governing coalition, criticized him strongly, and the opposition Social Democrats said he was no longer capable of keeping peace. Demonstrators chanted "Coward!" and threw eggs when he appeared a week later in Berlin.

It was up to President Richard von Weizsacker, whose position was largely ceremonial, to decry the violence. Speaking in Cologne, he said the firebombings in Mölln and Solingen grew out of a climate created by the extreme right that was intended to weaken Germany's democracy.

Four young men were arrested for the arson. Three had been drinking in a Solingen pub and had attacked patrons who they believed, apparently mistakenly, were Turks. After they were thrown out of the pub, they met a fourth man who suggested they set fire to a Turkish house. They ranged in age from sixteen to twenty-three.

Arsonists continued to attack Turks the following weekend. A woman and her five children were burned out in Hattingen, thirty kilometers from Solingen, barely escaping with their lives. In Konstanz, on the Swiss border, a Turkish restaurant was burned. Arson attacks targeted Turks in at least two other towns.

News of the Solingen firebombing was still fresh on June 15, a steamy day in Washington, D.C., when the press and many young Capitol Hill staffers crowded a hearing room in the Rayburn House Office Building. The occasion was a hearing of the House

Foreign Affairs Subcommittee on International Organizations and Human Rights, chaired by white-haired California Democrat Tom Lantos. The four witnesses on European nationalism and anti-Semitism included Hier, Svoray, Abraham Foxman of the Jewish Anti-Defamation League, and a former State Department official named Paul Goble.

The hearing was part of Hier and Cooper's calculated strategy to draw a reaction from the German government. After weeks of silence, they had approached Lantos, a Hungarian Jew who had survived the Holocaust in Budapest before immigrating to the United States. Lantos had agreed to convene a hearing.

As listeners loosened their collars and hung their coats across the backs of chairs, Hier launched his testimony by reminding the committee members, "Not since the days of the Third Reich has Germany been witness to the wave of violence currently eating away at her social fabric." In light of the results of Svoray's investigation, he questioned Germany's determination to crack down on right-wing extremist violence.

Svoray suggested that the problem was larger than Germany's leaders were willing to admit.

The hearing produced the first reaction from the German government to the Wiesenthal Center's evidence. A government representative attended and took notes, as did a member of the Social Democratic opposition.

In the wake of the hearing and the publicity it generated, under pressure from its embassy in Washington, the Bonn government invited the Wiesenthal Center and Svoray to present their findings to authorities in Germany.

Two black BMWs and a pair of large black Mercedes sedans arrived in front of the Hyatt Regency Cologne at about nine on the morning of July 8. They disgorged a group of men in sport jackets who glanced around the parking lot as they stood together talking. Svoray looked down from the hotel's glass-walled restaurant and was reassured by the obvious security. He was nervous about being back in Germany. He had slept the night before in a blocked-off wing of the hotel with a German shepherd on patrol outside his door and a loaded Beretta under a rattan footstool. Now he had a headache that he felt was about to kill him. Soon he emerged with the rabbis and Eaton from the hotel and entered the black cars, which took them to federal police headquarters in Meckenheim.

The building was a modern suburban office set off by security gates and a guardhouse. A veteran cop with a wry expression and short salt-and-pepper hair met the entourage and took them upstairs to where their hosts waited.

Gerhard Siegele, the director for internal security in Germany's Interior Ministry, sat at the middle of a long white table, his back to a wide window. He was a handsome man, with a snowy mustache and a shock of gray-white hair swept back in a pompadour. He was dressed in a navy blue suit, striped shirt, patterned tie, and gold-rimmed glasses. On either side of him, in addition to a translator, were officials from the federal police, the Verfassungsschutz, and Hessen state prosecutors. The translator and a petite, dark-haired Wiesenthal Center staff member named Michelle Eisman were the only women in the room.

There were handshakes all around. The table was set with drinks and snacks and arrangements of dried flowers. The room's stark white walls were hung with well-chosen abstract lithographs and drawings. Green plants lined a long shelf under the window. Given the German resistance that had preceded the meeting, such hospitable appearances were beside the point.

Hier sat down across from Siegele, Cooper and Eisman to his left, Svoray and Eaton to his right. All of them squinted as they faced the window light.

"I suggest you start by giving us any information we may not have," Siegele said, speaking through the translator. His tone implied strongly that there was no such thing.

Eaton handed over three massive binders. Two contained transcripts of tape-recorded conversations, the third photocopies of documents. These ranged from Svoray's canceled check to Juchem and Godenau's faxes to Ron Furey, to catalogues of extreme-right posters and T-shirts for Meinolf Schönborn's Nationalistic Front, Schönborn's plan for starting the Fourth Reich, and Reinhard Kops/Juan Maler's tracts distributed by Godenau.

"We're just here to pass on information," Hier said. "We believe this information is worthy of investigation and in some cases prosecution. But this is up to you."

What followed was a six-hour game of cat and mouse.

Siegele said that Svoray's contacts with Republikaners gave the government new reasons to look at the party. But when Hier urged strict measures, Siegele said the Republikaners already were being monitored and that a court ruling just the day before had limited the types of surveillance allowed. When Cooper asked why no one had managed to trace neo-Nazi computer games like KZ Manager to their source, Siegele said that the games must show Nazi symbols or incite hate and violence to be illegal, that children were good at hiding such things from their parents, and that it was difficult to stop such things now that Europe had no borders. When Svoray described the Nazi-oriented literature he'd seen, the stiff-armed Nazi salutes, the homage to Hitler, and the swastikas he'd witnessed, and the plans to consolidate the right that he'd heard, the prosecutors asked for proof.

"Would you be willing to testify in court?" asked an investigator for the Verfassungsschutz. He was at once the sharpest and the most skeptical of the Germans listening to the presentation. He smoked Marlboros and spoke with his head tilted forward, blue eyes peering from underneath his eyebrows, with a challenging expression. His hair was fashionably long and his clothes eclectic: a dark checked jacket, blue and white striped shirt, and dark-patterned tie.

"Of course," said Svoray.

"We don't want to prosecute any innocent people," the investigator said. He took issue with the figures Büsse and Schönborn had given for their membership, saying, "They don't agree with our intelligence."

Svoray shrugged. "They tell me figures, I tell you. Does this prove Friedhelm Büsse has a thousand members in his movement, or Schönborn seven thousand? I don't know. Their friends and comrades and followers may be what they consider members. But to argue about the figures is beside the point. The Büsses and the Schönborns are not the danger to the republic. The danger is the professor and the ex-policewoman. These are the people who stood by when Hitler ran wild.

"If I had to be scared of someone, it would be Juchem," Svoray added. "He's presentable. When he speaks, he is magic. He is very smooth. He doesn't do the Hitler thing. When he went in public he never exhibited any signs of Nazism. Privately he's the worst Nazi you ever saw. He's subtle, preying on nationalistic fears. He's probably the most dangerous one. He is a Nazi for the nineties.''

"If he doesn't make public statements about what he believes or intends to do, it is very difficult," the investigator said.

A digital clock hung on an end wall. The officials glanced at it as they occasionally jotted in their notepads. They passed Svoray's books of photographs around the table. Svoray said, "I think I've touched the edge of an iceberg. It is up to you to go below the surface."

Around four in the afternoon, Siegele placed a hand on the binders Eaton had handed him that morning and began to rise, as if to close the meeting.

Svoray leaned toward Siegele and said, "Wait. I want you to know why I did this."

Siegele sank back into his chair. The translator spoke simultaneously as Svoray continued.

"I didn't do it for money, nor because I am working for the Simon Wiesenthal Center. My grandfather served in the German army in the First World War and my father was born in Berlin and when I was a boy he read to me from the works of Goethe and Schiller and to this day he speaks Hebrew with a German accent. My grandparents survived the Holocaust. Many of my relatives died.

"I believe the Germans are a decent people. I came to Germany at a bad time and I saw bad things, but I do not say the Germans are a bad people. But these people are bad people. They want to turn back the clock fifty years. I do not believe that this meeting today will result in fifty of these people being arrested tomorrow. That is not the way democracy works. Democracy is something you have to work very hard for and it is always at risk. It is at risk from the right and from the left. Today it is right radicals, tomorrow it may be people who paint their heads green. There will always be such people. I regard them as criminals, and I only hope that what I did will help stop them."

Siegele looked up and down the table. "Well, Mr. Svoray," he said, "we have to thank you. I can only say this has been very interesting for me. You can rest assured that all of the material you gave to us today will be examined and analyzed carefully. After that we shall see which measures we can take in the framework of our law.

"On my part, I would like to give you some material which you may already be familiar with. As I said in the morning, the federal government is taking a whole series of measures against right-wing violence and xenophobia, and I have here a summary of these measures."

He pushed across the table a handful of pamphlets and brochures, Germany's official response to Svoray's investigation.

At the end of the meeting Svoray accompanied the Hessen state prosecutors into a borrowed office. They were attached to the public prosecutor's Department of Political Affairs, which considered cases involving public expression in violation of the anti-Nazi laws. They had asked if he would file a criminal complaint.

One of them, a thin and dour young man with protruding eyes and hair already turned gray, paced restlessly. The other, Dr. Ralf Köbler, with an oval face, dark blond hair, and glasses with thin gold rims, launched a series of questions.

"Just a minute," said Svoray, perched uncomfortably on a hard office chair. "You're only asking me about one person. What about Juchem, or Godenau? What about Schönborn, who wants to start the Fourth Reich? Or Büsse, with his skinheads?"

"But you told us you witnessed criminal acts by this man," Köbler said. "Have you ever heard Heinz Reisz deny the Holocaust, or seen him make the *'Heil Hitler'* salute?"

Köbler did not reveal, nor had any other official at the meeting, that less than a week earlier, on July 2, the young district attorney had successfully prosecuted Reisz for denying the Holocaust in an interview with the newspaper *Frankfurter Allgemeine* in December 1992. Reisz had acted as his own attorney. Köbler, listening to him ranting in the courtroom, said later he thought Reisz sounded "like one of those people from the forties." Reisz was convicted in the nonjury trial of offending the memory of the dead and was sentenced to five months in prison. He had filed an appeal and avoided immediate imprisonment. Köbler nonetheless was ready to take a new complaint.

A secretary whose blond hair was twisted into a chignon and

pinned with a barrette typed Svoray's statement into a computer. He said, "I witnessed thirty times Heinz's salute and *'Heil Hitler'* to his picture of Hitler on the wall. It was a thing he did. He would always introduce Hitler to his friends, and I was one of them."

July 1993–
June 1994

Epilogue

GERMANY TIGHTENED the asylum provisions of its constitution, effective July 1, 1993. The most liberal asylum law in Europe became one of the most restrictive. Germany began automatically denying asylum to refugees from countries Germany considered safe from political persecution. These included all the countries in the European union as well as Poland. The new law halted all asylum seekers entering Germany by land, since all countries abutting Germany were considered "safe." Refugees from other countries crossing Poland to apply for asylum in Germany, for example, were returned to Poland.

The change in Germany's treatment of asylum seekers had an immediate effect. Ten thousand fewer refugees applied for asylum in July than in June. By September, state governments were making plans to close refugee hostels.

The U.S. Federal Bureau of Investigation announced on July 15 that agents had arrested eight white supremacist skinheads in Southern California who were planning to blow up a black church and kill Jews and prominent blacks in an effort to set off a "racial holy war."

The Simon Wiesenthal Center offered the skinheads lessons in tolerance.

German Interior Minister Manfred Kanther, appointed the month before, said late in August that prosecutors and police needed more powers to crack down on both right- and left-wing violence.

The *New York Times* reported on August 30 that a group of German politicians, artists, writers, museum directors, and theologians were pressing for the establishment of a Holocaust museum in Berlin.

A power struggle that began in the fall split Willis Carto from the Institute for Historical Review and led to accusations and lawsuits threatening the existence of the Holocaust denial organization.

On October 29, a member of the United States luge team training in Germany for the upcoming winter Olympics was attacked at a discotheque by a group of skinheads. The luger, Duncan Kennedy, had come to the aid of a black teammate, Robert Pipkins, who was the skinheads' original target. The skinheads, who chanted "Nigger out!" at Pipkins and his teammates, said they were only "having a little fun." Two were later sentenced to prison terms.

Friedhelm Büsse was attacked in November in downtown Bonn near an information booth of ANTIFA, the antifascist organization. Büsse, seventy-three, had teeth knocked out and bones broken.

The Verfassungsschutz, meanwhile, was tracking an increase from two hundred twenty to four hundred thirty members in Büsse's FAP. The figure remained far below the membership Büsse claimed in talking to Svoray, but was enough for the domestic security agency to tag the FAP as Germany's leading neo-Nazi party.

The name of Vladimir V. Zhirinovsky joined the list of hate-mongering nationalistic politicians in mid-November, when his Liberal Democratic party won roughly twenty-five percent of the vote in Russia's parliamentary elections. Zhirinovsky, a virulent anti-Semite who is in fact Jewish on his father's side, had advocated dividing eastern Europe between Germany and Russia and retaking Alaska from the United States. His German ally was Gerhard Frey, the nationalistic Munich publisher who headed the German People's Union.

Wiesenthal Center contacts in Europe informed the research department that Wolfgang Juchem had begun appearing openly at neo-Nazi rallies.

In December, the *Liberty Bell,* a pseudo-intellectual hate sheet published in West Virginia by neo-Nazi and former Hitler Youth member George Dietz, announced that "the indefatigable Juan Maler has added a fourteenth volume to his series of books on the destruction of our world by Freemasonry." A note added that orders for Maler's books should now be sent directly to Argentina rather than a previously listed address in Germany. This led Aaron Breitbart at the Wiesenthal Center to speculate that Maler had dismissed Roy Godenau as his distributor and had severed their relationship.

In December in Germany, federal prosecutors began looking into a "hit list" of opponents of the right published in a neo-Nazi magazine from Denmark.

A German television documentary on Ewald Althans, a neo-Nazi whose name had frequently been mentioned to Svoray, was prevented from airing because it failed to rebut Althans's neo-Nazi views and denial of the Holocaust.

Twenty-six-year-old Michael Peters, an unemployed handyman who was the older of two confessed Mölln firebombers, was sentenced to life in prison for arson, attempted murder, and murder in the deaths of the Turkish woman and two girls who had died in the previous November's firebomb attack. His twenty-year-old companion, Lars Christiansen, a grocer's apprentice who was treated as a juvenile by the court, received a ten-year sentence.

The stiff sentences were seen as a sign that German courts were losing their tendency to be "blind in the right eye."

The year 1993 ended more peacefully than 1992. Acts of right-wing violence had declined slightly, from over twenty-five hundred to two thousand two hundred thirty-two. Arson attacks dropped from six hundred ninety-nine to three hundred eleven. Deaths dropped from nineteen—a figure the Verfassungsschutz had revised upward from seventeen—to seven, including the five victims of the Solingen firebombing.

German authorities were quick to credit a policy of increased vigilance. However, the total of reported right-wing criminal acts, proven and alleged, ranging from murder and arson to racial taunting and insults, rose thirty-seven percent to ten thousand five hundred sixty-one. Part of the increase was due to outraged Germans reporting such activities. At the same time, police expressed alarm about growing links among right-wing groups, including computer networking.

In January 1994, authorities raided Curt and Ursula Müller's home and compound outside Mainz. They failed to find, however, the swastika banner that had flown above the backyard shrine where Svoray was photographed with Büsse and Heinz Reisz.

Also in January, Reisz's conviction for offending the memory of the dead by denying the Holocaust in his December 1992 interview with *Frankfurter Allgemeine* was upheld. Reisz appealed again, however, and remained out of jail.

On March 3, Germany's ombudswoman for foreigners' affairs called for laws against discrimination, which for the most part did not exist. Cornelia Schmalz-Jacobsen also said that immigrants should be given greater access to German nationality.

In Geneva on March 9, the United Nations Human Rights Commission condemned anti-Semitism as a violation of human rights and expressed concern about its persistence. It was the first such declaration by an organization of the United Nations in the forty-nine years of its existence.

NPD head Günter Deckert's 1992 conviction for inciting race hatred by distributing Fred Leuchter's denial of the Holocaust was overturned by Germany's highest appeals court, causing an outcry for strengthened anti-Nazi laws.

A firebomb attack on a synagogue in Lübeck, Germany, on the eve of Passover at the end of March was the first such attack on a synagogue since Kristallnacht in 1938 during the Nazi heyday, officials said.

Heinz Reisz was never prosecuted on the basis of Svoray's complaint. The prosecutor, Köbler, said that Reisz's Nazi salutes and *"Heil Hitlers"* all were done in his home. To violate the anti-Nazi laws, such things must be done in public, with political intent.

As for the rest of Svoray's evidence, it languished in a bureaucratic limbo. It had not even been translated more than nine months later. Without a translation, Köbler said, nothing could be done. Rabbis Hier and Cooper were frustrated and angry that the Wiesenthal Center's long and costly operation, in which Svoray had risked his life, apparently had failed to move the German government.

But on April 14, when Interior Minister Kanther presented the annual domestic security report of the Verfassungsschutz, it became clear that the government *had* moved. For Kanther said what had not been said before: extremist forces were out to disrupt Germany's democratic order, and the threat came especially from the right.

The Verfassungsschutz began saying publicly for the first time that right-wing and neo-Nazi violence presented the greatest danger to Germany's internal peace. Right-wing rallying cries of "Germany for Germans!" and "Foreigners out!" amounted to incitements to riot.

In those small semantic increments lay victory, for they contained what the center's investigation had sought from the beginning. It was the admission that German history was something to be feared, even by the Germans. Svoray and the rabbis, and many others, had conveyed the deadly menace of the neo-Nazi resurgence after all.

The investigation produced its most dramatic result the following month, in May. ABC television's "Prime Time Live" reporter Sam Donaldson traveled to San Carlos de Bariloche looking for Nazis in Argentina. Following the Wiesenthal Center's lead, he turned a camera on Reinhard Kops/Juan Maler. Maler denied he was Kops until Donaldson produced a recording Rick Eaton had made when he visited the German. Then Kops drew Donaldson to one side and said, "I'm only small fry. Why don't you look for Priebke?"

Erich Priebke, an SS captain, was the second-ranking Nazi at a massacre of more than three hundred civilians, including seventy Jews, in the Ardeatine Caves near Rome in March 1944. Earlier, he had helped free deposed Italian dictator Benito Mussolini from jail, an act for which he received the Iron Cross. He had escaped from a detention camp in Italy after the war. War crimes charges against him in Germany and Italy were dropped in the sixties when he could not be found.

When Donaldson confronted him, Priebke, eighty-one, said that it had all happened long ago. He had only followed orders. Donaldson was not a gentleman.

Rabbis Hier and Cooper immediately pressed for Priebke's extradition and trial. The government of Argentina, its files of ex-Nazis opened in 1992 after years of secrecy, placed Priebke under house arrest and said it would extradite him if asked to do so. All that remained was for either Italy or Germany to ask that Priebke be returned to stand trial. The rabbis focused on Italy, the site of the crime. They arranged a meeting with Prime Minister Silvio Berlusconi. His cooperation was by no means assured since he headed a newly elected right-wing government that included neo-fascists. But on June 7, the Italian Ministry of Justice filed its official request for Priebke's extradition.

Later the same month, Argentina announced plans to create an Office of Special Investigations aimed at identifying other living Nazis.

As he waited to learn if Priebke would be tried, Svoray found an elusive, added satisfaction. The trail to Priebke had started with Roy Godenau. Perhaps the last war criminal, and the secure world in which he and Reinhard Kops had taken refuge, had been exposed by the unraveling of a single thread, woven by Svoray in the course of his investigation.

Index